TONY SACCA

LAS VEGAS AMBASSADOR OF ENTERTAINMENT

A 50 YEAR JOURNEY

Biography by Arlene Krieger

DEDICATION

My mother Carmella (Millie), father Joseph, brother Robert, and Uncle Nick who have passed away.

To my sister, Marie and her husband Ed Tully, my family members who supported me throughout my career. Joan Gentile, my English Teacher, and to the folks that helped train me in the art of entertainment.

To the people who challenged my dreams.

To the people who have influenced my life through their trials and tribulations.

To friends and acquaintances who have come in and out of my life.

Copyright ©2014, Tony Sacca

All Rights Reserved. No part of this publication may be reproduced,
stored in a retrieval system or transmitted in any form by any means
electronic, mechanical, or photocopying, recording or otherwise without
the permission in writing from the publisher.

Requests for permission to make copies of any part of the work
should be submitted online at info@mascotbooks.com or mailed to
Mascot Books, 560 Herndon Parkway #120, Herndon, VA 20170.

ISBN-13: 978-1-62086-791-4
CPSIA Code: PRB0514A

Printed in the United States

www.mascotbooks.com

TONY SACCA

LAS VEGAS AMBASSADOR OF ENTERTAINMENT

A 50 YEAR JOURNEY

TABLE OF CONTENTS

City of Las Vegas

Office of the Mayor

Proclamation

By virtue of the authority given to me by the
laws of the State of Nevada and by the
Charter of the City of Las Vegas,

I, Oscar B. Goodman,
Mayor of the City of Las Vegas,
do hereby proclaim

January 20, 2003

as

Tony Sacca Day

in the City of Las Vegas
and I ask all citizens to acknowledge Tony Sacca
as he celebrates 40 years in the entertainment industry.
He has been named the Entertainment Ambassador of
Las Vegas and is adored by our community.

IN WITNESS WHEREOF,
I hereunto have set my hand
and caused the seal of the
City of Las Vegas to be affixed
this 20th day of January, 2003.

Oscar B. Goodman
Mayor, City of Las Vegas

FOREWORD

I first laid eyes on the good-looking Sacca Twins when they came to town in 1981 as lounge headliners: when the lounges were viable mini-showrooms and plentiful, and I was an entertainment newspaper reviewer. Little could I have imagined that one of the two men, who I seriously couldn't tell apart, would become a best friend and close business associate.

Socially, over the years we ran into one another at many regular media events. In the late 1990s, we got together and became close as couples with our spouses: especially after his brother Robert passed away. After the turn of the century, which makes one sound old, I worked as a marketing director at the former Sahara Hotel and Casino, and then the Imperial Palace Hotel & Casino and turned to Tony for his business acumen and filming services. While Tony loves to perform, he has always been business and work savvy. There are few people who can pack so much energy into any given day and accomplish so much. Like a human Energizer bunny, he exhausts most people around him. He is a real force to be reckoned with.

After I left the hotel world, our relationship morphed into me becoming his personal publicist. Tony has an innate ability to foster PR so needless to say, he keeps me busy.

Combining his business sense and his singing and stage talent, Tony has produced and hosted the television show *Entertainment Las Vegas*

Style, for 28 years and interviewed most every star who headlined in the city. His video archives are of tremendous historical value, and last year, he celebrated 50 years in show business.

Tony is a one-man Las Vegas promotion machine. He has created his own line of trademarked Las Vegas Rocks souvenir items, including his musical clock with the song, "Las Vegas Rocks" that he penned. The clock has been voted a best Las Vegas souvenir. Tony's love for his adopted town, Las Vegas, prompted former Las Vegas Mayor Oscar Goodman, to name him, "Las Vegas Ambassador of Entertainment," which he surely is. He was the 23rd recipient of a star on the Las Vegas Walk of Stars and has received seven city proclamations and Certificates of Recognition from every judicial office in the State of Nevada, including a Certificate of Recognition by US Senator Harry Reid.

Tony is courageous and adventurous. After a divorce, he found a new love, Chef Josette: and during the country's recent Depression, they were ahead of Las Vegas' downtown resurgence and opened the Las Vegas Rocks Café, with dining and entertainment. They took the plunge too early and made an amazingly auspicious start, but were dramatically derailed. It was one of two times that I've seen Tony truly down, depressed and dejected; but Tony's determination and perseverance is amazing and the next day he was tackling new challenges and conquering new dreams.

While some may find him self-absorbed, they fail to remember all his charitable contributions and how many entertainers he has promoted and helped. Tony has booked his cohorts at special events and on his television shows, including his newest one, Las Vegas Rocks Variety Show. When a fellow performer is having financial or health troubles, he's the first who wants to help with a fundraiser, etc. Appreciating learning his craft as a child, Tony founded the Youth Foundation for the Performing Arts and produces an annual fundraising Christmas television show for the group. He's also taken the talented students to Washington, D.C., several times to perform at the White House at Christmas and at the U.S. Capitol Building.

Tony is never at a loss for new challenges. It's been a lifetime pleasure for our friendship to evolve on so many levels, including confidant: but as well as I know him, this book tells so much more of his story. Seldom does Tony dwell on the past. He's very goal driven and always seems to try to be proving something to himself. This book will help you to get to know the son of hardworking Italian immigrants whose love of Philadelphia (Philly), where he was born and raised, still prevails. He's kept the home he was raised in with his family. While he was born an identical twin, there's no question he has found his own identity.

Jackie Brett

PROLOGUE

As I entered the hospital room at Methodist Hospital in Philadelphia, where I was born, after flying most of the night from Las Vegas, I knew in my heart that I was not going to like what I was about to see. My twin brother was lying in the hospital bed in a coma after fighting a long battle with leukemia. He had an oxygen mask securely fitted on his face, which appeared lifeless as he took in each breath. I slowly walked closer to his bed to see if he might awaken and recognize me but he didn't. I walked even closer as he was silently lying there. I was three inches from his face, something I have done with him thousands of times during our 48 years together. As I stared into his motionless face, we were nose to nose. I began thinking back on the wonderful life and career that I had shared with him as a brother, a twin, a partner, and a friend. Lying there immobile I realized that his life was fading away and I turned my head 180 degrees only to be staring into a mirror, seeing us once again side by side. His face was withdrawn, his headed bald from the chemotherapy treatments, and I was as healthy as could be. We were no longer the identical twins that people from around the world had admired, two talented good looking young Italians born in the city of Brotherly Love. That was all about to end....

Tony Sacca

From the office of the Mayor

Proclamation

BY VIRTUE OF THE AUTHORITY GIVEN TO ME BY THE
LAWS OF THE STATE OF NEVADA AND BY THE
CHARTER OF THE CITY OF LAS VEGAS,

I, CAROLYN G. GOODMAN,
MAYOR OF THE CITY OF LAS VEGAS,
DO HEREBY PROCLAIM

September 27, 2013

AS

Tony Sacca Day

IN THE CITY OF LAS VEGAS AND ASK ALL CITIZENS TO JOIN ME IN
CONGRATULATING YOU ON 50 YEARS IN SHOW BUSINESS,
ESTABLISHING YOURSELF AS ONE OF THE CITY'S MOST SUCCESSFUL
ENTERTAINERS AND BUSINESSMEN, WHILE PRODUCING
OUTSTANDING TELEVISION AND COMMERCIAL PROJECTS, THAT
HAVE GARNERED NUMEROUS AWARDS.

IN WITNESS WHEREOF:
BY THE POWERS GRANTED TO ME,
I HAVE HEREUNTO SET MY HAND
AND CAUSED THE SEAL OF THE
CITY OF LAS VEGAS TO BE AFFIXED
THIS 27TH DAY OF SEPTEMBER 2013

HONORABLE CAROLYN G. GOODMAN
MAYOR, CITY OF LAS VEGAS

1929 – A young scout named Rafael Rivera is the first person of European ancestry to look upon the valley. His discovery of a valley with abundant wild grasses growing and a plentiful water supply reduces the journey by several days. The valley is named Las Vegas, Spanish for "The Meadows."

Tony and Robert
were both altar boys

CHAPTER 1

He is never alone. As he stands on stage, he feels his presence: he knows he is with him. He is a part of his heart, his soul, and his mind. Even when he stands naked, he clothes him with warmth, he will never leave: his love will never set him free. That soul is his identical twin brother Robert.

It was as brilliant red as he had envisioned, when Tony walked the red carpet in celebration of his fifty years in show business. Already situated inside the theatre, the local television stations had their camera crew preened and ready for the star to make his auspicious appearance. Dressed in a deep purple jacket, with a deeper purple shirt and matching tie, the star made his solitary entrance. A hub of celebrities and guests stood in line, parading down the red carpet, they each shook Tony's hand as the photographers snapped hundreds of pictures. Tony's effervescent smile overshadowed the missing components of his life: his twin brother, his mother and father. Paying homage to the other half of his psyche, rather than a remorseful opening, he ran clips of their television talk show, where he and Robert sat on either side of the guest making it impossible for the celebrities not to laugh as they looked into the mirror image of the twin hosts. One of the film clips captured a celebrity declaring he was getting whiplash as he gazed from brother to brother. The video ended with Tony hugging Robert as they signed off with their bright wide smiles.

"Fifty years in show business, what the hell was I thinking?" he jested as he prodigiously opened the live show; "Growing up, I was always beside myself, and the girls said I had double stamina," the audience was in stitches. It was later that evening, after Tony had opened the show for Louie Anderson, a world famous comedian, and had gone home and made love to his wife, when he shed pent up tears for his other soul mate, his twin, Robert. Happy to be alive and celebrating a half century doing what he loved the most, he would have traded it all for another moment with his brother.

It was more than Las Vegas who celebrated this auspicious occasion, as reported in the Los Angeles Times Travel, with headlines reading, "Las Vegas: Tony Sacca Marks 50 Years in the Biz With Free Shows." Written by Jay Jones, "Free old style variety shows will return to Las Vegas on September 3, 2013, as longtime entertainer Tony Sacca celebrates 50 years in show biz. Sacca, a singer and TV host who has been on the Las Vegas circuit for three decades, will emcee three free shows on consecutive Fridays starting September 3, 2013. The 2:00 pm performances will be in the Railhead at Boulder Station, a hotel-casino five miles east of the strip." Little did the columnist realize at the time, these three free shows would turn into a nationally syndicated program, streamed into over one hundred fifty million households.

He could hardly wait to return home from school, quickly gobbling a sandwich, he escaped down the cement stairs into the basement. Grabbing his guitar, he began picking at the strings, slowly creating a melody line. Even though he loved playing, he was often frustrated with the dedication it took to perfect the chords and the sounds. At just ten years old, his father had already convinced himself that Tony was destined to become a star, and the rigors of guitar lessons would point the way.

The low ceilings and the constant dampness of the basement made some of the notes muffled, but Tony didn't care, he just wanted to hear the sounds. A few minutes later Robert, with remnants of a bologna sandwich still clinging to the edges of his mouth, flew down the steps, picked up his sticks, and began banging the drums to the melody his brother had begun. A daily ritual, the twins practiced and practiced. Sometimes they would throw on 45's and accompany The Drifters, or the Temptations, or The Coasters. Singing and playing along, the two began carving their way into the world of music and entertainment as their voices bounced off the basement walls.

They lived in a modest red brick home in South Philadelphia, trellised with ivy surrounding the gleaming white window panes. Nestled within the middleclass Italian section of the inner city, their neighbors shared not only the same ethnic background, but values of hard work. With just two bathrooms, the twins had to learn to share with their older sister. From the day they were brought home from the hospital, the twins never slept apart, they were their own best friends and often ignored their older sister. Their dad owned a butcher shop, and worked hard to put food on the table. Six days a week he left the home early, often in the inky darkness of the winter months, opened the shop, prepared the meat for the glass showcases, and then waited on customers until dusk had settled. He spent many twelve hour days on his feet and he didn't want that for his children. With three mouths to feed, and a husband who was determined to make his sons important, their mom went to work as a seamstress in one of the many clothing factories. Now with two salaries flowing into the household, whatever dreams their father saw for the twin boys, they would have the means to make it happen.

What this butcher believed was that his children would find their destinies in music. Ironically, one of Tony's jobs was to help deliver the Saturday meat orders with Ronny Rags, who was an accomplished drum musician. Sometimes, when they finished early, Ronny would invite Tony back to his home, showing off his skills and teaching the twin the fine art of playing the drums. When their daughter was born, he became obsessed with the accordion and upon her sixth birthday, presented her with the awkward instrument. It took a very short time for the parents to realize their daughter not only hated the accordion, but had little talent to sustain a musical career as an accordionist. It was when his wife gave birth to identical sons that the butcher's dreams would be answered. In their matching faces their father was imbued with a sense of power that would carve out the sons' musical destiny.

Nobody cared about the constant reverberations disseminated throughout the household, because that banging and guitar playing was the family's ticket to security and fame. With an unbroken stalwart will, their dad believed the twins had a trajectory straight to stardom. The family would put up with the cacophonous sounds until one day, those sounds would be perfected, and the boys would be famous.

"I'm done for today," said Robert as he tossed the drum sticks to the floor.

"Please stay," asked Tony, "I just want to practice this run a couple more times. My fingers get twisted up and I need you to help me out."

"Naw, I'm done practicing for the day," and up he leaped up the steps, through the kitchen and hurried out the backdoor in search of some buddies to keep him company. Left alone, Tony put a pile of 45's on the simple record player, and spent the next hour playing and singing to his favorite groups. Gulping down a few sips of soda, he cleared his throat and then reloaded the RCA Victrola and continued until his mom called down that dinner was ready. Reverently laying down his guitar, he turned off the fluorescent light, galloped up the basement steps and joined the family. Their father sat at the head of the table, the mother at the other end and the three children in the center. Ritualistic, they momentarily prayed, and then dug into whatever meat was unsold from the butcher shop that day. With little time, and little preparation, they ate simply, but well each day.

Between her job and taking care of the household, their mom wasn't much of a cook, and Sunday was the one day she relinquished the cooking duties and allowed her husband take over. He shined, making specialties from his childhood. The children looked forward to the smell of tomato sauce and roasting chickens wafting through the house. After Sunday church, their dad would set out a large pot, douse it with olive oil, toss in spices and chopped garlic and hours later, after he had poured two glasses of Chianti, they would eat a most delicious meal. Wrapping their napkins around their necks, they devoured the spaghetti: the tomato sauce cascaded down their chins. It was the one day of the week their father seemed relaxed. Drinking the wine, he smiled, turning to each child, he would ask each of them questions displaying genuine affection. Usually carrying a gruff exterior, he knew that hard work and dedication was the only way anyone could succeed, and he used that exterior to push his children in that direction. One day of the week, Sunday, he let down his defenses and allowed himself to simply enjoy his wife and family. Those were the days that Tony tried to remember most as he grew into early adolescence.

"Please stand still," demanded Millie as the boys tried on tweed pants with matching jackets. "The tailor has to fit the jackets so you look nice when you are up on the stage." Twisting and turning, they were a handful for the older man, stooped over, pinning up the raw bottoms. "No cuffs, I don't want them tripping over anything when they walk around the stage."

On a blue velvet stool seated in the corner, their sister sat with chagrin on her face as she noted the boastful gleam in her mother's eyes while preparing the boys for the performance. Her mother would never reveal that same proud look to her daughter: she was a disappointment to them. Or so she thought.

"It's Saturday. Can we do something fun?" asked their bored sister. Casting a quick look out the shop windows, dark clouds had gathered, threatening a snow shower. "It's going to be awful out." Sometimes it did occur to their mother that the oldest child was left too often to her own devices, and needed some personal attention. Noticing the first buds of snowflakes whirling down from the blackened skies, she suggested a movie. Two blocks away, the cinema was playing cartoons and children's movies in the afternoons, and entrance was only twenty-five cents. The tailor, whose watchful eye sensed the daughter's displeasure at being there, suggested she look at the paper. Drawing the newspaper from the coffee table, he gently handed it to her and with a caring glance, he told her to turn to the entertainment section. For the first time, he noticed a glint in her eye as she reviewed the choices.

"Old Yeller is playing an hour from now."

"That gives us just enough time to have lunch, and then we'll see the movies. Everyone agreed?" asked their mom. With that, the twins scampered out of their suits and into the comfort of weekend jeans and flannel plaid shirts. Always dressed alike, and the same exact size, neither knew what shirt belonged to whom. The family buttoned up their thick woolen coats, placed knit caps on their heads and ventured into the storm. The wind picked up as they turned the corner and ducked into a small candy store. With deference to her daughter, Millie asked what she would like to eat, knowing full well the answer would be a grilled cheese with a soda. With three hot dogs and orange sodas, they sat at the counter and watched the snowflakes thicken as they continued to shower onto the gray pavement. She looked down at the children's feet and realized none of them had thought to wear galoshes. She was concerned about the walk home. Their mother didn't want to disappoint them, she was confident they would find an easy way home despite the weather.

She paid the box office attendant and took her children to their seats, then went back to the lobby and purchased three boxes of Cracker Jacks and three more sodas. Her only worry was that each toy inside the three boxes was the same; she couldn't handle a fight over something so trivial. Hopefully, their attention would be drawn to the movie, not the snacks. As the deep red velvet curtains parted, she sat in the middle of her children and began thinking about their lives. Unlike her husband, she thought it way too early to mold their destiny: that it would come naturally to each child when they were ready. This was a thorn in her side, and the basis for many an argument with her husband. She didn't share her husband's obsession for music, nor the need to push the children when they weren't ready. The boys were barely twelve and had time to ponder their own passions. Music was something you had to love and that love could never be instilled by any doting parent. It was a gift from above and if the Lord saw fit to bequeath that to you, then it was a sealed fate. She wanted her kids to be kids, to enjoy their childhood. Perhaps she was resentful that to satisfy her husband's goals, she had to work. Thinking about most of the mothers in their neighborhood, she was one of the few who worked outside the home. As she got off the bus, and saw the clutch of boys playing ball in the street, she could feel the leer of the mothers' eyes. It made her feel less than a perfect parent, but one day she would show them. One day when her twins were famous, she would shove the photos and the news clippings underneath their noses and take on the haughtiness she worked so hard to obtain.

The movie ended and she prepared the three children to face the fierce elements. With tears trickling down their faces, they didn't quibble about the toys at the bottom of the box, instead they showed compassion for the loss of the hero in the movie, Old Yeller. Had Millie known the ending, she probably would have thought twice about taking them to see this film: but then again, she was keenly aware that all three children were able to offer empathy, and that wasn't such a bad thing.

"Sweetheart, dad and I are going out, can you please watch the boys tonight?" asked Millie. It wasn't five minutes after the front door had slammed shut that the twins were wrestling around the living room floor. Marie yelled to stop the shenanigans, but that went to deaf ears: after several more threats, her patience had worn thin very quickly. She couldn't take the twins constantly running around and fighting with each other. Grabbing a hanger, she threw it directly at the two of them but instead of hurting them, it became airborne knocking into the crystal chandelier, shattering it into a hundred pieces. "Oh, mom is going to be angry now!" screamed Marie. It served to get her brothers' attention and they ceased fighting and scampered upstairs to the bedroom, leaving their older sister to clean up a major mess.

A couple of weeks later, Marie was again put in charge of a Saturday night. Millie had extracted a promise from both boys that they would listen to their sister and behave. Shaking their heads in agreement, the parents left the three kids quietly seated in front of the television watching Ed Sullivan. "Click," went the front door. Marie got up to get a glass of soda but when she returned, Tony had put his hand on the footstool; the very one she was just sitting on. An argument ensued, whereupon Marie won back her place and plunked herself squarely back down on the stool. She heard a slight cracking sound and Tony let out a blood curdling scream; she had inadvertently sat on his thumb. Holding his hand up above his head, she could see it was bent all the way back and she ran to get ice. Somehow they got through the rest of the evening as her little brother let out intermittent whimpers of pain. The next morning, Millie took him to the emergency room where they splintered his thumb and told him to return in two weeks. A quick stop at the pharmacy for an ice-cream cone seemed to be the best cure.

The following Saturday night, Marie had to do double duty as her parents pranced out of the house for yet another party. Millie wagged her finger at the twins and reminded them to behave and listen to their older sister. That night a scary movie was playing and the boys were frightened. To distract himself, Tony went into the dining room and practiced walking on his hands around the huge table when his foot got caught underneath, and again there was a cracking sound: much louder than the sound of his thumb. Tony screamed with pain. Marie rushed in to see her brother sprawled out on the floor writhing in pain, this time he had broken his ankle. There was nothing for her to do but wrap her arm around his waist and drag him to the sofa. No one knew how to explain that mess. Back to the emergency room, the same doctor put a cast from Tony's ankle to the tip of his toe and then examined his thumb. "See the two of you in three weeks," the doctor laughed as he watched the little boy trying to figure out how to use the wooden crutch. He got another ice-cream cone, with words of warning from Millie that he needed to be a lot more careful. After hobbling home, Tony was so tired he fell asleep and was perfectly behaved the rest of the day.

Later that night, the familiar sound of footsteps grew louder as Joseph entered their bedroom. He took off his thick leather belt, snapped it in the air, and then beat Tony several times on his back. Joseph never uttered a single word, he just slapped his son until he shrieked with pain, and then he left the room. Lying in bed, Tony starred up at the ceiling praying for the day he could take out his revenge; it couldn't come soon enough. Robert, who had been spared, was also crying. He felt his brother's pain just as much as if had he been beaten.

Tony didn't have to be happy to play his guitar, in fact the deep sadness of the welts on his back spurred him to climb down the dimly lit basement steps and play music. Strumming the guitar, he picked at the strings until he created a melody that would reflect his pain from his father's abuse: for Tony, music could respond to all human emotions and feelings. It took the ravages of an angry father to keep him riveted in the basement for hours, playing and singing a proper tribute to his pain. There was no banging on the drums from his twin, who had disappeared into the yard and was busy constructing a snowman.

"Stop it, no it's okay, I don't want the train set, please don't hit me anymore. Please stop, stop!" screamed Tony in the middle of a nightmare.

Robert shook him awake and turned to his brother, "Another nightmare? The same one? Go back to sleep and stop screaming, this is the second time this week you woke me up."

He was sweating and trembling from the nightmare. Tony closed his eyes and returned to sleep, but the images were already ingrained in his mind. The slaps to his temple, the belt undone from his father's pants, whipping him furiously on his bottom, the ceramic dish placed on top of his head. All these punishments simply for asking for a train set. He vowed he would never ask his father for anything ever again. It wasn't even the beatings that were so intolerable it was the fear of the beatings: the unexpected turn in his dad's mood, never knowing when he would put forth his diatribe.

In the morning the boys dressed quickly and arrived hungry at the breakfast table. It was Sunday, the one day of the week their dad was home and the four were seated together. The box of cereal was next to his dad, the kind Tony loved to eat. Robert got up and took out the Sugar Pops, they were much more to his liking, but that box of Cheerios stood as if it were three miles down the road, stationed next to his dad's elbow. For the longest time he sat and stared at the box, unable to ask his father for the cereal, unable to ask him for anything; the words just wouldn't come out of his mouth. Finally, he pushed himself, but instead of a clear sentence, he stuttered until his father finally passed him the cereal. He filled up his bowl and he sat mute until he was full and then disappeared into his room. Robert ran outside to play while Tony stayed in the bedroom trying to figure out what had happened that made his voice change.

Later they prepared for church; their mom dropped them off at Sunday school class while she attended services. Saying the prayers and singing the psalms, Tony was just fine. He felt safe and at peace. The teacher asked a question and Tony, who had read the short passage, shot up his hand in the air first, but when he began to speak the stuttering had returned. Embarrassed, the answer finally came out, but at a high cost to his young ego. This new thing with his voice scared him; he didn't understand where it was coming from or how to undo it.

"Boys clean up your room and come down to dinner," requested their mom. Lethargic, Tony moped around, too listless to move. The door to their bedroom slammed open and their father stood there with a belt in his hand slapping it against his wrist.

"You heard what your mom said, now get up and clean your room." Before Tony could make a move, he felt the belt slicing into his forearm, and then his back, and onto the other arm. When his father was finished, both arms were filled with red puckered welts, and he was in hysterical tears. He wanted to run and hide, but instead, he took out a long sleeved shirt to hide the damage from his mother. That night, and the night after that, the nightmares continued, and his stuttering escalated from an acute, to a chronic problem.

After weeks of enduring the pain and humiliation, Millie finally took him to a speech therapist who was all too familiar with the problem. She cleared up Tony's stuttering, but it was through surreptitious psychological insight. She got him to talk out his problems and share his insecurities with someone he could completely trust. The culture of the times accepted parental beating, a legacy handed down from the immigrant homeland, but when kids like Tony ended up with stutters, it was time to rethink those barbaric behaviors. Although the beatings continued, Tony was able to cope with the affects, circumventing his father at all costs. If he needed anything, it was his mother he turned to. The therapist gave him the strength and courage to put up with the abuse, and helped him change his thinking. It was decades later that Tony was able to forgive his father. The beatings had taken a heavy toll on his mind and self-esteem, leaving him with deep seeded feelings of insecurity that would take him years to understand, and longer to overcome. The beatings were senseless, taking a strap to a preschooler for not cleaning up a bedroom? The punishment didn't fit the crime. In later years, Tony was able to figure out that it wasn't he who instigated the problem: it was the insecurities of his father transferred onto his kids.

Joseph, too, was a child who was punished physically, and he suffered his own nightmares. He relived the horrors of being tied up in a dark, dank basement for hours, or thrown in a tiny overheated closet for an afternoon. Whether Joseph rendered those punishments right or wrong, he thought that was the way a father raised his sons. In spite of his deeply seeded emotional pain, it was all he knew, and he never questioned the authority of his parents, back then you took the abuse. With a third grade education, he didn't have the intellectual skills needed to understand how he was wrongfully treated, and how he should treat his own children. Yanked out of school before the age of ten, all he understood was working and putting food on the table.

Wounds so deep and so cruel, were cemented in his psyche, simmering from early childhood to adulthood. One thing was for sure, Tony would break that link set from his father's cultural legacy; beating kids was not acceptable in any shape, kind, or way. If he got the chance to be a parent, he was damn sure he would never perpetuate the harshness of his childhood.

Most of the happy memories were crafted by their mother, who celebrated the holidays with a fervent passion. Her three sisters lived within a couple of blocks from each other and took turns making the Thanksgiving and Christmas' feasts. Tradition was a big thing at the Sacca household. Christmas Eve they bundled up and headed to the grandparent's home to celebrate the Seven Fishes dinner. Their grandfather would play the accordion and Millie would always accompany him with the spoons: an Italian tradition using tablespoons as a substitute for a drum set. After the presentation they would sit down to a huge, delicious, customary meal. The meal combined seven types of fish, prepared in at least seven different ways: they feasted on salad, soup, pasta, crab cakes, cod, smelts and an array of homemade pastries. Stuffed, the family would make the short walk home in the frigid evening air, in hopes of tiring the kids so they would sleep deeply. While Millie stood guard to make sure the three children were tucked into their beds, Joseph would put together a train set in the middle of the living room, decorate a huge evergreen tree, and set piles of toys at the base. Christmas morning would begin with present opening, a big breakfast, and then off to church for a short service. Millie would drop off the kids at the movie theatre with at least a half dozen of their cousins. They bought bags of popcorn and cups of sodas, to stave off their hunger until dinner. Afterwards the cousins would emerge from the movies, form one group and tour the neighborhood, singing carols for all of the neighbors. After making the rounds up and down the street, it was home for the family Christmas meal.

"One year in the midst of caroling, Tony crossed the street. It was dark, and he didn't look and neither did the oncoming car. We heard the screech of car brakes and saw Tony flying into the air. We all rushed across the street, but he just dusted himself off, got up off the ground, and continued singing with us," remembered Marie. "He was like a cat with nine lives, and it seemed as though he was using them up pretty quickly." Unperturbed, Tony continued on with his cousins, never giving the incident another thought, he was a tough kid, it was Christmas and nothing bad was going to happen to him.

It was those rare times when they family would come together, relax, drink, eat, and play music, that stamped pleasurable childhood memories into his mind, helping to cloak the evil memories. His mom gave him precious joyful thoughts he could take with him on his life's journey that would serve to temper all the horrific violent scenarios unleashed from his father. The three aunts, Yola, Rose, and Antoinette, each with kids of their own, were spectacular cooks, bringing with them the family secrets handed down through generations of Italian cooks.

The following year at Thanksgiving, Aunt Yola's house was immaculately set for twenty-four people as the sisters, spouses, and cousins streamed into her living room. While her husband liberally poured the crystal glasses full of Chianti, the kids ran around the backyard playing kickball and soccer. There were always two tables, one for the adults, set with fine china and extra wine glasses, and one for the kids, set with scraped melamine and plastic cups. The long mahogany dining table, covered in a cream colored laced cloth, was laden with both traditional American and Italian dishes. The turkey, golden brown, was stuffed with handmade sausages, and sat prodigiously in the center of the table while the aunts ladled out food: portions of lasagna, mashed potatoes smothered in garlic, roasted sweet potatoes, sautéed spinach, roasted peppers, and veal scaloppini dripping in white wine sauce. A memorable meal, and one that kept them full until the next day. Clearing away the plates, their mom offered up the twins' services to entertain the crowd, and a moment later, they were situated at the piano, singing one of the top cover songs. Taking a quick bow to a smattering of applause, they adjourned to the backyard and started up a kickball game. "My cousins were sick of us always entertaining, they hated the fact we were always in the spotlight. Maybe they were jealous, but they couldn't care less about our success," lamented Tony. "Our parents were proud of our accomplishments and put us on display whenever they could, but my cousins never cared about our talent; they were more interested in tossing a football."

It was Uncle Nick who settled family disputes when problems arose. He held court, making the decisions that kept the members of the Sacca family at peace with each other. He stepped into another yelling match between Robert and Ralph, and he forced the boys to shake hands and get over it.

When he heard the loud shouting, he hoisted himself up from the tapestry sofa and lumbered into the backyard. Tall, with a splash of gray threaded through his thick curly hair, he was a person to be reckoned with: or that was how he appeared when viewed from a child's perspective.

"So what if the twins could sing," said Nick, "You, Ralphie, will do great things in your life, and they may not be as annoying as your cousins' singing. So keep your head up, and stop the damn fighting! Remember when you were a little kid, and I would put you in the palm of my hand and hold you up the air? Well maybe I can't do that now, but I can put you in your place. Stop being so jealous, you'll show them all one day." For the moment, the fighting stopped and everyone got back to polishing off the cannolis and freshly fried zeppoles dredged in powdered sugar. Uncle Nick had made peace, the boys had listened. As the twins ate the last remnants of the desserts, they wondered why their own dad couldn't be a lot more like Uncle Nick, settling fights with words of wisdom.

As they walked home, the family laughed and joked about the evening, critiquing the food, the family, and the weather. It was tranquil, for once; it felt like they were just like any other family on the block. That night when Tony put his head down on the pillow, the bad dreams were replaced with the joy he felt singing with Robert. In the morning, he grabbed the Sugar Pops; he was beginning to learn to survive.

When the summer months rolled around, the children were the happiest, they loved their vacation. With the commencement of the season, the family would rise early every Sunday morning and drive down to Atlantic City, where they would spend the day with their extended family. Millie would pack an excessively large lunch, and they would spend the early part of the day on the beach, walking the boardwalk and playing in the waves of the warm Atlantic Ocean. Joe Sacca would strut with his identical twins on either side of him: the quintessential proud father. The boys were always dressed alike, and always beautifully dressed because Millie, with her tailoring background, made sure when papa Joe was showing off his sons, they were immaculately groomed. Later in the afternoon, they would gather at a boarding home where they rented the basement, and prepare a clambake or a large family picnic with up to one hundred people. Millie, who had spent many evenings sewing costumes, would put on a show with her sisters and cousins, entertaining the crowd with vaudeville style singing, dancing, and humorous skits. Watching their talented mother acting so professionally, inspired the three kids; they could be anything they put their minds to. The glint in Joe's eyes as his wife performed was rarely witnessed by the children. Later, when she returned to their table, he uncharacteristically kissed and hugged her in front of everyone. He loved her no doubt, and he loved who she was when she was performing.

"I'm hungry," said Robert, "shall we do it?" The twins snuck down to the kitchen, opened up the pantry closet, stuck two pieces of white bread underneath their fireman footed pajamas, and snuck back up to their beds. Munching on the wonderful bread, they fell fast asleep, full, happy, and content. Not so for Marie, who was plagued with a horrible nightmare. Too old to seek solace with her parents, she climbed into bed with Tony, sleeping on top of the sheet with her feet dangling in his face. "Marie? What are you doing in my bed?"

"I had a bad dream and I was afraid, do you mind?" she said. "I can't sleep underneath your sheets because I know they are filled with bread crumbs, but don't worry, I won't tell anyone. Go back to sleep." That night, the three slept soundly in the one room, safely and securely. The younger brothers realized that their older sister shared their same fears and anxieties.

A week later Marie, crawled back into Tony's bed. He took one look at her and screamed to leave the bedroom: her face was covered with chicken pox. Robert didn't care. He brought her soup, sat in her bedroom, played games, and listened to the radio while Tony stood outside in the hall. Ironically, it was Tony who ended up with a face full of chicken pox: not Robert.

"I have the outfits, boys," shouted Joe returning home from the butcher shop. "Please try them on, we want to make sure they fit you perfectly. As perfectly as you will sing this coming Saturday night." Dutifully, they grabbed the shopping bags and went upstairs to change. Joe kissed his wife and asked her to check on the length of the boys' pants to make sure they were just right. As she ran down the wooden steps, she couldn't help but radiate a broad smile as her two sons appeared in their comely tweed suits. The tailor had measured meticulously and the pants and sleeves were the perfect length.

"Oh," sighed their mom, "my beautiful young men. I know you will do these suits justice when you play this weekend. We can't wait." From the living room, Tony shoot a furtive glance at his sister and couldn't help but notice the pout on her face. Yet again he and Robert were the center of attention and although he felt badly for her, there was nothing he could do to make it better.

Later that night, after the dishes had been put away and the boys were dressed in pajamas, Tony knocked on his sister's door. "Can you keep a secret?" he asked. "I have to tell you, I am scared to do this performance. What if I sound bad, what if they don't like me, what if my voice cracks, or I trip on the stage or…." and he began to cry. She assured him everything would be okay, and she hugged him.

"I'll be there, just sing to me," she said.

Before Tony could take another breath, he and Robert were lined up back stage and preparing to go on. His mom and sister were seated in the audience and their dad was standing next to them waiting in the wings.

"Dad," Tony tentatively said, "I don't think I can go on. I'm scared, what if I goof up. I don't want to do this." Angry, his father grabbed him by the hand and took him to the men's room. He punched Tony in the face and threatened to do it again if he didn't perform.

"I've given you everything, now get out there and play your music, the crowd is waiting." Luckily the punch didn't draw blood, but his white face was swollen with red blotches. When you're twelve, you do what your parents say, so Tony walked slowly back stage, joined his brother and went on to perform that night. Tony wondered why his twin showed no signs of fright, they always felt the same, why tonight did his feelings overwhelm him and not seem to bother Robert a bit. He could only surmise that there was a certain safety net when you sat at the drums and never had to worry about strumming a sour note on the guitar, or singing off key. Still shaking from the sharp slap to his face, Tony turned his head and nodded, Robert nodded back, hit the sticks together and counted off - one, two, three - and banged on the drums. Tony picked up the beat, strummed the background score and began to sing the melody. There was no crack in his voice and when Robert joined him with the harmony, they were perfectly in tune. That night launched the career of the Sacca twins. As they took their bows, the small audience gave them a hefty round of applause. Tony winked at his sister as they left the stage; he knew she had his back that night.

When the crowd applauded for the Sacca twins, it wasn't for their handsome appearance, or even the fact they were twins, it was because they had talent. For the first time in a long time, Tony tossed away his resentment and began to embrace the future with his brother. He found he could be his own person, yet when teamed up with Robert, they could rule the world. He felt he needed his brother, and that they were truly a part of a team. That night was a turning point for Tony.

That night was different for Tony it was the first time he and his brother had been gawked at, paid attention to, and shown affection, for their talent, not for their startling good looks. His entire life, well before a tangible memory could imbed itself in his infancy, people were attracted to the twin boys. They were arrestingly beautiful as babies, and turned into gorgeous young men. What they lacked in height was more than made up for in their perfectly oval faces, deep round eyes, symmetrical chins, light olive complexions, and thick wavy hair. As a pair they were striking. From the moment their parents brought them home from the hospital and placed them in a perambulator, people were drawn to these two as if they were magnetized. Dressed alike, the parents proudly paraded their twins throughout the neighborhood, taking them everywhere. Convinced at birth these boys were destined for fame, their father designed every aspect of their lives.

On the drive home, the parents bestowed kudos on the boys, but Tony remained silent as his father raved about the music. The slap was too prevalent on his mind, and he couldn't understand why his father had been so cruel. He had to admit, without that slap he probably would never have garnered the courage to walk out on that stage. Maybe his father knew something he didn't, maybe his father believed in his talent so much he would go to any lengths to make him perform: maybe. Tony had a lot more to ponder before he went to sleep that night. Perhaps instead of hating his father for the punishment, he should have thanked him for instilling in him the courage to go on.

Joe Sacca and Carmella D'Angelo, Tony's parents, were captured by the associated press in 1943 when Joe laid a farewell kiss on Carmella before leaving to go overseas

Las Vegas Rocks ®

*Late 1800s – The discovery
of minerals, including
precious metals, leads to
the beginning of the mining
industry.*

Tony and Robert in South Philly

CHAPTER 2

It was time to broaden their horizons. The twins could sing but they needed a band, and with their parent's blessing, they gathered a friend and formed JT & The Twins. They practiced religiously in the basement; they spent hours rehearsing cover songs. Robert continued playing the drums and they formed a singing trio with JT. Together at the microphone, they had a stronger stage presence; three handsome young men who sounded like song birds. Several days a week, JT would drop off his book pack at home, grab a soda, and then join Tony and Robert in the basement. Sometimes, when the spring weather allowed, they would crack open the small windows near the ceiling in the basement, and the sounds of the band flooded the neighborhood. The more they practiced and the better they got, the more confident they became. As time progressed and they could play a cover song flawlessly, from start to finish, friends began to trickle down to the basement to listen. The parents didn't mind the intrusions: quite the contrary, the more friends, family and acquaintances who heard the group, the more their notoriety. The three boys were having fun, it was obvious from their smiles and the manner in which they attacked the music. They learned to sing and play with passion, they felt the music, as the rhythm and the melody flowed through their ears and onto the tips of their tongues and through their fingertips. Sweating and moving to the beat, they would learn to translate this passion to the audience.

"I was hot into being a Sacca twin, and I knew this was all I ever wanted to do. The three of us were committed to practicing every day. The basement became our home as we sang and danced: emulating the look of the Beatles." The group didn't have a manager, or even a band leader and no one who could act on their behalf to obtain gigs. It was one of the older boys a few houses over who had heard the sounds coming from the basement. Curious, he walked closer until he could hear the music clearly. Impressed, he knocked on the front door, and Millie ushered him down the basement steps. He obtained the group's first professional gig at a sorority house, a dream come true when you are at the inception of adolescence. He made the arrangements and handed the twins' parents the address.

Spring in Philadelphia can be beautiful. The roses and geraniums were budding, the bushes laden with heavy winter snows had morphed from brown to an emerald green, and the cries of newborn birds permeated the evening air. When they dropped off the preteens at the designated address, the parents sped away so as not to embarrass the boys. With a deep sense of pride and determination, they carried their instruments into the sorority house and set up at the foot of the massive brick fireplace. It was hard to concentrate when the room was filled with beautiful, fully developed college girls, all offering to assist the young musicians. Tony looked at the clock, nodded to Robert, and the performance began. Unlike the first time he performed, Tony was confident as he, Robert, and JT pushed through cover song after cover song. It was just like they rehearsed. There were no hitches, they sang and sounded just like they did when they were in the basement. With each song, the feelings of insecurity melted away as the small crowd gathered to dance and sing along with the band: raising their hands in the air and twisting to the left and the right. The trio put on a great show. Their harmonies and sweet voices took the college crowd by surprise. Turning to Robert, then back to the guitar player, Tony sensed everything was under control, and the best part was, he was having fun. Tony fell in love with performing that night, and that feeling would stay with him for decades to come. To celebrate their great success, the boys enjoyed their first glass of beer, which went right from their mouths to their heads. When the parents picked up the three little musicians, there was hell to pay when they smelled beer on their breaths.

Word spread quickly in the small neighborhood and soon the preteens, finally turning to teenagers, began booking gigs at a variety of places. At thirteen, the three boys weren't choosey where they played, as childhood labor laws were ignored. They picked up one-nighters at local bars, teen night clubs, school dances, VFW halls, and local pubs. If anyone would listen and paid them nominally, then off they went. It wasn't a startling fact that the more they played the better they got, and the more in demand they became. Performing in the smoke filled bars, it never struck their parents that perhaps that wasn't the best of situations, but at that time, when medical doctors touted the value of smoking cigarettes on the nightly network broadcasts, there was no need to worry: back then, everyone smoked. At least the bar owners had enough sense to make sure the young men weren't allowed any alcohol. Sodas were on the house.

The twins' parents, acting as chauffeurs, dropped the group off wherever they had a gig, never questioning the venue. By now, the musicians had become proficient at handling the instruments and setting up the sound systems. Trooping into the various locations, they quickly found the outlets, adding extension cords if necessary, set up the microphones and the drums, and ran wires across the stage for the guitars.

Marie often tagged along, watched the performances and supported her brothers. She had made a decision, instead of liking them, she would join them. She created a fan club and acted as their publicist. She put together lists of followers, printed up postcards announcing their gigs, and handed out buttons with the Sacca twins' names embossed. Marie recalled:

"I remember one time, we were at a high school auditorium and the twins were on stage performing to a packed audience, when several girls found out I was their sister. They started grabbing my sweater: they wanted a piece of the twins and they thought a few shreds of my sweater would give them a token. I was really scared and ran out. In my heart I was actually proud to be their sister and watch them climb the ladder to success."

"This place makes me a little nervous," admitted Tony as they walked past a couple dozen Harley Davidsons parked outside the rustic style pub. "Who picked this place?"

As they prepared the stage, he became more nervous because of the patrons seated at the tables. They had never played in a biker club, and rarely saw an authentic biker riding through their neighborhood. The men were huge, as wide as they were tall, sporting hair from the top of their head to their ankles. Their weather beaten black leather jackets, heavy jeans, and scuffed boots, reflected a tough life, hardened by crime and fighting. Tony looked down at his pristine white shirt and crisply pressed pants and suddenly felt like he didn't fit into the scene. He feared that if the bikers didn't like the music, they would be tossed out on their ears. Hesitantly, he nodded his head to begin the performance as a large beer swished down the length of the polished wooden bar and shattered on the floor.

"What the hell!" screamed the bar back as he grabbed a mop and dust pan. Another few bikers strolled in took seats at the bar and turned to the mock stage. Jibing each other in the ribs, they made fun of the three young rosy faces.

With the usual affirmative nod, the group began the first set with an upbeat song, singing and banging away as loud and as fast as they could. Not realizing there would be such hardhearted customers, Tony rethought the play list and removed the ballads, this wasn't a ballad crowd. Even at thirteen, he had learned how to read the audience well enough to know when to adapt at a moment's notice. As the evening wore on and the pub filled up, the musicians were sweating as they constantly pounded up tempo beats on their instruments. Much to their surprise the men stopped making fun of the young boys and began tapping their fingers to the music. Before they knew, it a few of the men even joined in the chorus. Turning to his brother Tony gave him a thumbs up: yep, they would make it through this rough and tumble night. "Yakety Yak," ended the set and the night as Tony mumbled to himself, "and don't come back." The four boys gathered their equipment in record time and stood in the cool damp evening air, waiting for their ride home. They smelled of smoke and beer; the once immaculately dressed crew looked motley. Tony was never so happy to see the family car pull up, and before the ten minute ride was over, the three young men had closed their eyes and were sound asleep. Looking at his sons, Joe could hardly sustain a loud roar, "Guess the crowd got the best of these guys tonight."

The following Saturday night, they were booked at the Aquarama, an aquarium that doubled as an entertainment center for teens on the weekends. Open to the city, the venue attracted top acts who were making their way up the ladder.

"I remember seeing the Supremes perform there and when we got the gig, we were really happy. It was always a packed house." Arriving an hour early, the three teens were dressed in white suits, black patent shoes, and had freshly tuned guitars. The stage was long and narrow, with a sturdy gray cement floor that had been highly polished so they could slide around and effortlessly glide through the dance steps. They set up the instruments, did a quick sound check, and at the stroke of eight o'clock, they began their first cover song. The dance floor was filled with teens dancing wildly to upbeat classical rock, and then the group cued the lighting director, slowing down the tempo, creating a romantic scenario for the young audience. The couples paired off, but in the back opposite corners, Robert noticed two separate clusters of guys snickering and glaring at some of the couples on the floor. Afraid of gangs who often showed up, the group quickly adjusted the tempo back up to a strong rock and roll beat. The two groups of guys dispersed, grabbed partners, returned to the dance floor and everything seemed copacetic.

During a ten minute break, the three singers refueled with sodas and potato chips, quickly rebounding for the last set of the night. After another three upbeat cover songs, they again tried a ballad, and as the kids paired up those two same sets of gang members returned to their predetermined corners. This time the snickers escalated. One of the guys walked onto the floor and tapped another guy on the shoulder, he wanted to dance with the girl wearing a red dress, and a yellow daisy clipped in her curly brown hair. Startled, she took a step back while the two guys began shoving each other. There was a slap to the head, and as Robert gazed up, he nudged his brother. The two groups of gang members had become one big bunch of brawling men, punching each other in the middle of the dance floor.

"Shit, we need to get out of here," said JT. No one even noticed when they grabbed their instruments, threw the pieces of the drum set together and ran to the back of the stage. Robert called his parents to come and get them as fast as they could. Robert stood shaking behind the curtain and peeped out, the entire dance floor was filled with screaming kids running to the exits, while the others were still duking it out. The security guards blew their whistles and began breaking up the fights. As the three young singers dove into the family van, the sound of sirens filled the air. Back up was on the way, and the jails would be filled that night with gang members who refused to lose a piece of their territory: and in this case it was all because of one innocent lovely brown skinned girl.

"Drive as fast as you can mom," said Robert. "Tonight the crowd was ugly."

"I don't even think they noticed us leaving," said Tony, who was still shaken from the scene. "Two weekends in a row with rough audiences. I think we need to find some safer venues."

"Yes," said JT, "Like maybe a convent!"

As the boys grew through their early teens, so did their appearance. They were extremely handsome and between their music and their looks, the girls flocked to the young men. It wasn't their fault they were blessed with gorgeous faces, and had great musical talent. The neighborhood boys went from jealousy to outright loathing of the Sacca twins, who seemed to have it all, including the girls. Late one afternoon when the twins got home from school, they tossed their books on the floor and were about to dive down the basement stairs, when they noticed a small clique of boys outside their front door. Tony recognized the classmates, who all belonged to the same gang. The twins didn't want trouble, but Tony didn't want to appear weak. He knew he had to face them, so he went into the kitchen and grabbed the largest butcher knife he could get his hands around. He opened up the front door and screamed at the kids to leave them alone and go home. They held their ground, but Tony would not be deterred. He took a big breath and then began running after the boys, brandishing the knife. Shocked, the group scattered instantly in every direction and never returned to bother the twins again. As he set the knife down on the kitchen counter, the young teen was shaking from his head to his toes. He had shown them a thing or two, he thought: but his mom, who had witnessed the scene, admonished her brave son and relegated the two down the basement for the rest of the school year. They practiced that day, and every day after that for the balance of the school year: and none of the boys who were at their house that day ever bothered the twins again.

For some of the neighbors it wasn't the fact that several pretty young teenage girls hung around the modest brick home, it was the perpetual sounds of the rehearsals, and the cacophony from learning how to be performers. Big Bob, who lived in the corner home, put an end to the complaining.

"Leave the kids alone," he said, "They have a right to practice their music, even if it doesn't always sound so good." Owner of the local bar, The Teddy Bear Lounge, Bob envisioned the twins entertaining in his little pub one day. The neighbors took his advice and stopped complaining.

Failure was never anything Tony would accept. At a very young age when his English teacher Mrs. Gentile threatened summer school, he thought he could fall back on his good looks and highly skilled negotiating powers, but in this one instance, she couldn't be dissuaded. Without so much as batting an eye, she scribbled an, "F" on his eleventh year report card. He had a reason which, in retrospect, lacked a preponderance of rationale as to why he had skipped her classes, never turning in the required homework. It had all boiled down to one sad state of affairs; racism. Between the Irish and Italians, a fomenting hatred boiled, often diffusing itself through gang fights. Tony had weightlifted, and learned to run the mile at a racer's pace, he would be ready to rumble if, and when the time arrived. During his sophomore year at high school, he found himself, along with several classmates, embroiled in those racial wars. Despite the fact there was bruising, an occasional broken arm, or concussion, there were never any deaths. "Kids didn't carry guns back then," noted Mrs. Gentile, "all those weapons were saved for the gangsters who were smart enough to keep them away from the young punks."

South Philly had its cross to bear in the spring of that year when a huge fight rampaged through the city streets in the middle of the St. Patrick's Day parade. Parents stood in horror as they witnessed their sons doing battle for their homeland, and it knocked some sense into their stubborn heads. Just what were they doing to cause such a stir in the once congenial neighborhoods? There was a sudden change of heart, and those battles were laid to rest.

The following fall, racism returned in the form of Black versus White, but this was where the twins drew the line. Neither one would take part in any of those useless fights, they had their careers and couldn't appear on a stage with a bloodied face, or a broken arm that could no longer clash the drums or strum the guitar. They tried to sit this one out, permanently.

Malcolm X, the fervent Black leader was assassinated, setting off a fuse of racial riots throughout the South Philly area, especially at the integrated high schools. It was 1965 and the boys were in their freshman year at high school. The only thing weighing on their minds was their next gig, and their next girlfriend. School was done for the day. Tony threw his backpack over his shoulder, heading home, and Robert went with a friend in another direction. As Tony walked through the corridors he heard a kid yell out, "Malcolm X is dead and now we are going to kill all the white guys." Before he could blink an eye, Tony was surrounded by twenty-five Black kids, most he had never seen:

"They began chasing me, and threatening me. All I could do was run, and run I did. I unstrapped my belt, and flung it in the air like a gladiator. The heavy metal buckle flew off the end of the belt and into the crowd of boys, hitting one of them in the face. I kept running and the threats kept coming until I reached the door to the parking lot, and pushed it open. At that very moment, I felt the tip of a knife hit my back, and then drop to the floor, I had missed being stabbed. Racing through the lot, I threw the backpack over the chain link fence and then leaped up and over, just in time to get away. I kept running until I reached the front door step of my home. Scared, I went up to my room and reran the scene over and over in my head. 'What did I have to do with Malcolm X's death? What was wrong with the world? Why did the Blacks hate the whites, and didn't they realize these violent scenes would make the whites hate the Blacks?' This was an awful time."

A week later the police were called to the high school. It was lunch and kids were milling around the yard waiting for the bell to ring for the afternoon sessions. In one corner, four guys were singing a cappella, and in another, the girls were practicing a cheerleading routine: all quite innocent, banal activities:

"I looked up and saw two hundred Black kids coming after us with knives, chains, bats, and belts. Using threatening language, they screamed they were going to do us in, and began beating up on the guys, but left the screaming girls alone. I guess they felt that all of the problems were caused by white men. I saw my friends get hit, beaten, but again I ran, scaling the fence and into safety of the city streets. The sound of police sirens, and ambulances rang out loudly in the air as mothers opened up their front doors to see what was going on. The race riots became official and I was terrified to go to class, as were most of my friends. How can you think and learn when you are worried about getting beat up at lunch time, after school, or for that matter, any time. By the grace of God, no one was killed, but then, no one had a gun, and perhaps that was the saving grace."

Skipping school became a routine for many kids, the threats were too frightening to face, the sounds of the chains rattling along the floor, and the slap of the bats was too potent a memory to dismiss.

Thanksgiving was traditionally a family day, except for the local high schools entertaining family and friends with a mid-morning football game. Catholic High versus Public High, the two teams played a decent, honest game, while on the sidelines, the Black and White teens held their own battle. One of the parents had noticed a kid walking to the edge of the turf with an unusual gait and intuitively sensed he was hiding a weapon. The tall, heavy set forty year old jumped from the stands and accosted the kid: grabbed his pant leg and extracted an axe. Instead of admonishing the punkie teen, he took away the weapon, remonstrating him in front of hundreds of people. Mortified, the rebellious kid ran away and never returned. Although a tragedy had been averted that day, it did little to dampen prejudice. In the public schools, boys were afraid to use the bathrooms, or eat in the wrong place in the lunchroom. Mrs. Gentile said,

"One day I was looking out my fourth floor window and saw one of my students holding out a car antenna as six other boys encircled him. He took the antenna using it as a weapon like a lion tamer, and thrust it into their faces. As I stood there helplessly watching, within three minutes, that brave student had scared off all those other boys. Neither Tony nor Robert could imagine themselves so involved with fighting and racial strife, they saw themselves only one way, as entertainers. When the young students sat in my classroom, I made them feel safe and it was through this tight sense of security, I was able to pull out the best in them. We read plays and I encouraged them to delve into the roles becoming actors. Some were great, especially the twins. Perhaps that was what I remembered the most, they both had so much innate talent. They didn't see the point of all this interracial strife"

Every Saturday morning, the three Sacca kids took turns scrubbing the front porch, and when it was pristine, they would sit on their favorite step, contemplating the world, or watching the other kids wash down their porches. It was a self-contained community, and everything they wanted or needed was within walking distance. When the sun faded, the older boys would meet at the street corners and sing a cappella until their parents returned from their dates and rounded them up. Music was everywhere: in the streets, the bars, on the radio, and thanks to Dick Clark, television had become the one soothing ingredient that helped to rebuild the city of Brotherly Love.

"Hey boys, you about ready?" asked their dad as he peeked behind the front door. "Even though you're playing down the street, we still have to load all your instruments into the car, so let's get a move on." Joe grabbed his tweed jacket while the boys piled into the van. They picked up JT, and drove two short blocks to a neighborhood pub. Their dad grabbed a seat at the bar and ordered a beer and a round for the other people seated next to him. They all knew each other and were there to have a drink, relax, and support the local talent. Proud of his sons, Joe couldn't do enough to fulfill their dreams, which in fact were his own. If buying beers for the crowd meant another few gigs at the pub, then his money would have been well spent. After the first set, he drove home, they were hosting a card party and his hand was needed.

"Call me when you're ready," he yelled to the boys, taking care not to kiss them in front of an audience, that wouldn't seem terribly professional. Oh how he loved his sons, and yet Marie, was the star in his life. She was smart, beautiful and in his heart he knew she would always keep the family together and the boys in check. It was as if she were the alter ego of the next generation. He plunged the key into the ignition, smiling; he had done a good job raising his family. If he died the next day, he knew they would survive.

The three boys continued to rehearse and play local gigs throughout Philadelphia. However, money was tight at home, and Tony took an afterschool job stocking the shelves at a small family owned grocery store. The pittance they earned playing in the bars, even with cash tips tossed their way, wasn't enough to sustain the household.

"Hi, first day on the job? Don't be nervous, the old man who owns the store is a friend of my dad's, so just listen to what he says and it will be fine," advised John as the two began stocking the shelves from the busy weekend sales. "I'm John Colarelli, and I know you are Tony because I hear all about you from the kids at school." As Tony took cues from his new friend, he mastered the art of stocking shelves, mopping floors, cleaning out refrigerators, and delivering groceries. Although it was a physically grinding job, at least there was a tip when he handed over the packages to the stay at home mothers. Tuesday afternoon, heads turned as Tony walked into the store singing the Beatles, "A Hard Day's Night." Stretching out his arms, he took in the grocery store performing as if he were in a Broadway theatre, "I should be sleeping like a log." Splitting open a box of canned beans, he finished the rendition to a smattering of applause of a few surprised shoppers and his friend John.

"I think that song just about sums up our job," he laughed as he slicked back his thick black hair.

The two boys had become close friends and John began accompanying the twins on their gigs acting as an unpaid stage hand. Although he envied their talent, he was never jealous except when it came to Tony's hair; Tony was blessed with thick black waves, while John's straight hair wavered in the wind with a cowlick so stubborn even the heaviest of creams would never tame its peak. He felt like a part of his head was always standing at attention. In reverse from the grocery store training, Tony led the way on their performances, while John took his commands. His friend didn't mind not getting paid; he was having way too much fun, especially after the shows on the weekends when they didn't have to get up early for school. Robert and Tony knew how to party and there was always a bevy of cute girls who followed their every move.

Between school, work and music, Tony barely had time to breathe; homework was last on the list each night as he flopped into bed wiped out from the long day. This exhaustive routine continued through the rest of his high school year. South Philly was a tough place, even at a young age you had to learn to make your own way; there was great pressure to keep up with your peers. If your friend had a new transistor, then you went out of your way to make sure you had one. Life was all about earning a living, the parents never had a pot to piss in, so the kids would pitch in and help make ends meet. Working at twelve was typical in the Italian section: as were oversized families.

Tony needed a change, some recognition, a chance to become well known and make more money. One day he opened up the, "Philadelphia Review Journal" and spied an advertisement; he thought he saw the light at the end of the tunnel. "Send in your photo and try out for the title as the best looking kid in Philadelphia."

"What do I have to lose," thought Tony, as he selected the best photo from a pile his mom kept in a drawer next to the bed. Holding up the shiny black and white head shot, he placed it inside an envelope, along with the application and secretly mailed it to the modeling agency. He never gave it another thought.

"Tony," yelled his mom, "There is a letter for you, come down and open it."

As he began to read, his eyes dilated and his heart began to churn. The modeling agency had reviewed his submission, and he had been selected as one of the finalists for the contest. He threw his arms around his mother, jubilant; he couldn't believe he had a chance at the contest. As he celebrated the moment, he felt a pang of guilt while Robert looked on. Should he have shared this with his brother, well, maybe, but he was his own person, and his brother could have also applied. Tony's reality set in, he was insecure, he needed someone else, other than his family, to tell him he was good looking, that he was talented, and that he was a worthy, valuable human being. This contest would help him carve out his own identity, and perhaps diminish his insecurities. It was scheduled for the following month and he could hardly wait. In preparation, he zealously practiced his singing and guitar playing, he got a new haircut, and his mom had the tailor make him (and of course Robert) new white suits.

"You look so handsome, my Tony," whispered his mom so Robert wouldn't hear. He stood in front of the mirror, anxiously turning around as he critically took in his physique, hoping he would stand up to the other contestants. Tony kissed his mom, grabbed his guitar, and took the bus downtown, riddled with anxiety and insecurity as it neared the store front. Vacillating, he almost got off the bus and went home, but then he remembered the slap his dad had given him when he was too scared to perform. He would do this, he would be brave and he would show them all how talented he was. He walked confidently into the studio where he saw eleven other teens standing around, who were also vying for the title. He quickly lost his confidence and began slinking back to his insecure self. Smiling, the teens introduced each other and then an assistant met with them and provided direction. They marched behind the young instructor, and pinned numbers on their jackets. As she explained the procedures, it wasn't unlike beauty pageants his mom had forced them to watch on television. First, they simply paraded in front of the judges, gave their names, ages, and a sentence or two about their backgrounds.

"I got this," thought Tony. The second round they would show off their talent, and the final round they would answer questions from the judges.

"Don't worry," joked the instructor, "There isn't a swimsuit contest." Twelve young voices broke into laughter. They were each given a number in the line-up and would keep that position until the end. Tony was second to the last to go, which gave him plenty of time to calm his nerves and to study the competition.

His hands started to moisten as he watched the contestants give their names and background. He was so nervous, he hated himself for trying out; but, he thought, if those other eleven guys could do this, then so could he. As his internal pep talk became harsher, it was his turn at the microphone. He knew how to use a microphone, he used one every single weekend, he would pretend he was at a gig and everyone was drinking beer and ignoring the band. With composure, he stated his name, age and gave the name of his band and of course talked about his twin brother. With a smattering of applause, he walked off and began contemplating the next round. He picked up the guitar, slung it around his neck, and rehearsed the song silently, all the while watching the other boys. He had this. None of the others were as talented as he was, he knew he could out sing any of them, but then he reminded himself that it was a beauty contest, and the best looking face was the winner.

He sang a romantic ballad. Closing his eyes he felt the music from his toes to the top of his head and through his heart. When he was done, he looked up and the tiny audience was on their feet. A smile slowly crossed his lips as he took the requisite bow and thanked the audience. Slowly walking off the stage, he knew he had them in the palm of his hand. The power of his voice had brought the audience to its feet and he felt on top of the world. He didn't have to win the contest, had already won what he wanted. In that moment, he understood the power a performer can have over the audience, and he relished it.

The instructor lined up the boys for the final round of questioning by the judges. Again, they gave their names: then they waited for the question, and when the bell went off, they had to cease talking.

"Who is the most important person in your life" asked the judges. Tony didn't even hesitate or draw a nervous breath: he talked about his twin brother and their close relationship. An impeccable, heartfelt response, he confidently left the stage, waiting in the wings.

"May we have the final four contestants," asked the master of ceremonies. Taking the envelope from the first judge, she read off the names, and Tony was among the finalists. Shocked, he took his place with the other three teens and waited for the next round. They were to walk around the stage, as if they were modeling, provide their name, and then state why they wanted to win the contest. This time Tony didn't have the luxury of watching the other contestants; he would have to wing it on his own. Strutting to an upbeat tempo, he walked across the stage, did a quick pivot, put his hands on his hips and sashayed to the microphone.

"I love this town, and I would be proud to be the most handsome face in the city of brotherly love," Tony stated. Standing at the edge of the stage, the four teens waited for the results. When he was not the first runner up, he knew he had lost, but then, with a hush and a dramatic pause by the announcer, he heard his name called. Tony Sacca had won the contest. He had the most beautiful face in the city. Handing him a huge bouquet of red roses, he humbly took the obligatory winner's walk through the crowd, and returned back to center stage. The eleven boys, shook hands, hugged, and congratulated him for winning.

Tony collected his guitar and boarded the bus to his grandmother's home. Proudly carrying the bouquet of flowers and trophy, he presented them to his astonished mother. She kissed him and showered Tony with praise and lots of attention. Robert, keenly observing the scene, was livid and quite jealous, so much so that he began choking his brother. The grandmother had to separate the two and then scolded Robert for his poor behavior. Before the night ended, Robert apologized and they shook hands and made up.

"Oh," thought their mother, "when they were babies they fought over toys, now as they get older, they are still fighting. When will it ever end?" She knew the answer, when you have twins, the fighting never stops.

To make matters worse between the twins, the next evening their mom excitedly brought two papers to the dinner table which depicted Tony, beautifully dressed in his white suit, announcing he had won the Most Beautiful Face contest in Philadelphia. Even their father was uncommonly happy over the contest. "Most handsome face in the city?" he said as he kissed Tony's forehead, "What a surprise, who would have thought?"

That reopened his wound from the day before and Robert was seething with jealousy, but at least he held his temper and didn't smack his brother in the presence of both parents.

When he observed the anger in Robert's eyes, Tony felt compelled to make this up to him; there must be something he could do as a peace offering. Finally, he came up with the perfect solution; being twins sometimes had its own unique advantage.

"A speeding ticket," yelled their father as he chastised Robert for taking the family car and then driving through the streets carelessly. Holding the ticket in his hand, he made Robert promise to repay him and diligently spend the next four Saturday afternoons licking his wounds at traffic school. Tony took Robert aside and told him he would be happy to help him out, and for the following two Saturdays, he sat in his brother's place, diligently listening to the instructor discuss the perils of bad driving. The only saving grace was the two young girls who gave him lots of attention at the breaks.

With the end of the school year around the corner and a long hot summer ahead, the twins, along with JT, landed the perfect gig: playing at the swim club.

"John," said Tony as he tossed some oranges from the box into the produce case, "How would you like to hang around with us at the swim club for the summer? I promise there will be more babes than you can handle."

"Ya, sure, but I'm kind of over the babes, I actually think at the end of this year I'm going to get married," said John.

"Are you crazy? You will barely be eighteen, and there is a world of uncharted territory out there. How could you tie yourself down so early? I think you are crazy. You must really love this girl."

When John didn't answer as he continued to pick up heads of broccoli and toss them haphazardly into the empty bin, Tony realized his friend was probably in love, and nothing he could say or try to do would sway him.

"Oh hell, come to the club, help us out, and if you get lucky, you can swim in the pool at the end of the day when it's closed." Extracting a smile from his closet friend, Tony dropped the subject.

The contract covered Memorial Day through Labor Day, with no days off in between, save for the occasional rain out. They were set, a summer of fulltime work, surrounded by bikini clad girls, fresh air, and plenty of junk food at the concession stand. The private club limited the membership to two thousand, that way everyone would have a chance to cool off in the huge swimming pool, with two other, smaller pools for the babies and preschoolers. Late every afternoon, the pool emptied so the older folks and aspiring athletes could get in an hour of uninterrupted swim. The life guards would pull out a series of ropes creating lanes superimposed over the water, a horn would sound and off they would race at a tiring pace, up and back, for an hour. It all seemed so futile as Tony and Robert looked on, there had to be something else better to do than watch these people sprint from end to end. Distraction came in many forms at the club, but for the twins, it was in the form of an endless parade of girls: ladies playing cards, reading, knitting, eating, or attending to their infants.

Their play sets began after lunch, ending around eight, but on Friday and Saturday nights, they played until ten. A half hour set and they were off for fifteen minutes with a full free hour for dinner between five and six: which translated into an hour for sex. The problem was there were few places to indulge their loins around the openness of the club. Sleuthful, they quickly discovered places to satisfy their carnal hankerings: a broom closet, a car parked at the back of the crowded lot, in the kitchen pantry, the storage garage at the back of the pool, or sometimes at a nearby home.

The night before, Tony had met one hot babe who was instantly drawn to his good looks and singing voice. Stuck with a cousin visiting from out of town, she suggested that Tony come over the next afternoon. When most of the girl's family, including her cousin, was in church, Tony crawled up the ledge of a house, hopped into the branches of an eighty year old oak tree, and through the window of a waiting young girl. She was standing in a red dotted bikini. It was passion at first sight as they began to kiss madly. Suddenly the familiar sound of the electric garage door opening dampened the moment: she pushed Tony back out the window.

"My father will kill you if he finds you in my room." He jumped back into the tree, suspended twenty feet in the air while he waited for her to whisper it was all clear. He made it down to the grass but snagged his shirt on a lower limb, ripping off half the buttons. He ran back to the club. He was just in time. Robert looked at him and laughed,

"Bet you didn't get any from the looks of your shirt." Making the best of it, Tony undid the rest of the buttons and played as many Caribbean sounds as their repertoire allowed, he was in the moment, they had become a reggae band, and he looked just the part! He couldn't fool John either, who was forever warning him about having too many girls at one time,

"It will come back to bite you in the ass," he promised. For the moment that prophecy had yet to come true, and he continued on his lascivious pattern until the stroke of six o'clock on Labor Day. The bikinis disappeared and senior year was about to commence, what's next hadn't crossed the twin's minds, but whatever it would be, they were sure it was playing, singing and performing.

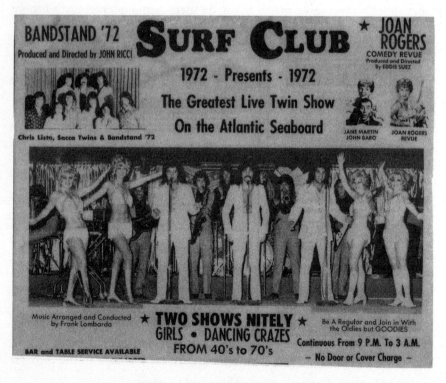

A newspaper ad promoting Bandstand 72 at the legendary Surf Club in Wildwood, New Jersey

*Tony and Robert as Bebo and Babet, two
characters that were a part of their act*

Las Vegas Rocks ®

*1844 – John C. Fremont
arrived in Las Vegas and
kept a journal describing
two springs he found. These
writings were very popular
and lured many individuals
to the area.*

Robert and Tony on graduation day with
Joe, Millie, and Marie

CHAPTER 3

The proud parents dabbed at their eyes as the twins strutted across the stage to accept their high school diplomas. They both rejected college in lieu of pursuing their performing career, but they first had to answer to Uncle Sam. In 1969 the two walked into the Marine Corps and enlisted as reservists. An anomaly, the boys were allowed to serve together, and after passing the physical were shipped off to Parris Island, South Carolina. There was no doubt, the Sacca household became eerily quiet as the boys packed their bags and boarded the bus to an unknown future. They hugged their parents and sister good bye. All of their lives would change forever.

"What I didn't realize at the time when I signed the contract with the service, was that I was signing away my rights and becoming an entity of the government. When you are a Marine, you become a Marine for life and it is

part of you until you die. Their motto was, 'attention to detail,' which I guess boils down to watching the little things because in the end those are the things that could save your life, or set the standards for a way of life. I think the hardest part was no longer holding my own fate: it was held by the hands of others, and my very survival was dependent upon strangers. I was surrendering my personal identity. As a twin, already lacking a complete identity, by joining the military, my sense of self became more diffused, until I was worried, I would never get it back."

"What do you think we will have to do?" asked Robert nervously as he looked at several other young men seated on the bus.

"Just be patient," advised Tony. "Remember, we are only in for six months and then after that we will be free as birds. I'm not happy about being here, but it beats being drafted and having to serve for two or three years. We'll be fine. They promised to keep us together."

"Yeah, together peeling potatoes for six months."

Early the next morning they arrived at Parris Island, groggy from the long bus ride. As they shielded their eyes from the bright sunshine, the sticky, humid air announced they were in the Deep South, at the home of the Marine Corps installation: the training site for enlisted men. They grabbed their bags and anxiously waited for the instructors to give the first commands. For Tony and Robert, they would be, until the day they left, in culture shock. They were so ingrained with a sense of freedom and independence; although their parents set some limits, for teens, they were allowed great leverage. After all, they were musicians.

"One of the most life changing experiences was being herded off by the drill instructor with the demeanor of complete intimidation. One could only image what it was like to go from being an individual to becoming a Marine in time of war."

Learning to stand at attention, they dutifully followed the platoon leader to the barracks, then gathered their uniforms, and within ten minutes were back in line for their initial training. The twins had a lot to learn when it came to getting dressed in a hurry. As performers they spent hours preening in front of the mirror, but in the military, they were lucky to have five minutes.

"My hair," said Robert quietly to Tony, "What about my hair? How is it going to look after wearing this cap all day?"

Tony just looked at him and laughed, "That will be the worst part of basic training. On the first day you are brought to the barber and your head is shaved down to the skin, very traumatic to say the least, it was as if they are erasing our individualism and putting us all on the same plateau: we are all the same, all part of the whole."

After a week using the issued deodorant soap, Tony broke out in a rash from head to toe; his body was used to Ivory soap. This was super embarrassing, he had to ask for a different soap and this could only be done in front of his bunkmates. At reveille, the next morning, in front of his entire platoon, he asked to speak, but averted the officer's eyes,

"Sir, the private can't use the soap, sir, may I please use Ivory soap, please, sir." Boy did that take a lot of nerve, but his entire body was filled with a rash, and if his drill instructor looked closely, he would see the dire need. While the rest of platoon was laughing, the officer became benevolent, and allowed Tony's wish. Beads of perspiration boiled up underneath his cap, this was the most difficult request he had ever made: probably served him right for making fun of Robert's hair. He became personified as a pansy, and that would be a hard feat to live down, but he found a way out.

For years when he was stuck in hotel rooms, often with no exercise room, he religiously did push-ups: two hundred on any given morning had become routine. So when the Marine Corp held their physical training competition, Tony was first in line for the push-ups. One man counted while he grunted through until he completed two-hundred-sixty-five, a base record. After that, the pansy term was dropped, replaced with the king of push-ups, his buddies no longer considered him a weakling, he was just as tough as the taller heftier guys, but in a quieter way. Redeemed for using Ivory soap, some of the other men made the same request.

They survived the eight week inauguration, even in spite of themselves, and they were better young men for it. They learned the art of discipline, getting dressed in a hurry, learning to care for others, getting up before dawn, and paying stringent attention to orders. The men in the platoon were handed their orders; the twins would be continuing onto Camp Geiger, North Carolina, where they would spend the next twelve weeks learning what it is like to do battle outdoors, in all sorts of weather conditions. Maneuvers didn't stop because it was hot as hell, or they were being pelted by rain; they ran, shot, and took orders every single day. Following infantry training, the twins were transferred to their given MOS, which was to acquire the fine art of driving military trucks.

"Not such a bad thing to know," said Tony. "At least it's not peeling potatoes for the next few months."

A dozen men boarded a bus, and off they headed to complete their military training at Camp Geiger, part of the Marine Corps Camp Lejeune. Over 20,000 recruits per year trained at the base, in the middle of agricultural fields surrounded by thick evergreens and magnolia trees and acres of emerald green grass.

"I miss mom and sis," said Robert sullenly. "And dad's cooking on Sunday."

"You know what I miss? I miss all the girls. I haven't touched a girl since we have left home. Do you think anyone in the Marine Corps has sex?" bemoaned Tony. Taking a seat in the middle of the bus, Robert started humming a song and Tony jumped in. The brothers hadn't given up their singing; they just had to give up the paying audiences. They sang in the shower, at lunchtime, in the barracks at night, and on the weekends in the mess hall. Everyone who knew the twins knew that they had great voices, and enjoyed the entertainment. They applauded loudly whenever they sang.

"It's so sticky here," said Tony, "I haven't been cool since we left Philadelphia. Brother, you gave me such a hard time when I won that beauty contest, just look at me now, look at my hair! I swear it will never be the same after months covered up with these awful caps." Standing at attention the small band of recruits followed the drill sergeant to a covered area where there were hundreds of trucks in varying sizes, parked in perfectly straight lines.

"Ah," sighed the sergeant, "I see we have a new group of drivers." The new transfers stood still as the leader eyed them up and down and then blinked his eyes twice when he saw the twins. "What do we have here gentleman?' as he scrutinized their name tags.

"Twins sir," responded the brothers.

"In all my years in the military, you're the first set of twins I have ever trained. Now don't pull any monkey business with me."

"No sir," they answered.

After that moment, their trainer was kind and patient. One day, as the dozen men were going through maneuvers, the trainer came over to the twins and told him he felt like they were lucky charms.

"My wife is pregnant, and I think training you might just bring me luck. I think my wife may be having twins." Fortunately, the boys put in their four months and were transferred out of the camp before his wife gave birth.

"What do you think would have happened to us if his wife didn't have twins?" asked Robert. "Am I glad they shipped us out!"

When the twins received their final three week orders, they knew the sergeant must have had a say in the matter, as they were shipped home to Philly, and spent the last three weeks driving five ton trucks throughout the city.

Millie heard them racing up the steps like a herd of buffalo: they opened the front door. Her eyes teared up when she walked down the stairs and saw her sons standing at the base of the steps.

"Oh my boys, I am so happy to see you home and safe. Just look at you, so handsome, and so thin," said their mom as she took their hands and lead them into the kitchen. She fixed them two filly steak sandwiches, which they ate with gusto as she peppered them with questions. There was no doubt they were happy to be home and back to their friends and their music. If nothing else, the military had taught them the importance to sticking to the rules and disciplining their minds.

After a fight, Robert got first dibs on the phone and called his friends while Tony canvassed the neighborhood searching for his old buddies. Six months away from home: at eighteen it seemed like an eternity. He walked into the coffee shop and bumped into a couple of old girlfriends, now holding hands with new boyfriends. That didn't stop the girls from smothering Tony with hugs and kisses, and the guys offering perfunctory handshakes. Tony smiled as he answered their questions and told them he would be busy putting together a band.

"Come listen to us practice," he said as he waved good bye. Now all he needed was a band. He climbed up the back steps, grabbed the phone out of Robert's hand, and began making calls to friends in hopes of creating a new band. Then he sprinted down the basement steps and began his career again.

The guitar had gathered a layer of dust, waiting patiently in the corner of the room. When he strummed the taut strings, he realized it was sorely out of tune and in need of a cleaning. Lovingly, Tony resurrected the instrument. He fingered a G chord and his ears told him it was finally in tune. Tony dropped the needle on a pile of vinyl 45's and began singing and singing. Not much later, a second set of footsteps came thundering down the steps. Robert wiped off the drums, picked up the sticks and accompanied his brother. The next two days, they practiced continually. They cracked open the basement window and the familiar sounds of the Sacca brothers permeated the air: their friends were drawn to the sounds.

They were like the Pied Piper, enticing a crowd with their intoxicating music. The teens returned to the house, some stayed in the backyard while others walked down the steps to watch the boys practice.

"It's time to get a real job," yelled their father at the dinner table. "You two have been home for a couple of weeks just fooling around, now you need to pull up your boot straps and get to work."

"But dad, we are busy trying to put together a band," they pleaded. He raised his hands in the air and said,

"I don't want to hear it. Get a job!" And that was the edict: set over a plate of meatloaf and creamy mashed potatoes. The next morning, Tony put on one of his suits, took the newspaper and began applying for jobs. The corner bank had just lost an employee due to pregnancy, and freshly out of the military service, Tony looked like a good prospect. He was hired fulltime as a bank teller. However, that didn't mean he was giving up on his dream.

"I want us to be front men for a band," Tony explained to his brother. "What makes us so different from all the other groups is that we're twins, and we should show that off when we perform. That is how we will make a name for ourselves. We sound as good as anyone, but as twins, standing together at the microphone, we will be remembered." That was one fight the boys didn't have, since Robert agreed wholeheartedly. They locating a drummer, bass guitarist, and a keyboard player, and initially they named themselves "Double Exposure." Later, they changed the name to "Gemini," after the astrological twins sign. For the next three years they performed throughout the Philadelphia area, playing at any venue that would give them a shot. It didn't take too much time before they started drawing in the crowds. Older, and even more handsome, when the twins stood center stage, the girls became instantly infatuated and the boys just loved the sounds of their music. The band played cover songs spun by the deejays, so the young audience was able to sing and dance along to the tunes. Whenever there was a dance floor it was always filled the nights, "Gemini" was in the house. The group became so popular they booked gigs seven days a week, allowing Tony to quit his mundane clerk job at the bank.

Hallelujah!

They kept busy because Ed Tully, Marie's husband, knew how to book gigs and manage the business. Joseph built them a touring bus, retrofitted with all the luxuries of a real Greyhound: complete with a small refrigerator and cots for sleeping. When they turned the magic eighteen they became of age to share a beer with their fans at the end of the performances. Ed drove them to gigs in Pennsylvania, Wisconsin, through Canada, and then South through Alabama. They were gone for over two months, during which time Marie learned how to become independent and proficient at her computer job. She knew if the twins were successful, then her husband would also be successful, so she suffered with the loneliness waiting for his return. With the knowledge she now had for using computers, she learned how to publicize upcoming events, expand the fan club, and help make their gigs successful.

"It was a family thing, each of us in our own way, supported the boys. We had faith they would make it big, it was just a matter of time. When Ed decided to become their road manager, it was because he knew they had the talent, the drive and the staying power to last in the craziness of show business."

In spite of the fact that Ed was an expert at getting gigs, each city and venue was different. They had never toured in some of these small, obscure towns and didn't know what the audiences wanted.

"When you are singing on the stage, you are hoping you get accepted. We were just getting started and people didn't know us, nor did they know what to expect. It was the unknown that created stage fright and a feeling of insecurity," admitted Tony. So it was, when they walked onto a small stage in a Quebec nightclub. Halfway through their first set, they were booed, and told to go home to America; they wanted to hear the cover songs from England, not America. Disheartened, they weren't about to stay and have bottles thrown at them so, Ed collected the cash and they hastily departed.

"Sorry about that guys," said their road manager, "I'm sure tomorrow night will be much better, we will be back on American soil." Sullen, the twins moped on the bus, while the musicians tried to cheer them up with their own horror stories of being booed off the stage. They told how beer cans and plastic sodas were strategically lobbed onto the stage, chasing their unwanted music out of the club.

Continuing their string of failures, they travelled south to Flint, Michigan. The winter roads were hazardous, filled with newly fallen snow, and unforeseen potholes. The window wipers were running at full steam, brushing off the blizzard like conditions, when they felt a sudden jolt and bounced off their seats, almost hitting their heads on the roof. There was a loud hiss and the bus came to an abrupt halt. Robert could see steam vapor rise from the front engine as Ed shook his head in disgust, the damn thing had run over something and they were marooned in the middle of nowhere. Their only saving grace was, they had crossed the border, and AAA would eventually find its way to their vehicle. As the night wore on, and the temperature dropped below freezing, the once confident musicians became quiet until one of them sprouted tears.

"We're all going to die here tonight. In this bus, we are all going to freeze our asses off and in the morning they will find our frozen bodies lying still," he cried. Robert would have none of that, so he walked to the back of the bus and tried to assure the whining trumpet player. As if he were a cheerleader, he convinced them they would make it through the night and would live to tell their families about the hard knock life of being on the road. Two hours later the AAA truck pulled up to the side of the road, changed the tires, restarted the engine, and off they went to Flint, where they would play at one of the biggest clubs in town.

Most of the cover songs were oldies, but the town only remembered their last claim to fame, which was Grand Funk Railroad, a blues rock band who wore ripped tee shirts and lots of biker chains. When the group finished their opening song, they could hear a pin drop, no one applauded and no one booed. They sat mute, waiting for the music the likes of earthy hard rock. Those were not the sounds the boys could, or even wanted to sing. It wasn't the Sacca Twins style. The following night they returned to the club, walked into the tiny dressing room and were shocked by two nooses tied around two paper mache heads of themselves.

"This is not a good sign," suggested Robert as he stared at the heads dangling from the ceiling. Incensed, they found the club manager, took him back to the room and showed him the handiwork.

"Look guys, I see you are unhappy. How about I give you five hundred bucks and you leave."

"Hell no," spat Robert. "Give us another night, and I think you will change your mind." The band huddled together, rearranged several songs, loosened up their costumes, and confidently returned to the floor. That evening there was actual applause and as the night wore on, and more women joined the blue collar beer drinkers, the place began to fill up. Word spread quickly, and soon the small club was filled every night, with the twins lasting out the full month. Not one beer was flung, nor any rowdy booing, rather the town embraced the act and a return engagement was in their future. Boarding the bus, which had been completely overhauled, the brilliant morning sun cast a balmy future for the crew as they headed to the state of Wisconsin, and eventually home to Philadelphia.

It was at a local watering hole that the producer John Ricci, for Bandstand '72, first saw Gemini. Staying until their last set, he was so impressed with their performance that he offered them a job with the show. Not only were their voices great, but he liked the way they moved on stage and interacted with the customers. Handing each of the singers his card they made a date to meet the following day and work out the details. As he walked out of the bar, the two starred at each other in disbelief. Three years doing the clubs, the bars, the halls, school dances and finally, they got their first break. Hugging each other, they were ecstatic.

It was after midnight when the boys arrived home. Trampling up the hallway steps, they woke their parents to relay the great news. Holding the business card, they showed their dad the person was real and they had an appointment in the morning. "Then I suggest you get some sleep," he said as he turned over on his side closed his eyes and let go a wide smile.

Dressed in dark well-tailored suits the singers shook hands with Ed Tully, the promoter. Leading them to a small conference room he offered them a seat and coffee.

"Frank told me you guys can really sing. He likes the way you move on stage and how you get the audience going. We have a big gig coming up, Bandstand 72, and we think you could be a successful part of the show, along with another lead singer Chris Lista: like Three Dog Night. The performances began in June and continue through the entire summer, down at the shore, at Wildwood. We have booked the Surf Club and plan on being very busy. There will be no dark night: that's days off. You know at the shore, it's a very short season so we have to make hay while we can. Do you understand?"

All three heads nodded yes in unison as he continued.

"That means you have to arrive at every show, every rehearsal, be on time and sound just as great as Frank said you were last night. No crazy partying, drinking, and absolutely no drugs. If you agree to these terms then we would love to have you come work with us." Handing each singer a contract, he left the room allowing them time to talk things over and sign on the dotted line. Chris was a bit apprehensive, but watching Robert and Tony sign away without reading one line of the contract, he followed suit.

"Our first big break is really happening. What could be better than three months at the Jersey shore surrounded by beautiful babes in bikinis?" said Tony. "It's like a dream gig come true. We have the entire day off to sit on the beach, and the evenings we will do what we love doing and get paid fairly decently." Since no one could possibly argue with that logic, they presented the three signed contracts to the promoter the moment he opened the conference room door. Shaking hands, he told them to see the secretary on the way out and she would provide them with all the details they needed. Batting her thickly mascaraed eyelashes, she handed each singer copies of the contracts, with separate instructions as to time, location and rehearsal schedules.

"What do we tell the band members?" said Robert "We all got so wrapped up in ourselves that we forgot that they only want us and not the band." The twins looked at each other and Tony realized he was right.

"Okay, we agree, you are right and they will probably hate us, but I, for one, would not want to give up this chance for the world. I say we have a meeting, be honest and explain the situation. It's only for the summer and at the end of the gig, we can get back together again," suggested Tony. "Look, we have a week before we leave. We are rehearsing with the guys tomorrow and we will tell them." The singers left the office with bittersweet feelings. They would have to face the music tomorrow and it wouldn't be pretty.

"It's not fair," spat the drummer as he tossed the sticks on the floor.

"It's only for the summer, and then before you know it, we will be playing gigs together," said Robert.

"Just tell us how we are supposed to be a band when we have no singers. We have to eat too," said the bass guitarist.

"We're sorry, we're all sorry, but if the tables were turned and the promoter only wanted the band, I'm quite sure you wouldn't turn down this chance," added Tony. With that, the musicians left the basement, lumbered up the dank basement steps and never returned to another Gemini rehearsal.

With the savings from his clerk position, Tony purchased a used sedan that was large enough to hold his brother, luggage, and his guitar.

Hurriedly kissing their mom and sister good bye, Tony tossed the keys to Robert. He turned on the ignition and eased the car out of the driveway, onto the soaking wet streets, and carefully headed directly east. After a couple hours drive, they arrived at the resort town. In spite of the gray clouds and constant drizzle, hundreds of people were walking on the beach, pushing covered baby carriages on the wooden boardwalk, surfing in the Atlantic, and riding the rides at the amusement park. What a town, what a place to be! They had directions to the house; Tony barked out orders to Robert as they slowly cruised through the town. The three would be sharing a summer rental cottage with three other musicians: that would make six young men in one tiny home and a refrigerator door that would be banging open and closed most of the day. At least there were two bathrooms: one on each floor, but again, miniscule in size. The front door was wide open as they walked into the cozy living room, carrying their luggage. They heard a shout from the kitchen,

"Come on in and join the party." Their housemates were sitting around a wooden kitchen table eating scrambled eggs and drinking orange juice. They were part of the band that would be backing up the newly arrived singers.

"Rehearsals begin at noon every day until around two, or until the production crew says we are good enough," explained the drummer, "but Sundays there are no rehearsals, I guess they figure we can run on the steam from Saturday night. After you guys get situated, we will show you the ropes. It's a great little town, and the girls are really hot." They shook hands and completed a round of introductions, and then the singers walked up the steep stairs, locating their bedrooms. For once, Tony and Robert each had their own bedrooms and they were quite happy. In his bones, Tony felt this was the summer he would find love: and lots of it. Having his own bedroom would at least guarantee some modicum of privacy.

Just before noon, the house emptied out as the six performers piled into two cars.

"Wait," said Robert, "none of us has the key to the front door." The drummer laughed and responded that no one had the key to the front door. Life down at the resort was safe and easy going. People would be filtering in and out of the house twenty-four hours a day.

"You'll get used to this very quickly," he laughed as they sped off for morning rehearsals. After a few short blocks, they wound around the back of a huge wooden structure, located a block off the boardwalk. The large marquee read, "Bandstand '72."

"I guess that's us," said Robert. The wide backdoor creaked open as they entered the musty smelling stage. A few other band members were milling around, puffing on cigarettes and awaiting instructions. Their first show was just three days away, and Gemini had a lot to learn. When the entire crew was fully assembled there were nine band members, four dancers and three singers. The scuff of footsteps hitting the wooden planks, announced the director as he entered the club with his assistant. He introduced himself and began spouting off a grocery list of orders to the various cast members. He handed the singers a play list and directed them to the keyboard player, where they immediately began practicing. After six long hours, they called it a day and reminded the crew to return the next morning. The four dancers were beautiful young women who would be headed off for college in the fall and looking for as much fun as the guys. The boys offered the girls a ride home, but they declined.

"Then how about a get together, tonight," suggested Tony as he scribbled down his address.

"Sure, why not? See you fellas around eight. Make sure you have a few six packs."

"Ugh," said Tony, "how are we going to put together a meal when none of us knows how to cook." That hurdle was easily solved when they returned to the cottage and handed over cash to the bass guitar player; for a few extra bucks, he was more than willing to purchase a home cooked meal from an elderly grandmother who made money in the summertime cooking for the college kids. Although tired from the rehearsal, the boys scurried around the home cleaning up cigarette butts, dumping out garbage, and wiping the table tops, they wanted to impress the girls. Right on time the four dancers arrived at their modest abode. Just as the boys admired the beautiful faces and matching bodies, so too did the girls admire the Sacca twins. They popped open several beers and sat around talking for hours, and then Robert threw on some records and asked a girl to dance: her name was Linda. The music had been predetermined; Robert had selected several upbeat songs, and then stacked the record player with a series of romantic ballads. Even at a tender age, he had learned how to set the mood for love. Within a half hour he had vanished to his bedroom with a petite blonde, and later Tony was holding another young woman in paradise inside his shabby cramped bedroom. At the breakfast table the next morning they were all sporting broad smiles.

"I know it's not nice to kiss and tell, but wow what a night," said Robert. They looked at each other and made concurring smiles. Tony's prediction of a summer of love was certainly looking up.

For the next two days rehearsals ran from noon until dusk, with Gemini staying even later. On top of learning the play list, they had to master an entire repertoire of dance numbers; there was no time for hanky-panky. Friday night was the first show of the season and they had to present a perfect show, so they put in the hours and practiced diligently.

The musicians took their places and began warming up. Tony peeked out from behind the curtain and saw every seat in the house was filled. The girls were all dressed up in summer prints, and the older men were wearing suit jackets. As they waited for the final drum roll, the production crew nodded and the three singers gallantly took the stage. Quite nervous, as soon as the first song was over, they became so immersed in the music, their nerves disintegrated. When they added the dance steps, the Sacca twins truly held their own on stage as they interspersed steps between the four dancers: by the end of the evening, they were actually enjoying the performance. They were smiling and relaxed as they seamlessly moved from one production number to another. The applause from the audience assured the performers they were on the right track and as the evening progressed, many joined in singing the songs. When they took their final bows, the entire audience stood up, cheered and whistled. There was no doubt the show had been successful. The production crew came around and shook the performers' hands and let them know they had a great show.

The boys were too excited to simply go home, so they walked over to the boardwalk and sucked in the damp sea air. It was a perfectly clear evening; the sky was filled with stars and a waning moon. Although most of the vendors had closed down, they found one pizza stand with a couple of freshly baked pies. They stopped at Mack's Pizza, a legendary pizza place that made their own blend of cheeses and dough, there was nothing like it anywhere. They purchased the entire pie and three large sodas, and animatedly discussed the show.

"I was nervous, especially when I saw the packed house," admitted Tony as he grabbed a large triangular slice.

"Me too," added Robert, "But when I started to dance with the girls, I kind of forgot the audience, I was too busy trying to impress the girls." Chris just laughed at them and boasted that he wasn't nervous at all. The weekend shows continued to improve as Gemini became more confident in their songs and stage presence. It was a small community, so many people would come back to see the shows several times before the close of the summer. The production crew would add new songs and dance numbers so as not to bore the returning locals. The two hour afternoon rehearsals were rarely that short, as they were constantly learning new songs and dance steps. It seemed that the shows had been sold out for the entire summer, and Frank wanted to make sure the customers got their money's worth.

Sunday morning, Tony got up at the crack of noon, put on a swim suit and tennis shoes, and hoofed it down the three blocks to the ocean. He walked along the boardwalk, removed his shoes, and then plunged his feet into the warm white sand. The cool breezes from the ocean water drew him to the edge of the ocean. Splashing in the waves, he felt like a young kid: and it felt great. A young girl, with long black hair, dark blue eyes, and a wide smile approached him and told him she had seen him sing in the show and thought he was quite good.

"Thanks," he said.

"Would you like to go for a walk on the beach?" she asked. The two began a very long walk up and back at the edge of the cool ocean water. They talked about school, their families, friends, where they were staying, and what they did for fun. In the fall she would be entering Penn State and studying pre-med, so this was her last hurrah before the fall semester.

"I intend to have the time of my life this summer," she boldly admitted.

"Me too," Tony said. "Maybe we could do this together." By the end of the walk those blue eyes had penetrated into the depths of his heart and he was enamored: and for her, it was quite easy to fall in love with a singer who had a gorgeous face. They agreed to meet the following afternoon after rehearsals,

"But if I am late, you will know where to find me," he added. Turning, he looked directly into her eyes and she leaned over and kissed him deeply on the lips.

"I hope you will remember that until I see you again."

They did meet again the next day as planned. At two o'clock, Tony looked up when the showroom door opened and watched Jenna slide into an aisle seat. He waved, but continued practicing for the next hour as she sat patiently watching his every move. When the crew announced it was time to wrap, Tony lunged off the stage, grabbed Jenna, and off they flew through the front of the theatre.

"I'm starving, how about a late munch?" Smiling she took his hand and they walked to a sandwich snack shop, one block behind the boardwalk. The overstuffed sandwich was filled with Italian deli meats, cheeses, and pepperonis, and came with a bag of chips and large drink. When Jenna saw the size of the sandwich she asked for one bite and then ordered a soda. There was no way she was about to ruin her bathing suit body she had spent the winter diligently working on. All those swim meets, and softball training sessions were not lost on her svelte body. She guarded every morsel so as to not ruin her shapely body. There was no doubt that Tony was a catch, and if she wanted him hook line and sinker, she had to guard her body with her life. He wouldn't give a fat girl a second look. Jenna took this friendship to be a summer fling and if she played her cards right, she hoped Tony would reciprocate. The cuckoo clock chimed six o'clock and Tony had to leave to prepare for the evening show. They kissed good bye and she began to jog out of the shop when Tony yelled out,

"When will I see you again? How about Monday night after the show? Meet me at the back door." She blew him a kiss and she skipped out to the street in utter delight. She would be hard pressed to study the books she had brought, with Tony constantly on her mind.

The summer commenced, as Bandstand '72 became extremely successful. With a filled house every night, the producer was thrilled he was making plenty of money. The Sacca twins, did as promised and arrived at every rehearsal, performed at every show, and did it all with the height of professionalism. In the small world of the entertainment business, word spread up and down the coastline about the rock and roll show. It became so popular that on the weekends, hundreds stood outside, just to hear the music ringing in the air.

Labor Day was upon them which cast a pall throughout the beach towns. Summer was ending. Jenna would be off at college, and all Tony would have were his memories of making love on the beach under the moonlight. He had truly fallen in law with Jenna, but he knew he had to face the reality that they would be travelling in different worlds. A first love for each of them, their memories would be held hostage in their hearts forever. It was time to pack up and return to Philadelphia.

On the drive home, the twins talked about their escapades with girls and their sexual prowess, each topping the other in the amount of young girls they had had their way with. When they each mentioned the list of names they realized the two had shared some of the same girls, but at least they were on different nights. Oh, they had all learned so much in the quaint town of Wildwood, and they would never be the same.

The local paper loved the twins, and promoted them in the entertainment section. Without a full-time publicist, it was almost impossible to get a story in the paper, but Bob Charger obviously loved them and followed their career closely:

"This was the real break they needed. The Sacca twins along with the fantastic full band are making it happen down the shore. They joined forces with a nine-man and four girl band to form Bandstand '72 with music directed by Frank Lombardo and producer John Ricci. All summer long they have been performing at the Wildwood Surf Club and will continue until September."

There was an attached photo of the three boys with one of the blonde dancers seated in the middle. This article helped explain why the shows were sold out. Every teenage girl who could steal the family car headed in that direction.

Shortly after the singers recuperated from a staggeringly successful summer, Chris decided to leave Bandstand 72'. He felt as if he couldn't compete with the attention brought to the twins, he felt like a third wheel and went to what he did best, hairstyling. They spent that winter playing local gigs and making a name for themselves throughout Philadelphia. With their handsome faces, versatile vocals, and spot on dance routines, they filled up the venues, and sold out most of the shows. As the New Year approached Frank and Ed, the producers of Bandstand '72, were looking to repeat the success of the prior summer, and they knew the key was the

Sacca twins. They called a meeting the five got together, including the twins manager, John Ricci, at the producer's office in downtown Philadelphia, and when they were finished, they had renamed, "Bandstand '73," to the, "Sacca Twins Revue." John had convinced the producers that the draw to the show was the twins and that a change in the name would guarantee another successful and profitable summer run. Ed and John began promoting the summer show and the twins. They believed in their talent and they believed in their ability to make a lot of money. Robert and Tony began singing on local television shows, and did live performances and interviews at numerous radio stations. This media frenzy helped promote the summer show and the tour. In the middle of May, the newspaper depicted a striking photo of the entire review, with the twins center front, and the nine piece band all decked out in white tuxedos with black satin lapels. The headline read, "From Bandstand '73 to the Sacca Twins Revue." The article stated that the name of the Revue had been changed, and that they were on to bigger and better things playing at the "500 Club" in Atlantic City: "Bandstand '73 was a good name the Sacca twins say, and it served its purpose. But now it's the Sacca Twins Revue who will seek future stardom. The name's changed but the talent is still there."

Music evolves, and at that point in time, show bands were all the rage. Audiences clamored to see singers with back-up dancers and a full supporting band. Television promoted several types of those shows, and soon showrooms cropped up across the country to cater to those types of reviews. John went full steam ahead and booked the twins touring on the road in 1973 for a solid year. The boys were twenty-two: in the prime of their lives and rearing to go.

Dressed in matching black tuxedos with sequin embellishments, the twins entered the stage at a popular venue in a wealthy Philadelphia suburb. The show went well as they harmonized perfectly to a series of cover songs in a myriad of tempos. Most of the audience was filled with teenage girls screaming at the end of each song. They felt pumped up and confident as they went through the act and the audience responded in kind. It was during one of the songs towards the end of the last set when Tony became annoyed with the girls on stage and the way the band was flirting with them. After the show he went back to the dressing room and complained to John. The two got in a fight and Tony, still very young and impetuous, grabbed a chair and flung it in their manager's direction. Luckily he ducked just in time, but he became incensed and told Tony he had a lot of nerve trying to hurt a made man.

"Just who do you think you are? You are nothing but a little punk, wet behind the ears. Trying to hit me with a chair? I got friends and they will come after the both of you and shoot you. You won't even know what happened," warned their very angry manager.

Tony was shaking in his boots: he had no idea the damage he had done and he was terrified. The next morning he replayed the entire story to his mother. Although she was angry, and told her son never to mess with John ever again, she was forced to hail the troops. She called her cousin living in Connecticut.

"Benny, I need your help," said a desperate mother trying to save her twins. "You see the other night, Tony got into a brawl with John and then John told the boys he was going to have them shot. Please help me. I don't know what to do. I know that Tony was to blame, he got angry after the show and took it out on John, but to have them both killed over a little spat? That's crazy, don't you think?" she cried. Benny who had known and loved his cousin his entire life, wasn't going to allow John to destroy her family.

"I'll be there, just give me a couple of days to get ready." And get ready he did. Two days later he arrived in a black sedan with four other guys, who were so large they barely wedged into the ample back seat of the Cadillac. They carried with them the appropriate tools of the trade; they were armed to the teeth. Benny called John and told he him wanted to take a little meeting; he wanted to see how the twins were doing and how the shows were going.

"Sure," responded John. Later that day Benny knocked on John's door and the manager's broad smile dropped a mile when he saw the four additional men standing at his front door. They walked into the small office, which was empty save for John, and Benny suggested they have a little chat.

"I heard about the chair incident from the boy's mother. Hey, I think we can all agree that Tony is still very young and has a lot to learn, but I heard that he was very sorry for throwing the chair." He nodded at the four henchmen, who on cue, pulled out four pistols of varying sizes. John felt his blood run cold and his heart race as Bennie continued. "I heard you told the boys you were going to shoot them. I'm here to tell you not to shoot them, you know, out of respect to their mother."

Starring at the four well placed guns, it appeared as though Bennie had made John an offer he couldn't refuse.

"Alright," he promised, "I will call off the troops, but I'm done with those two brats. They can find another manager, but they must work on the opposite side of Wildwood, and never sing in my territory again."

"Well John, I think that is an excellent decision. I'm not worried about the boys, they will have their choice of managers and agents, just stay away from them," Bennie warned. Turning to the four hulks he nodded his head; they holstered their weapons and walked out of the office. John never bothered the twins again, and Tony never threw a chair at anyone ever again. A lesson well learned as they sought a new agent.

That night Tony was itching his crotch fiercely, something was driving him crazy down there, and who could he turn to? Not his parents, it was his Uncle Nick: confident he would have the answer. When he took a shower in the morning he looked down and saw a tiny insect emerging from his mound of hair. "Shit, what is this?" Grabbing a large piece of toilet paper, Tony wrapped the thing up tightly and later that afternoon he paid a humiliating visit to his beloved uncle.

Tony knocked on Nick's front door and his uncle yelled out for Tony to come into the kitchen. Slurping on minestrone soup, he was engrossed in reading the horse racing results from across the country. A smile crossed his face, he had had a great morning and had picked a half dozen winners at Santa Ana. His bank roll for the day was primed.

"So what do I owe this visit to?" asked Nick who could read his nephew's face as clearly as the newspaper. "Trouble?" Moving out the chair, he motioned for the teen to take a seat. Tony cleared his throat: the words were hard to get out. "So just spit it out, what's the problem?"

"How do you know I have a problem?" asked Tony.

"Well, I just know." He held up the piece of toilet paper and slowly unfolded it, revealing a tiny black creature lying dead. He pointed to his crotch and began to cry. Uncle Nick, who was known for his great wisdom and decorum, let out a roar of laughter.

"You, my sweet handsome nephew, have been fooling around with the girls and now you have yourself a case of the crabs!"

"Crabs, what the hell are crabs, and how do I get rid of them?" Still laughing, Nick wrote down the name of two lotions, pulled five dollars out of his pocket and handed it over to his distraught nephew.

"And while you're at it, buy yourself some condoms. I promise you in a week, the crabs will be gone, and I will never say a word about this to your parents," he the back of his nephew's head. Nick was proud of the sexual prowess Tony possessed.

"I guess in a few years, you will make me some nice kids of your own," he added. A quick trip to the pharmacy, and Tony's problem with the crabs was eviscerated, but that didn't deter him from what romantic interludes would pop up in the very near future, he was fully armed with condoms!

The time was approaching when the boys had to begin creating their own music, it wasn't enough to just play cover songs, they had to carve out their own identity and it had to be more than just the concept of being twins. Hermie Dresel, who had managed Woody Herman, became their manager and hired Diana Snow, a writer from New York, to come up with some hit tunes. As networking goes, the twins were introduced to Gary Anderson, a gifted saxophone player and arranger. Anderson attended Berklee School of Music, where he later became a full-time professor. He was the musical director for Woody Herman, and after several years on the road, he settled down in Manhattan, working on television, film, and stage productions that eventually earned him a Grammy. A multitalented man, his initial arrangements for the twins proved to be very successful. Like many famous entertainers, he eventually found his way out of New York City headed to Las Vegas.

Anderson produced two original songs for the twins, "How Do you Pack Your Heart?" and "Tonight Tonight," but they fell flat, and never saw the light of day in the top 40. Tony attributed this to his inability to dissect the song, to be able to understand the meaning of the lyrics and then portray this to the listeners. He saw his twin act as performance art; it was in their performance and the fact that they were twins that brought the music alive. They didn't have to sing original songs to be successful, it was the arrangements and their stage presence that set them apart from all other groups and that was the career path, they decided to take. At the time show bands were trending, and in great demand, it was easy to retain the limelight if they stuck to that path. Although making music was their primary goal, making money came a close second, and catering to the current tide would guarantee a decent livelihood. As they entered their late teens, they polished up their act, incorporated choreography, tweaked the harmonies, and added more musicians.

The Revue continued to tour throughout the tri state area and they kept their word never entering John's side of town ever again. They played the local clubs under the Sacca Twins Revue, and then prepared to return to Wildwood in 1973 for another, what they hoped would be, successful run. The gig was more ambitious than last summer, there would be two shows each day, seven days a week and the shows would last for one hundred twenty days. Not one day off in four months.

As they practiced for the summer show, Robert and Tony had big plans for love. Although Tony's girlfriend had disappeared into her books, he eventually got over his first love and was anxiously seeking a summer more like the kind Robert had had: he would spread himself a lot thinner, dating more than just one girl. That way, he wouldn't have the heartache of breaking up when they returned to the tour. He was seeking a summer of a lot of fun. The two would work hard every day and he had every intention of playing as hard as he worked, taking advantage of his stardom.

This year, Tony and Robert would have their own bungalow, and wouldn't be stifled with the nine band members. With more privacy, they could have their own parties, especially when it came to entertaining the bikini clad, stunning girls. Carrying a lot more luggage than the last summer, they had an expansive array of new costumes. Their mother saw to it they were always well-dressed, in a conservative manner. They never sported the crazy flamboyant styles of other groups. It was their impressive handsome faces, and great voices that carried the show and brought the young girls back season after season. The play list was entirely revamped from the previous summers' tunes, with only current well-known cover songs. There was a wide range of tempos, from sultry ballads, to medium tempos blended with several upbeat dance songs. Doing away with the old standards, the twins wanted to appeal to a younger audience, they were the fans who used their babysitting money to come to the shows and later purchase the CDs.

That year as Robert drove into the town, they didn't need a roadmap; they knew every single street in the beach resort. When they opened up the car door, they took in the aroma of the salty sea air: it was intoxicating. The few puffy clouds promised a day filled with bright sunshine and cool ocean breezes. Two blocks away from the Atlantic Ocean, they could hear the low rumble of the waves as they grabbed the shoreline. Seagulls circled above and then flew east bound to fight for tidbits hidden inside clam and oyster shells that had been washed ashore.

"I feel so good about this summer, "said Robert.

"After last summer, I have no doubt you do. I think I will follow in your footsteps and not get too crazy about one girl. I don't want another heartache, I just want to have a good time. I will watch you and you can lead the way," said Tony. The white washed bungalow was one story, with two small bedrooms, a kitchen with a dining table, a bathroom and a small living room with a brick fireplace. There was a television in the corner, two oversized chairs and one, very well used dark brown corduroy sofa.

"I think it's nice it's just the two of us," said Tony. "I know that last summer Chris always felt like the extra, and we won't have to worry about that this year." They tossed their clothing in the bedrooms, hung up their costumes, drove down to the sub shack and picked up lunch, and drove over to the theatre. They knocked on the back door: the stage hand hustled over slid open the metal gate and unlocked the door.

"Hey Tony, Robert, great to have you guys back. I hear the girls are prettier than ever this summer," said the stage hand as he winked. The musty smell was the same as on the first day they opened the year prior. Another stage hand jarred open the back door, as the fresh air flooded the stage, replacing the stale air with the sweet smell of the ocean.

Their manager had prepared a large play set of fifty songs, all of which the nine musicians had to learn. But no one wanted to feel overwhelmed on the first day of practice, so the twins tightened up the songs to those of the first four shows, and then they would add an additional two to three songs with each rehearsal so by the third week, the band would feel confident with all fifty songs. The crew was well aware that many members of the audience would return more than twice throughout the season, and they knew they had to make it as fresh as possible. The more they changed the show, the more likely more people would return to hear songs not performed. Of course this meant new dance routines as well. The twins were up for the work; they loved it, and they loved to perform. To them, life couldn't get any better than when they were singing and dancing in front of a devoted audience. There would be time for fun after the shows, and in the mornings. Once they had the complete play list down, they would have even more time to frolic in the ocean, and if they got lucky, in the sack. To Tony, the smell of the ocean air was synonymous with a summer of fun.

Dressed in white, four dancers and nine musicians took their places, tuned up the horns and guitars, and then the drummer began crashing the drums and the cymbals as the twins confidently grabbed the microphones and began the first song: an upbeat version of Poison Ivy. The humorous lines were instantly received joyfully by the young teens. The twins followed this with several dance songs, a couple of new romantic ballads, and then pranced off stage for short intermission. The theatre insisted on a twenty minute break which was just enough time to sell a couple hundred drinks, snacks, and candy bars. Ice-cream was the only junk food not sold as it was too messy to clean up. Although the theatre was only open four months a year, the profit generated in those short summer months would carry them through the entire year. Every minute counted and every additional sale counted. As the first act of the performance was about to close, sodas had already been poured, all they had to do was rake in the cash. Of course, the theatre owners insisted on a cut of any items the Sacca Twins sold on the premises after each show. Both sides were quite content with the relationship, the twins were well paid, and the theatre was packed every night with a huge bucket of gold at the end of the summer: a perfect symbiotic relationship.

Sunday morning the sleepy town rose late after the tourists had drank, eaten, and played themselves out the night before. As he approached the empty boardwalk, Tony stretched, laced up his running shoes tightly, and commenced a half hour jog up and down the wooden planks. His ears were covered with the latest sounds broadcasting from the local deejays. He never wanting to miss a beat, so he would listen intently in case there was a red hot song that needed to be added to the play list. The sun was peeking out from behind scattered cumulus clouds making the run cooler than normal. He dropped by the concession stand selling fresh fruits and juices. He ordered a large orange juice mixed with pink lemonade, guzzled it down, and paid.

"Thanks Tony, or are you Robert?" asked Vita, owner of the stand for forty years.

"Tony." he answered, as he continued to drink.

"Here, have another, it's on the house. We finally saw the show Friday night, and we loved it: especially my two granddaughters. You guys are really smooth. I can see why all the girls love you."

"Thanks: and thanks for the extra juice," said Tony, "See you later this week." He walked another block or two and he stopped to pet a golden retriever just as the owner was taking him off the boardwalk.

"Such a great dog," said Tony as he gently pet his nose. He never had a pet growing up. It would have been nice to have a dog like this big fuzzy retriever. Maybe someday he would have a dog: he loved them but he also knew that all he did was tour and dogs just couldn't make the cut.

As the summer progressed and became hotter, the afternoon rehearsals became shorter as the band and the twins had perfected all the dance routines and songs. On Sundays they skipped rehearsals altogether giving the performers a partial respite. It was one of those days off that Tony met another beautiful young college girl. After he pet the dog, he walked to the edge of the sand and sat silently watching the waves lap to shore. An angelic girl who was walking by in a striped bikini, turned and looked at the lone boy. Just as she looked at him, he glanced up into her brilliant green eyes and was immediately transfixed. "*Boy,*" he thought, "*she really compliments that bikini.*"

"Hi, my name is Sherri, and you look an awful lot like that singer I saw last night and the night before, at the theatre."

He stood up and introduced himself and she suggested he join her on the walk. Since that was all there was to do in the early morning hours, began a long walk on the wide beach. The tide was out, and they moved toward the hard damp sand picking up clam shells and tossing them back into the ocean. She was in her third year of college and was waitressing at the clam bar, which never opened until noon.

"I guess we both work late hours," she said, "The place doesn't close until ten at night and then I have to clean up hundreds of shells and toss several other hundreds of empty beer bottles into the recycling bin. Then I go home and take a bath in lemons to get rid of the seafood smell."He grabbed her arm and smelled the back of her neck,

"I don't smell any seafood, just you, and you smell great." She blushed, then she pointed and said were at her street. Tony, the gentleman that he was, offered to walk her home.

"My show gets over around ten tonight, how about I pick you up afterwards and we go for a late walk on the beach?" It was a date. Tony could hardly wait until the show ended. He dashed home, changed into jeans and a tee-shirt, threw a blanket and a six pack in the car and was over at Sherri's cottage before the clock struck eleven. He knocked on the screen and heard the chatter of several girls inside, when he asked for Sherri. They knocked on her bedroom door and she quickly emerged with a bright smile, carrying two oversized beach towels. He took her hand, opened the car door for her, and slowly drove down to the ocean front. They used a street lamp for a guide and walked five minutes toward the ocean, until the light had diminished into a tiny speck. They spread out the blanket: they were completely alone underneath the stars and the crescent shaped moon. Tony popped open two beers and she happily accepted hers as they toasted their first date. They talked for hours and when Tony leaned in to kiss her, she put her arms around his neck and pulled him closer.

"I want to remember this night forever," she said as she slid out of her sundress and threw the towels on top of them.

"Me too," was all Tony could get out. He thought about how lucky he was to have found love again, as he returned Sherri back to her home. As much as he tried to be enticed by other women, she remained his solitary choice until the 120th show ended. A week later, she went back to college and he went on to bigger and better things, but he never forgot the passion and the intensity of their lovemaking…ever.

The twins continued travelling around the country performing as a show band in a myriad of locations. With their nine piece band, and dancers, they flew into destinations unknown, but all with nightclubs that wanted an outrageous band. One of the most bizarre remote cities they performed in was Eau Claire, Wisconsin, a small town located in the western part of the state. With a population around seventy thousand, it was the typical middle-American city, complete with the typical Main Street, turn of the century courthouse architecture, and mom and pop downtown stores. The town was hungry for entertainment and why was it so hungry? It was the absurdly frigid temperatures. In February when the band landed, the thermometer read sixty-five degrees below zero. It was so cold the engine on their van blew up and they had to rent a U-Haul to carry the instruments. Nobody in their right mind ventured to this town in the winter, but here they were stuck with a two week gig. They checked into their rooms: everyone was happy when they had warmed up enough that they couldn't see their breath anymore. With the room keys from the clerk in hand, they were on a mission, and the objective was to reach as many people as possible in the pursuit of their careers. Fame was what they sought, and if it meant playing in these remote, godforsaken towns, then so be it. They sucked it up, and gave it their all for the two weeks, and then departed as fast as was humanly possible.

As he stared out the window, Robert blew his breath near the pane glass, fogging up a tiny corner.

"I'm so bored, it's come down to me trying to warm up the damn windows. It's too cold to go outside, I'm afraid my best parts would get frost bite, and I'm not talking about my feet," he laughed. As if on cue, the phone rang and he sprang to pick it up. Their agent was on the phone with the best of news; they would be flying down to Miami Beach the next morning. Elated the two brothers knocked on the doors of the band and gave them the good news, it was time to break out their swimsuits. Tony called his mom and told her not to bother picking them up at the airport, they would be on the road for a two week stint. Everyone celebrated: they sang reggae music and formed a conga line in the halls of the motel.

"Sunshine here we come," they bellowed.

The Marco Polo Club set upon the pristine sands of Miami Beach was the place to play. The resort contracted the top entertainers in the country and luckily for the Sacca twins, they would be there for a heavenly two weeks. That first evening, as the crew took their positions on stage, Tony was already scouting the audience for babes. Unlike Eau Claire, Wisconsin, the women were scantily clad, their skins bronzed, and their bodies svelte.

"They all look like sweet candy to me," said Tony as he cast a furtive eye into the filled seats, imagining each girl was a different flavored lollipop. After the show, a buxom young woman with long blonde waves, blue eyes, and a wide smile, handed him a bouquet of white roses. Tony promptly invited her back to his room where she spent the rest of that night rearranging the bouquet. In the morning, the room smelled of roses, and he was as happy as a clam.

Several band members met for lunch at the deli the next day and each of the musicians had their own story to tell, but they decided to dub Tony, "Eagle One," the man who literally always came out on top. Although the others were jealous at the ease at which women constantly approached the lead singer, they got a vicarious thrill when he shared his escapades. An artist in every way, Tony had a gift for gab and the ability to describe carnal pleasures. Ah yes, Miami was number one on his list for gorgeous women: for the balance of the stint, Tony met a new woman each night, and in some way or another, they all ended up in his hotel room. No one had to be coaxed; they were infatuated with the singer and wanted a piece of him, a memory to take to their graves.

"I never spent a dime on any of the women I saw. They would pay for my dinner, or bring me a bottle of wine. The women took care of me, I didn't take care of them, and it made me very, very spoiled. If I would ask a beautiful woman out to dinner after the show, when the check arrived, she would grab it, and thank me for having dinner with her, imagine that," said Tony.

The crew rented a large black limousine and travelled to Ft. Lauderdale, where the women were just as hot, but the resort not quite as upscale. The entire atmosphere screamed college students out for a great time. They were booked at two different clubs performing the rigid six night runs. The shows were well received, as they offered a wider range of top 40s, and tossed out the standards and country western genres. The audience was there to party, and wanted upbeat tempos and dance songs. Tony would always make sure a couple romantic ballads were interspersed for fear of going to his room alone. He put his acting skills to excellent use: he would close his eyes and immerse himself in the sexual potency of the song and when he looked up there was always hundreds of pairs of eyes burning into his face, no doubt the girls in the audience were taken in.

One warm Thursday evening, an irresistible young girl came up to Tony after the show and invited him back to her home, she said she had made extra dinner and she thought he might enjoy a taste of her home cooking. Of course, Tony knew the only thing he would be eating that night would not be coming out of the oven in her kitchen. Her beauty was overwhelming: she was totally intoxicating. When they arrived at her apartment, she admitted that she had a boyfriend, but said he was out at the baseball game and wouldn't be returning for a while. She excused herself from the bedroom and Tony began nosing around. Right next to her bed, his picture had been torn out of the local newspaper and circled in red.

"I thought I was picking up this stunning woman, but in fact it was she who had plotted out the entire evening." That night was all about sex: about the best and the most physically pleasurable sex on this planet. Spent, he crawled home and spent the morning trying to extricate himself out of his own bed. Later that afternoon the guys met for lunch and the topic of conversation was the exploits of the night before. When it came time for Tony to divulge his adventure, true to form he won the prize and his title of, "Eagle One" remained intact.

"So how do you know which one you want?" quizzed the drummer.

"First, gentleman, I have to find her attractive but from the girls sitting in our audiences each night, that's not hard to do. Then I try to make eye contact with her, especially when I sing those romantic ballads. When the show is over, I try to walk in her direction, but I have to say, oftentimes I get waylaid and another beautiful girl approaches and you know the song: 'If you can't have the one you love, then love the one you're with.'" The lunch table was filled with laughter as Tony pontificated upon his journey through the world of love.

"I guess you better keep singing those ballads," remarked the drummer. The balance of the two week stay followed the same pattern; there was a new girl beside him every night. The fun wasn't over as their limousine carried them up the coast highway overlooking the pale blue Atlantic Ocean, into Daytona Beach. The bright sunshine was masked by the tinted windows, but there was a joyfulness lingering with the boys. They were unabashedly happy; they were living the lives that most young men dreamed about, and at times it was surreal. To hold so much power in their hands, to have everything they wanted, which at that young age was simple enough, was fulfilling, in every way. They didn't think about getting older, putting money into a savings account, they were living in and for the moment, and relishing every moment. Happiness was a commodity they were fortunate to obtain. With their health intact, their comely looks, talented stage presence, and golden voices, life was about as perfect as any human could conceive. They were riding the peak of the highest waves and enjoying every second of the adventure.

One afternoon they received a call from a newspaper critic who had been following their act and had fallen in love with their talent. He met them for an early lunch, carrying a newspaper which had placed an ad for an open casting spot for a military short film. Excited at the chance to break into acting, they asked the entertainment director at the resort for one day off and hopped on a plane to Manhattan. The twins were such an anomaly that they were offered the parts. This was their first entrée into the world of acting, the trip had been worthwhile. The name of the short film was, "The Two Henry Gordons" featuring just the twins. One brother was the actual Army recruit and the other brother played his alter ego.

The movie took place after a day at work: the real Henry collapsed on his cot and lay there, starring at the ceiling. The alter ego suddenly appeared in his room and began suggesting a profuse amount of ideas as to how to use his extra time wisely. At first Henry fought the alter ego and didn't want to do anything, just lay on his bed and sleep ("It's my free time, and if I want to kill it doing nothing, then I will."); whereupon the alter ego explained, between sleep and killing time, he would be left with a life devoid of value. He then took Henry on a tour of the campus, pointing out the library, sporting facilities, and the learning center where an abundance of classes were offered. As they continued walking, the alter ego mentioned the abundance of clubs, groups, and societies: *Open up your eyes Henry, there is a whole world of opportunity here on the base.* The last scene pictured Henry back in his room, determined to investigate the opportunities. The film doesn't mention exactly what Henry selects, just that he would be doing something with his life. As he makes this decision, he turns and the alter ego has disappeared from the scene.

That was their premiere acting video, and it was very impressive. Both neophyte actors came off as credible in their roles, which might have been the ease they had interacting with each other, but anyone watching the video was readily convinced of their acting ability. The true reality of the video could be found in the extraordinarily handsome faces of the twins, on screen they came off as competent movie stars on the way up. Not only were they believable in their roles, but they had the timing and the stage presence to serve as the basis for successful acting careers.

Their manager, Hermie Dressel, found the perfect spot for Easter Break, "The Other Place," a club also lining the ocean front, with its large dance floor, massive bar and huge stage, it was the number one nightclub in town. The crew located their three cottages within walking distance of the venue, threw down their possessions and took a long rambling walk on the wide beach. The air was warm from the salty sea breeze, which had a calming effect as they stretched out their legs and cleared their minds. It was one of the few places in America where one could drive on the beach. They rented small beach buggies and sped across the hard ocean soaked sand, waving their arms in the air as they raced up and down the ocean front.

"We have to add some beach songs tonight," suggested Tony who always had an affinity for the Beach Boys' sounds. The crew dusted off the sand and gathered together to walk to the club, while one of the guys drove the limousine. The smiles seemed to be permanently etched upon their faces as they galloped into the prestigious theatre. Their conversations alluded to the beach and fresh songs for that night's play list instead of their sexual escapades, for once. After the sound check and extended rehearsal, they walked home, grabbed a late lunch, dressed for the performance, and waited for the limousine to cart them to the show.

"This Easter break, I believe the Easter egg hunting will be very easy, everywhere I look, I see beautiful, sweet eggs," joked Tony.

It was one in the morning and Tony's conquest had already slipped out of the cottage. He was hungry, so he threw on a pair of shorts, brushed back his waves, and meandered into the kitchen when a hand touched his arm. He turned and beamed into the cherubic face of a young woman,

"Robert," she whispered, "I didn't know where you went." So Tony, who was never one to pass up a chance, responded that he was right there all of the time, and then led her into his dark bedroom and took advantage of being an identical twin. In the morning she scrutinized the face of her lover and realized that it was the other twin who she had made love to, but she didn't seem to care. With his adeptness, it was crystal clear he knew exactly what he was doing and it felt as close to heaven as anything she had ever experienced. His soft touch, his prolonged patience, his deep kisses and his hands gently kneading her body, brought both of them to a grand ecstasy. When they were finished, if she had slept with Rumpelstiltskin it wouldn't have mattered, the sex was close to ethereal, and she wondered if she would ever find such a man ever again.

"The Other Place" was quite happy with the bottom line, the band was pulling in a full house every night and they were raking in the dough. Between the hordes beating a path to the beaches over spring break, the optimal weather, and the attraction of the boy band, the nightclub enjoyed a bountiful bottom line. Before the group left to less interesting places, the owner wrote up a contract booking the boys for the next several spring breaks. Tony and Robert, along with the band were only too happy to make return engagements: the Easter Egg hunting was exceptional!

This was a period of time when making love was in mode, and no one worried about sexually transmitted diseases: it was love in the moment, free, unattached and recreational. The motto for many was "why not?" but Tony used this as it spelled his name backwards. There was one category of women that Tony would never touch no matter how beautiful or attracted he was, and that was a married woman.

"There were so many frustrated women whose husbands treated them horribly, taking them for granted, ignoring them or abusing them, and they sought physical love in the arms of other men. I didn't want to be their solution to an unhappy marriage, nor did I need to have sex with a woman who had committed herself to another man. There were many times when I would listen to their stories and my heart would ache for the way they were treated, but I was a firm believer in the wedding vows. When a couple pledged their love till death do us part, I believe it refers to the soul of the marriage, not the physical death. When love dies between a couple, that is the death of the marriage." These thoughts were premonitions about the loves he was about to experience and he held those values dearly and truly.

In the blink of an eye, the Floridian engagements were finished, and it was on to less glamorous locations: Norfolk, Virginia, Huntsville, Alabama, Altoona, Pennsylvania, and three major cities in Michigan. Wherever there was a nightclub, the band showed up and played six out of seven nights a week. With steady incomes, they had plenty of money to spend on extravagant personal items: they still lived at home under their parent's roof, and they didn't have to worry about paying mortgages or utilities.

When the summer rolled around again, the show was back in their side of Wildwood, where they were all having the wild time of their lives. With gigs hit or miss, although they made a decent living it wasn't sustained, and being young and carefree they blew the money on cars, clothing, and travel. At this point in they lived the, "dream sequence of attaining stardom," said Tony.

"All we cared about was becoming famous and having lots of girls." The show was all about cover music, neither their parents nor their agent, took the time to yank them off the stage long enough to record original music, turning them into recording artists. That seemed to be the only regret in Tony's life. They had they voices, the following, the looks and the talent but the one thing that was missing from their lives was a decent agent who could have, and should have, catapulted them to the next level. Young, all they could think about was having a great time doing what they loved to do: perform.

Robert was off and running with two hot numbers in his hot car, leaving Tony in the dust with his very unsexy Ford Pinto. *What the hell*, thought Tony, *we both make the same money, but my brother sure seems to have a lot more stuff, especially that great sports car.* What Robert had that Tony didn't was control of the business bank account. At the end of each week, when the band was paid, Robert would fold the cash into his brother's palm, and supposedly bank the balance of the money. From where Tony sat the money was ending up in his twin's personal account, otherwise how could he possibly afford the car, and the extra bling he wore on his fingers and neck. In a call to Uncle Nick, Tony complained bitterly about Robert and they agreed the three of them would sit down and take a meeting.

A few miles away, the family had rented a bungalow for the summer, alternating weekends with different cousins. With a series of tiny bedrooms, a small kitchen, and cozy living room, a family of six could enjoy a couple days of cool ocean breezes, gentle Atlantic Ocean waves, and a spectacular star studded night, at a very reasonable amount of money. Uncle Nick was seated prodigiously at the only chair in the living room when the twins walked in. They hugged and kissed and took seats on the adjacent sofa. They sat mute while Tony mustered up the courage to discuss the problem.

"Uncle Nick," he lamented, "I just don't get how Robert has such a nice car and I don't. He always seems to have more money than me, but we are supposed to be making the same amount. So please help me solve this problem. You see, Robert also has control of our business bank account, and hands me my money, but I never see what he takes. I'm thinking it has to be a lot more than me, otherwise how could he afford that sports car and all that jewelry he wears?"

Uncle Nick, the family confidante and advisor, was privy to every problem, and had a solution for each one. Slicking back his thick, curly black locks, he pondered the issue carefully. Standing up, he began pacing the floor, acting as if this were a truly important matter. His dark brown eyes grew intense as he turned, arched his thickset eyebrows, pointed to the sky and announced he had a plan.

"You, Tony, will now take control of the books. You will use the money wisely and not squander it away on silly things. You will learn how to pay bills leaving enough funds in the account for emergencies and capital expenditures. Is that agreed?" he asked, but it really wasn't a question. When Uncle Nick stated a solution that was that and there was no backing down, it was a pronouncement, and mattered as much as if he were both judge and jury.

"Now shake hands and have a great show tonight." Giving each of his nephews a bear hug, Tony turned and asked,

"What is a capital expenditure?" Laughing, Nick sharply retorted, "Condoms."

A postcard of the Sacca Twins Revue promoting their appearance at the
500 Club in Atlantic City

1855 – Members of the Mormon Church choose Las Vegas as the site to build a fort halfway between Salt Lake City and Los Angeles, where they would travel to gather supplies. The fort was abandoned several years later. The remainder of the Mormon Fort can still be seen at the intersection of Las Vegas Boulevard and Washington Avenue.

Tony and Robert take a Marine photo - they allowed the brothers to take the picture together because they were on the buddy plan

CHAPTER 4

After a few days of relaxing and catching up with old friends and family, the twins met at their agent's office.

"Boys, I see you had another great summer. The theatre manager told me you packed them in every night and there was always a full house. Good for you. The time has come: as in all acts, if you want to continue, you must upgrade and polish your act. It has to evolve with the fickle winds of the industry. You stagnate and you die. I think you realize that, just look at your friends and the bands they put together. How many of them have survived and are still performing? Not too many, I'm quite sure. You two are special, we all know that and we should continue to take advantage of that, but at the same token, evolve."

"What are you trying to tell us?" asked Robert.

"First, I have booked you for the rest of the year in the Hilton Hotels throughout the state. You will have five performances per week, Wednesday through Sunday, but if things are heating up, say on a Saturday night, you will be paid extra if you play another hour or two. Because of your local success, the hotel chain was confident you would bring in the crowds, people know who you are and follow you, so they laid down a substantial contract. The next thing I have arranged for you is acting lessons, but the lessons are in Manhattan."

"Manhattan!" the boys screamed together. He held his arms in the air to quiet them down and explained that they needed to hone in on stage presence, and the real possibility that they would be offered roles in television and movies. There was nothing like the present to secure future possibilities.

"To be honest, I had to pull a few strings to get her, but she is one of the best acting teachers in the industry." He handed them a business card. It simply read "Maria Greco," with an address and phone number.

"I know you have a tough year ahead, but if you really want to make it in this industry you will have to pay your dues. You're fortunate that the best teachers are going to help you make your dreams come true. Classes begin Monday." He handed them the train schedule from downtown Philly to Times Square, patted each of them on the back, and promised he would see them at the first show the following weekend at the Hilton. He shook hands with Robert and Tony and looked them in the eyes,

"You have a lot of people in your corner cheering you on. Be thankful and show the world just how talented you two are."

Robert and Tony walked out of the office a bit stunned, although hard work was no stranger to them, this schedule seemed insurmountable, five days travelling to New York and five nights performing in Philadelphia.

"We can do this," said Tony. "I want to be the best I can be at this show business thing and if our manager says this is what we should do, then I believe him. Let's go buy the train tickets and figure things out from there."

They drove downtown and purchased five sets of roundtrip tickets to Times Square. They would spend almost six hours a day riding the train, making for a very long commute and at the end of three of those days, they would be performing in the evenings at the Hilton.

"I guess we will have to learn how to sleep on the train," said Robert. However, Robert had a problem with this, and was afraid to tell his brother. He had recently become engaged to Linda, one of the beautiful blonde Saccette dancers, and they were planning to wed Christmas. He didn't know how she would react to him working such a crazy schedule, but he would see her every night at the shows and they would go home together. Somehow it would work out, it had to.

"So Tony, I wanted to tell you that Linda and I plan on getting married."

"Married? Are you crazy? When you can have your pick of thousands of girls? I thought you loved to run around, add those notches to your bedpost."

"Not anymore. She is definitely the one for me. I already told mom we would be getting married over Christmas and from the looks of our schedule, it appears as though it's the only free date the entire year." Tony hugged his brother and wished him luck, although he had plenty of misgivings.

"I'll see her all the time, she is one of the dancers we use in every show, so things will work out swell, I just know it," Robert convincingly said.

Monday morning the twins boarded the express train to Times Square. Armed with a lunch from their mom, they wore light weight tweed suits to make a good impression on their teacher. They had never taken acting lessons and had no idea what to expect. The train made good time, the conductor announced Times Square, the doors opened, and everyone filed out of the cars. They joined the thousands of pedestrians pounding the Manhattan pavement. They had a short walk to 52nd street at the corner of 8th Avenue, the heart of Broadway. As they ambled through the side streets, the crisp early fall air allowed many of the brownstone windows to be open. They could hear dance instructors directing the steps, actors practicing their lines, musicians practicing with teachers, and singers rehearsing their lyrics. The entire area reflected the rudiments of show business; it was in this neighborhood that actors, actresses, singers, and musicians were molded into their professions. This was where they needed to be, and the air and lifeblood of the city was where they belonged. As they walked through the streets it seemed as though they were being carried on a red carpet to their destiny. The sounds from the voices and the instruments made them feel as if they were joining an elite group of people whose lives was dedicated to perfecting their performance art.

Tony rechecked the business card and looked at the address on the dark brownstone; they were where they needed to be. They buzzed the apartment, the front door grated opened, and they walked up two flights of steps. When she opened the studio door, Maria had a smile on her face as she greeted her new students.

"I understand that you boys came all the way from Philadelphia and that you intend to do this for the balance of the year. I commend you for your ambition and I promise to make each class worth your while. After a year with me, you two will have the knowledge and the confidence to take on almost any role thrown your way." She sat them down on a tapestry rose colored sofa, and asked her assistant to bring in three cups of coffee. The twins spent the next couple of hours listening to Maria's philosophy of acting and then she began the actual process. Maria turned to Tony and asked him to sing a song, he did so and then he bowed. Maria clapped her hands and asked Tony why he bowed.

"Because I was done, and that is how I know to end the performance," he answered.

"Very good," answered their teacher, "You bowed because you were in the moment and at that moment it felt right, it felt like that was what you were supposed to do to cue your audience that your performance is completed. And that is what we shall work on throughout hundreds of different acting scenarios. How many times have you heard that the actors change the script because in the moment, they feel something has changed or that a certain chemistry has altered the scene? You have got to learn to be attuned to that, and follow your instincts. My job is to teach you how to do this," she advised.

Maria began a short series of exercises to pull out emotions. She would read a small piece from a play or a poem and ask them to respond. Then she would have them read the same pieces and implement their own feelings. At the end of the two hour lesson, the boys were emotionally spent, but felt high from learning how to control their actions and reactions. In a formal manner, Maria said good bye and opened the front door to her studio. They could hear the sound of several footsteps climbing up to the second floor, for their time with Maria. She was a sought after drama coach, and her schedule was filled. One of the girls stopped and said hello to the twins as they met in the hallway, and then disappeared into the studio.

"No time for that," admonished Robert as he looked at the return train schedule. At least on Monday and Tuesdays their schedule was light, just the class, no performing until Wednesday night.

"Gosh," said Tony, "I could have stayed to talk with her, well maybe tomorrow." They retraced their steps through the side streets and plummeted down into the tombs at Times Square. The thousands of people scrambling about gave the city a bubbling rhythm of its own. Never had they been in a place with so many people, going in so many directions and so energized. The exhilaration grabbed at their heels like a young puppy, and once that feeling was tasted, it was contagious; they never wanted it to leave. After they boarded the train back home, they slept most of the way. There was a lot to think about and a lot to learn. The twins realized that good looks and great voices could only carry them only so far. If they really wanted this expansive world of entertaining there was plenty more to learn and discover.

"I really liked the class, and I like the teacher. She makes me do things I would never think or know how to do. I think this acting thing is a great idea," said Robert.

"Me too," said Tony as he closed his eyes and took advantage of the little time they would have to rest for the upcoming year. In his dreams he promised a mantra of, "I can do this, I can do this."

Dusk had settled early behind the thick black rain clouds as the boys emerged from the train station. That afternoon, their mom was at the station and drove them home. She was excited about their first day of acting school and badgered them with questions.

"I'm sure you boys are hungry, I will have a nice meal when we get home, dad brought back some thick steaks, how does that sound?" As dinner was served the boys heartily dug into the perfectly aged rib eyes, the home-made split pea soup, and baked potatoes smothered in butter.

"Great dinner mom," said both boys, and then they changed into jeans and tee-shirts and darted down the basement steps to practice for the Hilton Show that was just two nights away. The agent had suggested they lay low on the up tempo songs until later in the evening as most of the crowd was a bit older, and into drinking martinis, not Jell-O shots. They practiced a playlist filled with ballads, and a few standards, followed by upbeat tempos, but nothing too loud. They would be playing lounges, and the sound level had to be tempered to accommodate the size of the room.

The test of their stamina arrived on Wednesday. They boarded Amtrak in downtown Philly, and hours later stepped out into a blustering northern wind tunneling through the center of Manhattan. They walked confidently into the studio: the twins were ready to begin their third lesson. Maria put them through the paces, extracting more out of their psyche. They learned that, to act in the moment to any given stimulus took practice, perseverance, and dedication, all things that Maria would diligently teach them. In her several decades of instruction, she knew those abilities didn't come overnight, they had to be learned, internalized and then perfected.

"That's it for today, and good luck at your show tonight," she added, as the twins departed, intertwined with the four young actors entering her studio. Tony glimpsed the beautiful, thin, blonde girl with a perfectly oval face and penetrating baby blue eyes. Perhaps one day he would catch her name. *Ah, he thought, something to dream about on the long trip home.*

They both slept on the train as it rumbled from city to city. They had a big show at the Hilton and they didn't want to disappoint. It was a smaller venue, so there were fewer band members: a drummer, keyboardist, two guitars players, and one versatile horn player who could play the entire gamut from a trumpet to a saxophone, clarinet, and flute. As they emerged from the train station they saw their manager waving wildly. He smiled and put his arms around their shoulders as he guided them to his car.

"I promised you I would be there for your first performance. I brought your costumes and the band is all set," he said. He handed them the playlist and suggested they study it on the short ride to the hotel.

"Don't worry, the band has already received the scores, and the keyboard player has worked on the arrangements. I know it will go just fine tonight. You won't screw up, you never do, but leave the cuing to the keyboard player tonight, he will direct the show," said the agent.

"Not a problem," answered Tony, "With this hectic schedule you have us on, we are happy to give up anything." Ushering them through the hotel and into the backstage of the lounge, they changed, warmed up with the band and twenty minutes later they were on. It was early, just eight o'clock and the room was more empty than full, so it gave them a little wiggle room to perfect some of the old standards resurrected for the mature audience. The dance floor was small, designed for dancing face to face, and with a quick look at the patrons, they had designed it right. If they kept with the ballads, the few martini drinkers would be satisfied with the entertainment, especially after their second. At ten o'clock they called it a night, collapsed the instruments into their cases and headed home.

"Great show tonight," pronounced their agent.

"This audience looked like they were going to keel over any minute. I kept waiting for an EMT truck to appear. I couldn't rouse this audience with a cattle prod," said Tony.

"Yes, but be patient, on the weekends you are going to see lots of young hotties and budding professionals and then the place will be swinging. Tonight, just write it off as a little less work than normal." Their agent dropped the fatigued twins off at their home and wished them luck the following night. He handed them one hundred dollars and told them to use the cash for cab fare from the train station to the hotel until he could figure out something better.

"I called your mom and she is putting together several outfits that will be kept in the changing room. We want to make this as easy as possible. Basically with the train schedule, you will go from the station directly to the hotel. There will be time for you to change and grab a light bite before you go on. Look, boys, I know this will be tough, but if you couldn't handle it, I would have never suggested this regimen."

He dropped the boys off at their unpretentious home: the agent envisioned two huge pretentious Hollywood Hills mansions, one for each boy, in a few years. He truly believed in their talent, and with the pace he had set for them, the goal being complete dedication to perfecting their craft, they would all have their mansions. Time would tell, but he bet they would both stick out the arduous year.

As they became more proficient, Maria began sending the boys out for small parts. The twins' first commercial was with Fresca, the flavored soda company. They did well and were paid residuals for a year. They would have been perfect, but there was no room in their tight schedule. Tony was then cast for a Juicy Fruit Gum commercial in which he played guitar and sang their new jingle. They almost cut him because he was too good looking and resembled Elvis, and they feared he would distract from the chewing gum message itself. They kept regardless and it was financially profitable. However, when they discovered he was an identical twin they asked the Sacca twins to do a Doublemint chewing commercial. Because of their busy schedule they asked them to wait two weeks, but the company was too impatient and gave it to another set of twins.

Christmas Eve was a week away, as the groom's mother completed the wedding plans. The couple was to be wed at the Catholic Church two blocks away and the reception would follow at a family owned Italian bistro directly across the street. In spite of the holiday, the restaurant owners had known the Sacca family for decades and if they wanted a wedding Christmas Eve, then they would make the best wedding in the world. It was the first time the twins were dressed differently: Robert in sparkling white tuxedo, and Tony in black. This would insure the bride married the right guy, and give Robert the spotlight he well-deserved. Linda nervously walked down the aisle in her pristine white organza gown. She was fetchingly beautiful, if not heavenly. Her golden hair was twisted in curls framing her face as it trailed down the back of her neck, her soft pink lips, with matching nail polish and bouquet of roses gave her an angelic appearance. Robert held out his hand, and walked with her the last three steps to the priest, where they pledged their love until death do them part. As best man, Tony couldn't help but cringe when he heard his brother say, "I do." He was way too young. There were so many fish in the sea, why would he tie himself down?

After the short ceremony, the winter weather had been kind, and the harsh icy winds subsided for the next few hours. The wedding party and all hundred guests walked directly across the street, and enjoyed the essence of a true Italian wedding. The red wine flowed, as platters after platter of appetizers were passed and then hours later the main course was served. Between the veal, the lobster, and the steak entrees, everyone was sufficiently stuffed. The two sets of parents huddled in the corner and split the bill in half, all very cordial and all very civil. As he watched Linda and his brother kiss, Tony wondered how long this love fest would last. As the wedding cake was rolled to the center of the room, they fed each other a small slice and then Tony poured a glass of champagne and toasted the happy couple. When he gulped down the champagne Tony made a secret bet with himself, he gave them five years, tops.

The second wedding took place shortly after as Tony walked down the aisle with Dolores. A stunning young lady he met one evening at a local club. Tony was on a break and this beautiful woman caught his eye, they sat and talked at the bar for hours after the show. Young and impetuous, Tony wasn't into lengthy courtships, but with his brother taking the leap, the two young lovers followed suit. The fact that Dolores' father was in the record business was just another candle on the cake as they solidified their marriage. Her family had more money, so the nuptials were more lavish: the crowd was larger, the food lighter fare, with an emphasis on French food, and the bar was stocked with the top shelf liquor. This time Tony wore white and Robert wore black. Joe and Millie were not only happy, but relieved: both sons were married and now their wives could look after them. They were the first to hold up their glasses to toast the happy couple.

Like Linda, Dolores travelled on the road with Tony for a year. They seemed in love, at least that was how Tony felt, as he was physically drawn to her. Was it a higher love? He couldn't be sure, but how he felt in his loins each day was enough to make the marriage satisfying for him.

With too much time on her hands, she felt jealous of the constant attention drawn to her spouse, and Dolores became unhappy and unfulfilled in their marriage. In spite of her beauty, whenever the two of them were together, it was Tony who everyone gravitated to: she was ignored, just eye candy clinging to his arm. Very young, very immature, and probably not ready for marriage, she sought comfort confiding in others. Dolores simply picked the wrong person to lean on. During a twenty minute break at one of the Pittsburgh shows, the keyboard player left the stage and took the empty seat at the bar next to her. He whispered in her ear, she nodded and they began dancing to canned music played at intermission. Tony usually spent those twenty minutes changing, relaxing, drinking water and mentally preparing for the second half of the show, but that night, he walked out of the dressing room, peeked out from behind the stage and witnessed his wife being held tightly by the keyboard player. At first glance he didn't give it a thought, but then he continued to observe the two and it was painfully obvious that they were close, that this was not just a onetime occurrence. Unable to tear his eyes away from the scene, Tony grew angrier by the moment. This time the tables had turned and he was jealous, someone had grabbed his wife's attention, and from the way he was holding her, their relationship seemed to entail more than just talking and dancing.

He never said a word as they drove home in silence. He had only one thing on his mind and that was showing Dolores who was the better man. He slipped into bed, turned to her, kissed her, held her tightly, and took his time making love. He kissed her from her toes to her head, demonstrating all the passion within his heart. In the morning, he looked at her and simply said,

"I saw you last night, and I know you are not all mine. I saw you give away your heart to someone else. I'm leaving." Before she could offer a retort, Tony had packed his bags and left for good. Heartbroken, he wheeled his luggage through the narrow hallway, walked up to the front desk and took a new room, he needed time to think and recover from a short marriage that probably should never have taken place. He chastised himself for following in Robert's footsteps. When Robert walked down the aisle, he had given him five years: but looking at his own marriage, it had barely lasted a year. Tony had to face the cold hard fact that he had made a mistake and had fallen in love with the wrong person and for a while he would suffer the pangs of a crushed heart. At twenty-four, he would slowly pick up the pieces up and begin again.

The next night he was in bed by himself feeling very much alone. As he lay underneath the covers, all he could think about was fact that he there was no one next to him who loved him. He felt abandoned and deserted: for hours the same scenario ran through his mind and then out of the blue, he refocused,

"I'm the star of the show, it's my name on the marquee, and I'm free!" As those thoughts shuffled through his mind time and again, he went from depression to euphoria. He had made himself realize that by living without her, he was free to love again. Dolores was the fool not him, and now he would reap his just rewards. There was no doubt in his mind he would find another woman, and in seeking her he would have the time of his life. When he looked over at the other side of the bed, at the covers untouched, the pillow perfectly puffed up, he knew he would fill that empty space. This was a dawn of another person. He rose to the occasion, he threw on a pair of jeans, a long sleeved tee shirt and walked down to the bar. With twenty minutes until last call he surveyed the room, there was no one there he would hijack back to his room, but two middle-aged women called him over to the bar and boisterously flattered him on his show.

"Quite a voice, and quite a handsome guy too," they said. Maybe that was all he needed, and without ordering a drink, he took the elevator back to the room. A grin was stamped across his face, yes, he thought, I'm going to make it, if it's the last thing I do.

The twins somehow, through great tenacity, completed the year with Maria, while still entertaining the ever increasing crowds at the Hilton lounges. After their last acting class, they celebrated with champagne and then went on to a stellar performance that Friday night at the packed Hilton lounge. The entertainment manager was in the audience and was more than impressed with the Sacca Twins. He loved their songs, their impressive looks, stage presence and most of all, the way they interacted with the audience. He momentarily departed the showroom, went to his office, and flipped through the calendar to review future bookings. When his eyes landed on The El San Juan, Puerto Rico, he beamed with joy, as nobody of note was scheduled to perform there. He took his pen and put an x over the scheduled entertainer and wrote in the Sacca Twins for an initial four week stay. He knew those young boys, and he assumed they would jump at the chance to play at the world famous resort. After he jotted down a few notes, he waited for their final set of the evening, and then called them over to his table. The manager didn't mince words; he offered them the four week stint and then wrote the fee on the clean side of a cocktail napkin.

"Is this agreeable to you boys?" he asked.

The twins had to contain their elation. They simply responded yes, they would do the gig, but they would have to run it by their agent. The manager handed them each a business card and explained he would draw up the contract and it would be ready by the following afternoon.

"You would have to leave in a week," he added. As soon as he was out of sight, they hugged each other, the gig of gigs, to be playing at one of the trendiest night clubs in the southern hemisphere. The Revue had travelled around the northern states, in the most inclement conditions, and had not gone unnoticed by the booking agents as they noted the success of the shows. The Sacca Twins Revue had become one of the top show bands touring the country and with it came a strong demand.

"You know brother," said Tony, "This last year has been a bitch when it came time for women, I say let's go and have the time of our lives. I have a lot of living to make up for!" The twins marched back to the stage, gathered the Revue band and explained the offer. When the screaming finally died down, it was unanimous. Four weeks in Puerto Rico was just fine by them.

"Let's do this," agreed Robert. "In the morning, I'll call our agent and ask him to review the contracts. We only have a week, and I'm thinking there is a lot we should add to the show to really make it dazzle. Those people are coming to Puerto Rico to party hearty and we really have to step up our act. I think we should even throw in a couple Spanish songs. Even if we don't speak the language, I'm sure we could make it sound great."

"You know what else I love about this gig, is that our band will travel with us. Remember when we had to tell our first band to take a hike, that the promoters only wanted us? I am so thankful the manager has included our musicians," said Tony.

"Okay guys, as soon as we know the details, which should be tomorrow, our agent will contact you. In the meantime, if any of you can come up with a couple of contemporary Spanish songs, let's try to perform them. I think it would impress the audience that we sing a few songs in their own language," suggested Robert.

Tony and Robert were considered one of the top show bands in the country during the 1970s

Las Vegas Rocks ®

*1864 – Nevada is admitted into the
Union as the 36th state. This day is
recognized annually as a state holiday.*

Evel Knievel is presented with a birthday cake by the Sacca Twins in Puerto Rico where Evel performed a jump

CHAPTER 5

"I see it," said Tony as the jet began its descent into Puerto Rico. As far as the eye could see the deep blue water was calm, as the sunlight glistened at the edges of each wave before crashing back into the ocean floor. The smooth hum of the engines and the slow tilt of the wings as they glided into formation, announced a turbulent free landing. Perched at the opened cabin door, the twins could hardly wait to exit the plane. An immediate smell enveloped the air, it was the scents coming from the massive bouquets of red orchids, pale yellow hibiscus, purple orchids, and white poinsettias, all local rainforest plants, arranged throughout the tropical airport. They followed the signs and the vacationers and the crew collected their luggage and instruments and then nabbed a porter who quickly obtained a nondescript limousine to transport them to the hotel.

"Has anyone ever been here?" asked Tony and they all shook their heads, no. "Well from where I sit it looks awfully nice."

The black car slowly negotiated the sharp curve as they drove toward the front of the prominent hotel. The resort was imposing: it spread over acres of beachfront property. As they registered at the front desk, a constant cool ocean breeze blew through the lobby; it was the most paradisiacal place any of the guys had ever seen. After he handed over the keys to each guest, the porter led the way to each of their rooms. The resort wasn't fully booked, so every person had his own room for the entire four week stay; that would be heaven on earth as they were already glancing at the swim clad women.

Tony and Robert called a short meeting in the hallway and decided that they should take the rest of the day off as vacation and meet at noon the following day for rehearsals. There was no problem agreeing on that. Tony stripped down to his swimsuit and leather thongs, grabbed a bath towel and the room key, and headed for the pool. After a glimpse into the full length mirror, he was confident: he had religiously dedicated himself to a six day a week stringent exercise routine and it had paid off. He had the sought after six pack abs, muscular arms and back, and no loose skins hanging from anywhere. Looking around he had to find the perfect spot where he would most likely run into a beautiful babe. Nonchalantly circumventing the lagoon style pool he found the perfect spot, a lounge chair near the in-pool bar. Lovely girls in skimpy bikinis swam in the pool and then slinked up on the bamboo chairs ordering the fruit concoction of the afternoon. If he played his cards right, he would get a good look at a lot of those lush women. Painting himself with suntan lotion, he was ready. He plopped back on the lounge and squinted through his partially shaded eyes. Hearing a squishy sound he turned to his left to see an elderly woman had taken the vacated lounge next to his. This sure wasn't looking up, he thought.

"Hi," she said, "I'm Samantha and here on vacation, are you here on vacation?" Not wanting to get involved with an elderly woman he was polite but answered with a staccato response,

"Just a little work."

"Oh look," she said as her stunning daughter, wet from swimming, tossed her long red hair into the sky, caught it in her hands and wrapped it around her head, "May I present my daughter, Tricia." The lounge seat had definitely taken a turn for the better as Tony offered his hand. Unable to control his breathing, he was taken by her curvaceous body, ample breasts, cream colored, freckled face, and a mane of thick red curls. In his mind, he had been to paradise and the Lord had presented him with a princess. Standing up, he shook her hand and then offered to share his lounge, since all the others were either taken or had beach towels holding swimmer's spots. The minute she opened her mouth, he was completely infatuated. Tony asked Samantha if he could borrow Tricia and they headed for a quaint coconut bamboo bar on the beach. As they sat in the warm sand, they talked for hours as the sun began to close over the edge of the sea. Later they changed and shared dinner with her mother and then he took Tricia for a quiet walk on the beach, and later a slice of nirvana in his room, as he properly christened the queen bed. In the morning a layer of red hair was strewn across her pillow and a smile was on her face from a happy first date.

"You really know how to show a girl a good time," she laughed. He took her in his arms kissed her good morning and then she jumped up tossed on her dress and left. "I don't want my mom to think I was out all night," she said.

"See you after the show tonight?" he asked.

"I wouldn't miss it for the world!" As he stood in the shower, he was a happy man. He wondered if Robert, who had been married for over three years felt the same way after making love. Robert always seemed to be ahead of him when it came to quantity, but then Robert surprised them all and married one of the dancers he had met the first summer at Bandstand '72. This gig in Puerto Rico would more than even the score. He laughed and thought he might have to purchase a new bed, so he would have room for all those notches.

When he walked down to the café, Tony waved at Robert and Linda. He was joining them for brunch before rehearsals. The restaurant, which overlooked the pool and ocean, was light and airy with white canvas seats and matching wooden tables. The cool ocean breezes were a constant reminder of the resort atmosphere. Tony drank freshly squeezed juice and ordered the breakfast special, which contained half of the ingredients on the menu.

"You sure are hungry," said Robert dryly, "You must have had a hectic night." Before Tony could answer he noticed Linda kick his brother underneath the table with a scowl on her face.

"As you can see, Robert is eating very lightly. Guess he didn't have such an athletic night. What did you do Tony? Run fifty miles?" she jested.

Holding his tongue, he sensed trouble in their paradise. He glanced at a make-believe watch on his left wrist, and said to himself, *yep, five years just as I suspected.* He looked at Linda, the last five years had not taken a toll on her exquisite face or svelte shape, she was still as beautiful as the day his brother had married her. Robert tersely got up and excused himself,

"I'll see you in the showroom in a few minutes." He noticed the chagrin on Linda's face, it was obvious something was very wrong, but Tony was in no mood to listen to her tales of woe. She sipped on her black coffee, pensively placed the cup down, looked at Tony, and began to cry.

"I am so tired of being ignored. He treats me like I don't exist. We never talk and if we do it's usually a fight over something stupid. I don't know what happened or what I am doing wrong, but I feel like our marriage is falling apart. At night, after the show he says he goes out with some of the band members, but I no longer believe that. I think he is cheating on me, and by the way he ignores my advances, I'm almost sure of it. I'm way too young to live like this," she confessed. "And I'll tell you Tony, when this four week gig is over, I'm leaving him. I'm tired of feeling lonely. Can you imagine being married and feeling lonely? But that is exactly how I feel. I don't think he loves me anymore." She dabbed at the tears flooding her cream colored complexion. There was little Tony could say or do to console his sister-in-law.

"Give it some time," he suggested as he excused himself heading toward the showroom. In spite of being upset, he couldn't help but notice the grandeur of the hotel. Everywhere he looked there were huge sprays of multicolored flowers that complimented the white washed walls, cream colored tile floors, white plantation blinds, and restful light blue ceilings. The only dark space at the entire resort was the casino leading into the showroom. Just like in Las Vegas, the casino tried to grab the theatre goers before they settled into their seats for the show: or provide additional post theatre entertainment. Either way, as a ticket holder, the only way to enter the theatre was through the dimly lit casino.

Tony sat at the back of the showroom and asked the keyboard player to play a song so he could obtain an idea of the acoustics. Although the room was highly air-conditioned, the ceilings were low, the carpet thick, and the walls covered with a velveteen wall paper. It would be easy to misjudge the optimum volume. A few bars into the song he noticed the sound was immediately soaked in by the room, there was no echo, but the sound seemed a little too weak. He grabbed the drummer; Tony asked him to sit at the back of the room while he sang with Robert. Halfway through the melody, he asked for an opinion and the drummer also agreed the volume seemed too weak for the room. The band held a short meeting and decided to raise all the sounds up one level.

"I believe even with a full house, we might be too quiet for the acoustics of the room." The keyboard player insisted on a complete run through from beginning to end. With a full day of vacation under their belts, the rehearsal went well, and he pronounced them ready to perform. Tony and Robert stayed behind to practice two Spanish songs with the keyboard player. Extracting two CDs, they listened to "Matador," by Los Fabulosos, and "Clandestino," by Manu Chao and agreed those would be perfect songs. They were contemporary and well known.

"Now, if I just had a Spanish coach, I would feel a lot better," Tony commented. After several attempts, they had most of the pronunciation down pat, at least decent enough for the show. Tony turned around, picked up his pace and headed for the door, but a musician ran after him.

"Hey man, I could use some advice," he asked. Sympathetic Tony held his space and they walked into the warm afternoon air. "You see, I think my girlfriend is cheating on me and I think I can prove it."

"How do you know, how can you be so sure?" responded Tony.

"Well," stammered the musician, "I just found out I have a case of the crabs and I know I have been faithful, so I am pretty sure my girlfriend has been sleeping around." He held back laughter and broke the truth gently: he completely agreed with the musician.

"Sorry," was all he could add. After the show, the keyboard player hugged Tony, he had been right, his girlfriend was cheating and he was going to go out and celebrate. There were thousands of beautiful women and he was going to find one, even if it took him the entire night.

As the red velvet curtain parted, the nine piece band began a warm up medley of all the songs in the playlist, the dancers took the stage and began gyrating to the music and finally, the volume lowered and the Sacca Twins walked dramatically onto center stage. They wore black tuxedos and made a striking duo as they grabbed the microphones and began singing a romantic ballad. The skimpily clad dancers hovered around the twins creating sexual tension, which was readily picked up by the audience. After their first bows of the evenings, they began a series of upbeat top forty songs followed by the two new Spanish songs, which got them a standing ovation from the audience. The curtain closed announcing the first half was over. During the requisite twenty minute break, the twins quickly changed into new costumes designed especially for the resort show. They reentered the stage wearing flowered jackets, with pink satin shirts, and white patent shoes. When they received a round of applause before they opened their mouths, they guessed the new outfits went over well with the audience. The second half they stuck to standards mixed with medium tempo songs, two up-beat songs and then finished with Marvin Gaye's, "Let's Get It On," while the dancers erotically encircled the brothers. The women had to fan themselves as they extricated themselves from the seats.

"That show was hot, really hot," said many women as they staggered out of the theatre. Tony and Robert thanked the crew for a great show, and reminded them of the afternoon rehearsal the next day. Normally Tony would be quick to change out of his costume, especially one such as loud as the one he was wearing, but his mind was on making up for lost time and finding chicks. He figured he couldn't help but be noticed, so he walked directly out of the theatre into the casino. Two steps into the cash forest, he was accosted by a thin tall dark haired woman, with a light olive complexion and the juiciest lips he had ever seen. In a thick Spanish accent she told him she loved the show especially, the Spanish songs.

"All the Americans come down here to entertain us and they forget that half of the tourists are from South America. I thank you for thinking of us and including those songs in the show," she said. "But I can tell your accent is off." Still starring at her luscious lips, he absent-mindedly agreed,

"Perhaps you can help me with the accent. I come from and Italian neighborhood in Philadelphia, and meet very few Spanish speaking people. "How about a drink," he quickly suggested as she took his arm and he boldly escorted her through the lobby to the bar sitting on the edge of the beach. After ordering two Mai Tai's, she introduced herself,

"My name is Rosa and of course I know your name," she laughed. They tapped glasses and sipped on the rum infused drinks and chatted aimlessly about the resort, the weather, and their homes.

"Really," she continued, "I will be happy to help you with your accent." Tony looked into her dark brown eyes, and began singing one of the

Spanish songs. She stopped him intermittently correcting his pronunciation. He took her hand he led her off the bar stool, toward an empty lounge chair overlooking the ocean.

"If I'm going to practice, I don't want anyone else to hear," he said as he began serenading her. This time she didn't correct his accent, he had listened carefully and picked up on the subtle nuances making it sound authentic. They sipped on the drinks and he ordered another round as he continued to talk and sing away the night. As two o'clock approached and the bar closed for the night, they found themselves completely alone. She put her lips close to his,

"I think we are done with the lesson." he leaned in and finally kissed those luscious lips that had been teasing him for hours.

"I have an idea, why don't we go back to my room and I can instruct you in some American customs," he suggested. She took his hand and they strolled through the lobby and into his room. The windows were open and the thin white curtains were softly rolling with the gentle breezes, the bed had been turned down with the crisp white sheets folded back, welcoming sleep. He flipped off the lights and thoroughly instructed Rosa in the fine art of lovemaking, American style.

In the morning he reached over, and the bed was empty. He wasn't sure if he had just experienced the most lascivious encounter of his entire life, or if he had in fact, dreamed Rosa up. Later that afternoon, he took Robert aside and rehearsed the two Spanish songs.

"How did you become such an expert with the accent?" questioned Robert. Tony just looked at him and laughed hysterically.

Robert and Tony remained behind after the crew was dismissed from rehearsals and practiced the Spanish songs until they both could properly enunciate the accent perfectly. Robert was a quick study and after a few times, learned the accent as competently as his brother.

"Let's go grab some lunch," suggested Tony. After the crying spell with Linda, he wanted to get Robert's take on their marriage. They walked to the grill by the pool area, ordered two burgers with sodas and sat starring out at the ocean.

"How are things with you and Linda?" asked Tony. He could see Robert hesitate, as he looked down. Silence ensued and Tony was at a loss as to what to say next. "I guess what I want to say is that Linda was crying to me yesterday morning about your marriage. Can you be honest and tell me? I don't mean to pry, but your life is tied to mine and I don't want to see you hurting."

"To be honest, things are not so great with me and Linda. You might have been right when you discouraged me from marrying so early, but I was so in love, or so I thought. It's not that she isn't pretty, it's that I am bored, and I find myself eluding her whenever possible. I end up hanging out with the band members or,"

"Be truthful, are you cheating on her?" accused Tony. Robert didn't answer the question. His eyes moistened as he stared blankly,

"I guess I just fell out of love. I can't see spending the rest of my life with someone I don't love. She told me when we finish this four week gig, she is leaving me. I can't blame her. I feel horrible this happened but it's like I grew up and she remained the same." Tony hugged his brother and shed of few tears of his own.

"I'm so sorry, you think I would have seen you hurting. You really hid this from me." The tour continued on as the Sacca Twins Revue sold out night after night. The audiences were tourists, so they made few changes to the show and rehearsal time dwindled down to less than an hour a day. People flew down from the east coast and in from neighboring islands just to see the act. They were highlighted on local television, interviewed on radio stations, and given substantial space in the newspapers. They met the governor and city dignitaries and had become not only local stars, but heroes, adding to the coffers of the local businesses and the economy. Tony used his time wisely: he found many Rosa's, a Tina, two Theresa's, a Jennifer, Cathy, Lucile, Katherine and a Sonia to fill the void of empty hours. By the time he reached the states, his Spanish had been formidably perfected.

At the front desk of the hotel, a glorious Hispanic woman observed Tony escort a parade of beauties up the elevator and into his room; she decided then and there she wanted a piece of that famous man. So one morning, she zealously asked him if he would like to see what a local home looked like, and she could cook him some of the wonderful dishes of Puerto Rico. She was strikingly beautiful with her olive complexion, long black hair fraught with waves, dark brown oval eyes, the softest chin, and a perfect bikini body. Tony was not about to turn down such an offer. After the show she met him in the lobby and they drove back to her small home nestled at the base of a hill. Although the aroma of cooked food enveloped the home, she directed their attention to her bedroom where Tony enveloped her with his art of making love. In the middle of the night she said he had given her so much love her heart hurt and in the morning she drove herself to the hospital, she had suffered a heart attack.

After this setback and a slight ding in his chivalrous armor, he sought stronger women. The quest was resolutely answered in the form of a lustrous Puerto Rican lady who brought him the gift of ethereal sexual activity; transmutational sex. She lived in a hut on the sand in a cozy alcove overlooking the ocean. There was always a pleasant sea breeze sailing through her home as the smells of the ocean mixed with jasmine and hyacinths added to the exotic ambiance. She laid him down on a straw mat and massaged snake oils into his skin and caressed his face and hands. Her tender technique aroused him in a way no one on earth had done, yet she made him cease when his body was about to unleash the finale of the sex act- it was the power of transmutational sex.

"What!" screamed Tony. She put her finger to his mouth to quiet him down, turned him over and made him engage his sight at the brilliant blue sky, listen to the wind, and smell the freshly picked flowers.

"This sex will electrify you, give your mind power, give you a greater sense of creativity and enhance your brain's ability to think. Once your body is in a heightened state of sexual emotional intensity you become more aware, you are more sensitive to stimuli, you feel more alive, exuberant, more expressive and more inspired," she insisted. However she explained it, she became his sexual obsession, teaching him not only the art of lovemaking, but how to harness this energy into every aspect of his life. They were together for the next several months they. She brought him to a higher level of living and intensity. Sometimes they met before the show, sometimes after, but with each meeting, she brought him to a higher level of consciousness. At times it felt as if he were floating above the earth, she had altered his physical senses to such supreme heights in almost inexplicable ways. She had hypnotized him with her techniques. He never met such a woman again, but the impact of her art remained blossoming within his psyche, he would never forget her.

It would seem, at least for the average man with the average libido, that this experience couldn't be topped, but with Tony's remarkable looks, talent, tender nature, and bottomless sexual appetite, the impossible was a possibility. He had seen her many times, tall, perfectly portioned, with long flowing dark brown hair, high cheek bones, pouty lips, oval green eyes and perfectly rounded breasts. A dancer, her long legs were muscular, she was no weakling. They were both walking on the beach one morning, and their eyes locked as she changed speeds and jogged a mile up the shore, leaving a trace of her face in his mind. It was a small island and he was quite sure they would see each other again. Days later, after the late night performance had ended, this luscious woman approached him and asked him if he remembered her.

"I have been living with the memory of your face since the moment we saw each other on the beach," he confessed, "how about a drink?"

"I have a much better idea," she suggested as they wove their way through the crowd into the parking lot. "How about going to my favorite place in the city?" he climbed into the convertible, massaged her thigh, twisted his head, and looked intensely into her eyes,

"Take me to heaven," he said.

"Well it's my secret heaven," she laughed as they drove through the congested downtown streets. She pulled the car into an underground lot, pressed the elevator button to the top floor, and thirty stories later, they emerged at the roof of the highest building in the heart of San Juan. With a blanket and a bag filled with champagne, glasses, and hunks of local cheeses, she created a midnight picnic.

"This is a special place. You see we dancers like to sunbathe nude, and there is no privacy on the beaches, so during the day, we come here, take off our bikinis and get a complete tan." She popped open the bottle of champagne, they toasted, and then she took him for a short walk around the roof. It was a spectacular view of the entire city with the ocean meeting the edge of the beach and the skies filled with a canvass of twinkling stars. He placed a hunk of cheese in his mouth, held her tightly, and took in the endless view, with one of the most perfect woman he had ever met. After washing down the cheese with a glass of champagne, he took his hands and pulled her face close to his. Her lips were moist and her breath shallow as he drew her in for a deep kiss. As they lay down on the blanket, the two looked up at the sky, it was endless and limitless and in that quiet moment, they were overcome with passion. This wasn't their first meeting, she had been surreptitiously stalking him for weeks, and he had had more than one fading glimpse of her on the beach. This was a liaison that was meant to be, but with the perfection of the night sky, and the cool trade winds enveloping the air, this was a night of sexual intensity unlike anything he had felt before. They made love underneath the waxing moon, and when they were spent, she began kissing him again: she crawled down and her tongue lapped at the tip of his penis until he was spent again. The ultimate fantasy of the man whose arms she had dreamed of being wrapped in. He walked to the edge of the building and looked out across the ocean, happy and at peace.

As calm as the ocean waves silently slithered to shore, she came behind, grabbed his member, stroking gently, permeating him with a complete sense of sensual rapture. His eyes were closed and his heart was pounding as she adeptly anticipated his every need. When he had reached orgasm, he opened up his eyes and it was completely bright: it appeared as though the sun had risen. Was it the intensity of the lovemaking that brightened up the sky, or had they been so stuck in this transfixed state of intense sexual encounter that hours had passed, and the night had evolved to day? No, it was five in the morning and the sun had not risen.

When she put the gear of the convertible in park, she leaned over, brushing his ear lobe with her lips.

"I will remember last night until the day that I die, you are the tenderest lover I have ever known." He hopped over the edge of the car and blew her a kiss good-bye; he would forever keep last night in his dreams. As he stood in front of the El San Juan, he looked up at the towering marquee and saw his name plastered across the sign. He walked into the hotel and was greeted by several staff as he inserted the key into his second floor suite overlooking the ocean. *I have arrived* he thought. Life just couldn't get any better. Wherever he and Robert went, they were treated like kings: fed, offered drinks, asked to parties and clubs, they had become royalty on the tiny island. At that moment, he felt like king of the world, he was living out his dreams, reaching higher than he ever felt possible. He closed his eyes for a short nap and prayed this fantasy life would never end.

That night as Tony stood in front of a packed house, he scanned the room and saw her seated in the corner banquette. When the most romantic ballad in the set had begun, he set his eyes in her direction and received a smile in return. He pivoted around to cue the band and when he looked up the fantasy woman had vanished. She was the elusive butterfly he would probably never catch, but the one night they had together was a piece of heaven that would always be a part of him.

At the end of the four weeks, management was so thrilled with the success of the Revue, they extended the engagement for an additional seven months. Tony's Spanish would escalate from formidable to fluent. The show director ordered several new costume changes and added fresh choreography; the music director revamped the playlist, including three more Spanish songs, and the lighting director implemented new technology, making the show appeal to younger audiences. The combination of changes was nothing short of genius, as the money poured into the El San Juan. With less time spent on rehearsals, Tony joined some of the musicians at the Black Jack tables. They all took turns winning and losing, but in the end, each of them had left several weeks' worth of salaries in the hands of the dealers. A lesson learned, they vowed to stop but then Tony was introduced to a professional gambler who was only too happy to share his talent as long as they didn't play at the same table. Within a short while things were picking up and he was back in the winner's seat making a lot of money. However, in the end, when he was true to himself, despite of the expert coaching, he still left with less than what he had brought to the table.

Linda left Robert and went back to Philadelphia, later filing for divorce. Although he was remorseful, he was also young, famous, attractive and flush with money. The girls oozed out of the woodwork seeking his company and affection. Neither of the twins suffered from lack of love as their faces began to mature into suave comely young men. They had done their parent's proud, and had become the success their father envisioned.

Mel Tillis with the Sacca Twins during an interview

Las Vegas Rocks ©

*1885 – The State Land Act of 1885 offers
sections of land at $1.25 per acre. Farmers
move in and agriculture becomes the
dominant industry for the next 20 years.*

Mickey Gilley with the Sacca twins during an interview on their TV show, live from Las Vegas

CHAPTER 6

Eight months later, the deeply tanned crew emerged off the jet and scattered in several directions. The twin's mother waved as she caught the first glimpse of her sons. She held out both arms and hugged them together and cried that it had been so long since she had seen them.

"Let me look at you," she said gazing at their slim bodies, "So beautiful, so gorgeous, both of you." And then she proceeded to squeeze them again. They loaded every inch of the car up with luggage, and slowly made their way home through the congested highways. As soon as they opened up the side door, the pungent smells of marinara sauce impregnated the air. The boys spied a huge pot bubbling on top of the stove. Their dad held out his arms and warmly embraced his sons to welcome them back home. Eight months was a long time to be away and sometimes the silence was deafening. After lugging the heavy bags upstairs, they sat down to dinner.

"How is sis?" asked Robert who was prominently absent from the table.

"She's fine, you know she is busy with her life: doing a little of this and that, but she is happy and keeps herself busy raising her two sons Eddie Jr. and Christopher," said Millie in a saturnine manner, "She'll come around soon." She changed the subject and she insisted on hearing all the details of the trip. "How was the hotel, did you go swimming, did you meet nice people, and did you have a good time?" She looked at Robert: she knew the answers to some of those questions, as Linda had been by for a heart to heart visit and told her that she had filed for divorce. With a few tears welling at the corners of her eyes, Millie looked at Robert and told him about his wife's visit.

"I'm so sorry Robert. I didn't realize how unhappy the two of you had become. Look you have only been home a few minutes; we can table this conversation for another time. Now tell me about the show, did you meet any famous people, and how was the food?" their mom rattled on.

They hadn't gotten their sea legs back when their new manager, Gino Tonetti, called and asked for a meeting. Home just one day, the brothers drove downtown to discuss their next move. A svelte, dark haired man opened the door and escorted the twins to his richly decorated office; clearly this agent was doing a hell of a lot better than their last. He was sitting in a soft, black leather chair: the fifty-five year old agent pointed to the wall with hundreds of pictures plastered in a haphazard fashion.

"These are my clients," Gino bragged, "and as you can see, there are plenty of familiar faces. Trust in me and I can make sure your careers are always pointed in the right direction. I can make you international stars." He puffed on a slim cigar, glanced down at pile of papers, and then looked the brothers squarely in their eyes.

"I got a call yesterday from the owner of the El San Juan, Lou Puro, who was so taken with your performances that he extended the contract for another eight months. Can you believe that? You aren't home a day and they already want you back. I don't know what you did, but whatever you did, you sure wowed the crowds." Tony was numb, he wanted to spend some time at home and explore other avenues. He had fallen in love with acting and wanted to stay put and try to expand into other areas of the business. On the other hand, Robert was wildly happy. He was extricating himself from his first wife and wanted to go back to the resort and perform, and then make up for lost time. Tony had shared many of his sexual escapades and Robert wanted part of the action.

There was a lot more to Puerto Rico than their active sexual escapades, it was an old country with rich Spanish culture and kind warm people who welcomed the tourists. On occasions, friends would take them sightseeing through the countryside, up to the rainforests, or exploring underground caverns, there was a lot to see and do outside of the bustling downtown promenade. The country was absolutely beautiful, and perhaps Tony needed to take a second look, perhaps he should reconsider returning.

Gino sensed a rift, the brothers were not in agreement, but he really wanted them to sign the contract: it was a sweet guaranteed income for his own business for the next eight months and lord knew he needed the money. He choked on the cigar and looked around his office, it was time for another upgrade: maybe a new comfortable chair, or a better quality of cigar, or a Cezanne or a Gauguin to replace the cheap prints, either way, he had to get those twins to sign on the dotted line.

"I negotiated a great deal for you boys. More money, lots more money." He handed them each a copy of the new contract and he told them to take their time reading the fine print. He excused himself and gently shut the office door as he began pacing in the reception room. The dingy office, with scuffed linoleum floors reflected an agent whose time had come and gone. It was some luck when he received a call that the Sacca Twins were seeking a new agent. With that contract dangling in their faces, he was sure his ship had come in, at least for a while. The office was devoid of sound as he continued to pace up and back, covertly listening at the door for sounds of accord.

Tony wanted to stand his ground and not return to the resort, but he could see the hurt in Robert's eyes. Tony's brief marriage had left an unmended hole in his heart, and he was keenly aware that Robert was hurting as well. If he gave in to his brother, maybe that would be all it would take to revive his spirits after the divorce. He stared at the contract and then looked over at Robert who had already signed on the dotted line. His sparkling eyes and wide smile reflected a young man who had made his decision. *Oh the hell with it,* and copying his twin, Tony signed on the dotted line as well.

"Brother, I hope this makes you happy. It's another eight months in paradise." Gino abruptly stopped his relentless pacing when he heard the door crack open to his office. They offered their agent the two signed contracts, he shook their hands joyfully, and then immediately made two copies. Still sucking on the stub of the cigar, he stapled a copy of each contract, inserted them in two manila envelopes, and pronounced the deal was done.

"I'm telling you, this is your ticket to international fame, people from the ends of the earth flock to that hotel. With your names in lights you will be household names. Just stick with me and I will make this happen, but hey, another eight months at one of the finest resorts in the world isn't such a bad gig. I will try and make it down for one of your shows," he said as he ushered them out of the waiting room. He held his breath until the elevator door to snapped shut, then he jumped up and down and screamed, "Hallelujah!" Gino grabbed the phone and called the entertainment director at the hotel to relay the wonderful news, and then he mailed the new contracts. He sat back in his executive chair and took a few minutes to gloat before he picked up the phone to try and attract another upcoming star. As he looked at the photos on the wall, he reminded himself that he too was on the mend, and his comeback had just begun.

When the boys returned home, they gave their mother the news that they would be making a return engagement. She wrapped her arms around them hugged them and reiterated how proud she was of her sons.

"I barely have time to clean your laundry. Now empty out your suitcases and I will get started right away. How about if I call the tailor and make an appointment for you later today? You know he can make you some fine new suits and then he can ship them to you," Millie insisted. The brothers nodded in agreement, gathered their dirty, sand filled clothing, and dragged it down to the basement. Their mom was busy making them grilled sandwiches, and once again the house was filled with the scents of home cooking.

Tony took a few bites and then met his mom, who was busy sorting out the filthy clothes, downstairs in the laundry room.

"Tony," she said, "Did you finish your lunch so fast?"

"No, it's just that I was looking for a chance to talk to you, privately. I really don't want to go back to Puerto Rico. Yes, I had a great time and yes we were successful, but I wanted to try other things. I didn't spend a year of my life taking the train everyday to New York for acting lessons not to be able to use what I learned. I love acting and I would love to try and make a success out of it. I know I already signed the contract, but I don't want to go," he admitted. She put down the laundry and looked at her son with sympathetic eyes. She took his hand and hugged him.

"I'm sorry to hear that you aren't crazy about going back, but please just once, do this for your brother. Can't you see he needs you? With his divorce he must be hurting inside. When you get back then maybe you can go your own way, but please for now just stay with him. It wasn't such a short time ago when you were depressed after your divorce. Keeping busy is the best thing, and a cure for a broken heart," she advised.

"I guess you're right mom. I'll go, even though I don't want to and when I get back, I will try work on my acting career. We have this new agent, and hopefully he can put me on the right track."

"That's my boy," she smiled as she pinched his cheek. "Now go upstairs and finish your lunch and then we can all go visit the tailor." Lumbering up the steps, Tony looked over his shoulder at the room where the music all began, *funny,* he thought to himself, *that room seems so small now.*

"They will be singing in a tropical climate," Millie proudly announced to the tailor, "they need special, lighter weight fabrics. How about one black silk sharkskin tuxedo, one cream colored linen suit, and one silver single breasted suit." The tailor rummaged through piles of fabric swatches and pulled out a large selection. He laid them on the counter top and suggested they take their time deciding.

"Now, can these suits be mailed down to the boys once they are done?" she asked.

"Sure, no problem, but I want to take several measurements so the garments will fit them beautifully. With that he pulled Robert aside, took the tape measure that was draped around his neck and wrote down a long list of numbers and then he did the same set of measurements for Tony. The tailor laughed boisterously and turned to their mother and said,

"That was a waste of time, they each have the exact measurements!" They left an imprint of their credit cards and the mailing address, then Tony and Robert thanked the tailor and left the store.

"Boys, shall we do like we did in the old days and go for ice-cream?"

"Sure, why not. But this time it's my treat," offered Tony. They walked the two short blocks, and he looked over at his smiling mother. Her face had aged over the years, with an increasing number of crevices surrounding her eyes and mouth. Despite her hard life, she was always the optimist; all she ever saw was the bright side of any situation. With the boys out of the house, on their own and making a good living, she was finally able to quit the physically demanding seamstress job, but the rigors of a hard life had engrained themselves permanently in her once perfect appearance. It was times like this that made Tony realize how much he loved and needed his mother. Although a man in his mid twenties, he never outgrew his need to be coddled and cared for. Their dad was gruff, stalwart when it came to approaching life: there were no soft or forgiving edges surrounding his demeanor. With every problem, and every hurt, it was always his mother where Tony sought refuge. They talked often: when he was on tour, he called her almost every day. The sound of her voice reassured him that no matter what problems he faced, there was always a solution.

Robert ordered the, "kitchen sink," the house special. Ten minutes later it arrived in a large steel mixing bowl, piled high with several layers of ice-cream balls, sauces, peanuts, whipped cream and three bright red cherries. They dug into the delicious mess and ate until the last dollop of ice-cream was gone.

"I'm going to miss you guys, but I am so proud of you and what you have become. My sons, the famous Sacca Twins, so beautiful, so talented and so good," she said. "I know that your dad was tough on you, but look how you turned out, you're a success and they want you back." She began to cry and Tony took this as a cue to leave. He dropped several dollars on the table, took her hand, and the three left the café. When they emerged on the street, it was already dark: the day had vanished in the blink of an eye. Just one more day at home and they would be back on the plane.

As soon as they returned home, Robert was busy on the phone calling the musicians and the dancers confirming the flight and the new terms of the contract. The substantial raise in pay made the crew was ready, willing, and able to return. That night, a ton of laundry was loaded into the machines as everyone braced themselves for another eight months.

Robbie Knievel with the Sacca Twins during one of his performances

Las Vegas Rocks ®

*Early 1900s – The completion of the main
railway, linking Southern California with
Salt Lake City, establishes Las Vegas as a
railroad town. The availability of water
makes Las Vegas an ideal refueling point
and rest stop.*

George Maharis of Route 66 is one of many celebrities that appeared on Live From Las Vegas with the Sacca Twins

CHAPTER 7

It could have been déjà vu, but it wasn't: it was a return booking at the world famous El San Juan Hotel in beautiful San Juan, Puerto Rico, and the Sacca Twins Revue was boldly posted on the marquee. This time, as the plane descended onto the tarmac the ocean looked familiar. There was no surprise as the trade winds whipped up the waves in the Caribbean, nor as the birds dove perpendicular, down to water to catch a fish in their beak. The puffy cumulus clouds that shared the sky with the blazing sunlight appeared the same as when he had left. The adventure had gone. Depressed, Tony's thoughts reverted to his mom's advice, stick this out and when the engagement was over he could seek other avenues. He would be the dutiful son; he would stick this out, put money in his bank account and save for the future he dreamed of as an actor. He knew that acting was notorious for its unsteady income, so for once in his career, he would be ultraconservative with his earnings and save as much as he could. The rooms and basic meals were paid for by the hotel, which made living expenses nominal. *Yes*, he coached himself *he could and he would do this*. He had his own dreams, and they didn't include his brother. Damn, if he didn't finally want to be a whole person, not part of another.

The rooms were as spacious and as comfortable as before, with windows that allowed a panoramic view of the aqua marine colored water. Tony plopped down on the bed, spread his arms and looked out at the endless sky thinking, *well there are worse places on earth to feel sorry for yourself*. Rehearsals would begin early afternoon the next day. He could sit in his room and brood, or he could take a walk on the beach, which seemed the better option. After placing his freshly cleaned clothes in the drawers, he changed into a Caribbean patterned swimsuit, black thongs, and a white tee-shirt, punched the elevator button, and stepped in.

"Hi," said a voice from the back of the car, instantly recognizing Tony.

"Hi," he responded, but to whom he wasn't sure. When the doors opened at beach level, a gorgeous, tall woman carrying a beach bag followed him out. She offered her hand and introduced herself as Dana, the new lead dancer.

"It's a pleasure to meet you," Tony remarked as he noticed how well she filled out her black spandex bikini. "I was just about to take a walk, would you like to join me?" She didn't need any coaxing, she took his hand and answered,

"Sure lead the way." They tossed their few belongings on a lounge chair and they began walking along the shoreline. The weather was picture perfect, as it was almost every single day of the year, and the water temperature was ideal for swimming at a tepid eighty degrees. Dana ran into the waves, dove into the water, and then bobbed her head up. Tony was right behind. They swam parallel with the beach for a half mile and then back to the shore.

"You are my first swimming partner," he said. "I could never find anyone who would jump into the water and swim for more than a couple of minutes."

"I love it," she responded, "It makes me feel alive and relaxed. I love the way the waves make me feel like I'm floating on air." They walked back to the lounge and he was about to order a drink when she told him she couldn't stay. She slid on a pair of sandals over her pedicured toenails, shook his hand, and told him she looked forward to seeing him at rehearsals the next day. *The next day* thought Tony, *what about tonight? Hmm,* he wondered, *does she have a boyfriend?* With a body like that and a face that was arrestingly beautiful he already knew the answer, yes she probably did. Oh well, can't win them all. He opened the multi colored beach umbrella attached to the lounge chair he put on his Ray Bans, closed his eyes, and took a nap with Dana laying heavily on his mind.

Tony would feel the ocean beneath him later that night. Oh the girls were so beautiful on this Puerto Rican Island. With their lustrous long hair, tanned skin, deep brown eyes and statuesque bodies, one was more gorgeous than the other. Rehearsals didn't start for two hours which provided an ample window to scout out the local beauties. He took a beach towel from the room, walked onto the warm sand, took off his flip flops, and dove into the waves. As he emerged he found himself surrounded by three women, all wearing string bikinis, and smiles.

"We know who you are," they giggled as they playfully splashed water into his face.

"You are all so beautiful, but I'm afraid I only date women older than eighteen."

"I'm Lucinda," she said "and I'm over eighteen, so I guess that means you can buy me a drink." Tony was smiling from ear to ear as she lead him further into the warm salty waters of the Caribbean. As they floated in the waves, he asked her if she was free that evening after his show. She kissed him, which left a salty imprint on his mind as he anticipated the evening ahead.

"Where should we meet?" They swam to shore and he pointed out a small bar located a few feet off the veranda of the hotel. It was well lit and safe; he didn't want anyone stealing her away.

"Tony, want to go out for drinks with me and my squeeze," suggested Robert after the show. "Let's celebrate, we knocked them dead tonight, a standing ovation, it doesn't get any better than that." All that was on Tony's mind was meeting Lucinda, and perhaps the best part of the evening was yet to come.

"No thanks brother, I have made other plans, and she is a whole lot prettier than you." He haphazardly tossed his baby blue tux on the floor and pulled on a pair of linen shorts with a flax colored Bob Marley styled shirt. He emptied his pockets, save the room key, and he was ready for the ultimate experience. Seated in the center of the hut, her broad smile appeared as soon as she spied him walking toward the bar. She was sipping on a rum infused coconut shell. She nodded to the lone bartender who immediately prepared another.

"Let's go down to the beach. The moon is full tonight and the water is smooth, we will be safe," she suggested. Like a young duckling, he followed her to the edge of the beach, walking in her footprints. They sat down and quietly sipped on their drinks, soaking in the sounds of the ocean waters placidly slapping along the shore line. The moon was so bright it created shadows of the two of them seated on the beach. In the distance, a cruise ship sailed by lit by several strands of lights outlining the bow. He wasn't going to take another sip of rum, nor breathe another breath until he'd had this luscious island woman. He kissed her, and she kissed him and then she stood up and slowly walked him into the ocean. He tore off his shirt and she helped him out of his last piece of clothing, grabbed his hand, and took him for a swim in the inky waters of the Caribbean night. Making love in the ocean, feeling the warmth of Lucinda's skin next to his as the water cocooned their bodies was astonishingly sensual. He exploded with a sense of pure ecstasy as she guided him into her. He spun her around and around, they clasped each other until they became one entity, a single unit joined by divine passion. It was as though their two sprits had become as one. They laid on the beach and he wrapped her up in a beach towel and they held each other until the first rays of the morning sun propped up over the eastern shore. At that moment, Tony was happy he had made the decision to return. He could make love under the gray skies of Philadelphia, but nothing compared to the tropical breezes of Puerto Rico.

Dana took a quick shower and then headed down to the gym to warm up. As a lead dancer she couldn't afford stiff muscles that, when not stretched properly, could affect her precision. She washed her long blonde hair, and smiled as her thoughts turned to Tony. He was a catch, handsome, talented with money in his pockets, but she didn't want to be another conquest, she wanted a long term relationship that she hoped would end up happily ever after. She had watched his career, so she knew one quick marriage was already gone, and that he had quite the reputation among the single woman at the resort. Although she liked him, she would be cool; there was no reason to rush into any relationship, let alone one with a Casanova like Tony. Try as she might, she couldn't erase his face from her mind.

The twins met for a late breakfast and discussed the show and changes in the lineup. There were two new dancers, Dana, and Susan: both had arrived on the plane and were already busy rehearsing with music director.

"I met Dana," said Tony, "She is quite the looker, with a great body. We went for a swim in the ocean and I was really impressed, she is in great shape."

"Make me a promise you won't go near her, I think I might want her for myself," Robert joked.

"To be honest, I don't think she was that interested. We walked back onto the beach and I was about to order a drink when she disappeared on me. Maybe she was just checking me out and I failed the test."

"Don't worry, there are plenty of other fish in the sea, and they won't be that hard to catch," said Robert. They signed the check and walked toward the showroom, nothing had changed: not a light bulb, a maid, the color of the walls, or the smoky smell of the casino. The crew had assembled and was practicing with the new dancers, while the keyboard player handed out the new playlist. Although they kept a smattering of standards, the twins wanted to capture the younger audience, or at least play songs that were contemporary and upbeat. They added the number one single of the year, Blondie's, "Call Me," the sensual song by Captain and Tennille, "Do That To Me One More Time," and Billy Joel's, "It's Still Rock and Roll To Me." Tony, who had practiced his Elvis impersonation until it was perfected, insisted on doing a medley. He selected an eclectic group: he sung "Let Me Be Your Teddy Bear," "All Shook Up," "Good Luck Charm," and finished with, "Love Me Tender." Robert was fine with that; it got him off the stage for a few minutes.

The afternoon rehearsal ran longer than usual as the new tunes were placed in order, and the lighting crew was provided with new instructions. Promptly at eight o'clock, the first show of the new run began. Everyone was fired up, with a new contract and more money pouring into the crew's bank accounts, they were determined to put on a stellar performance. The twins appeared exhilarated as they took the microphones and began singing. After several duets, Robert sang a ballad allowing Tony to change into his Elvis costume. When he returned to the stage the audience was amazed at his transition and when he sang, they almost believed they were seeing a younger, thinner version of the king. With his singing and acting skills, he brought Elvis' image to life. When he finished the last song of the medley, the entire audience stood and cheered, as he walked off the stage with his hand flaying in the air.

They took their final bows and the entertainment director came back to the twin's dressing room to congratulate them on a terrific show, and then turned to Tony and told him how much the audience loved his Elvis impersonation. A sense of pride washed over his face as he took in the compliment. He had done it, had immersed himself in the character, and with his versatile voice, had impressed the audience with his ability to become another person. It was his love for acting that made it happen. It inspired him even more to continue on with his dreams: he would become an actor. As the entertainment director was leaving their dressing room, he told them a famous person was waiting for them in the showroom. The twins walked into the empty theatre and saw a man, with a thick head of blonde hair sitting at a table, nursing a drink. When they walked over, he stood, shook their hands, and introduced himself as Siegfried, from the world famous illusionist team of Siegfried and Roy. They sat down together and he told his story of how he had met Roy, moved to Las Vegas, and become one of the top headliners on the strip. It was not only the magician's great talent, but they were a unique act and that was exactly what he saw in the Sacca twins. He strongly encouraged them to come to Sin City, he truly believed they would be a hit, and he suggested he might be able to use them in his show, although that was a trade secret he could not divulge. He handed them his business card and told them if they ever came to Las Vegas to look him up. They shook hands and departed, but from that moment on, it put the idea of moving out west into the back of their minds.

Late the next morning, Tony put on his swimsuit and jogged down to the beach. In the distance, he could see Dana swimming in the water. He jumped into the ocean to join her, and they swam for a half hour before he followed her out of the water and onto the warm beach.

"That was quite a swim," he remarked, "I can see why you are addicted to the water, it really has a calming effect. Please join me for a drink: just a soda," he insisted. She nodded her head and they found two empty stools at the sand bar and ordered a mixed fruit drink, sans alcohol.

"At least it comes with an umbrella," she joked.

"Tell me about yourself," questioned Tony, "Where did you learn to dance?" Trying to be a bit elusive, she answered the easy questions and when he asked her if she had a boyfriend, she dropped her eyes, and stammered. "So many questions," she said, "and we just met."

"Look I'm sorry, I didn't mean to pry." He left it like that and didn't pursue that line of questioning. She put her empty glass on the bar, shook his hand, and then galloped off to prepare for the show. *Yep*, thought Tony, *I'm smitten, but I really need to know if she has a boyfriend, I would never intentionally tread on someone's territory.*

The keyboard player seemed to know all the gossip, and after rehearsal, Tony casually chatted with him until he extracted the answer. Dana was in fact a free woman. She had recently broken up with a guy and one of the reasons she took the job was to mend her heartbreak. Tony would go slowly, he would be smooth, he would wine and dine her, and hopefully they would both fall in love.

As he planned this happy scenario, Robert was on his own quest, the other new dancer, Susan. Her beauty took his breath away, as did her body, and when she spoke, his felt like an angel was in his presence. He was ready for love. After a three year marriage that ended in divorce, he wanted romance and a new person in his life; Susan fit the bill perfectly. After the second show, he asked her for a drink, and in the morning, she was curled up next to him in his king size bed. Love had struck him a second time and he prayed it would last. Before the end of the month, he had purchased an engagement ring and before the end of the run, he was on his second wife. This time he skipped the fancy wedding since all the parents were in the states. They hired a justice of the peace to marry them on the beach. With several bottles of chilled champagne and fresh seafood appetizers, Susan became the second Mrs. Robert Sacca.

Tony, as best man, stood next to Robert as Dana's eyes seared into his heart. All he could think about was *I'm next*. After Tony toasted his brother for the second time, he turned to Dana, took her hand and led her to a passel of palm trees lining the edge of a narrow beach.

"You know my brother and I always do things alike," he said. He looked into her eyes and with the reverence of a Sunday prayer, got down on one knee and proposed. Before she answered, he extracted a two carat diamond encased in black velvet, and slipped it on her finger. Tears flooded her eyes as she kissed him and simply said,

"Yes." They walked hand in hand back to the small wedding party, but Dana had requested Tony not say anything. It was Robert's wedding, and she didn't want to rain on his parade, this was his moment to bask in the sun. She never gave up her room, she wanted her space, but each night after the show they found each other, and spent the night together. They never gave up their swims together, it bonded their relationship: for her it was the trust factor, and for Tony it was all about having fun with a woman. He had never had a relationship with a woman that he could call a friendship, but this he felt with Dana. She became his lover and his best friend. As he shared his dreams with her, she too had a passion for acting, and they vowed once they returned to the states, they would pursue their dreams.

Two months later, the couple announced their engagement. Rather than copy Robert and Susan's wedding celebration, they decided to have an engagement party. They served champagne and a broad assortment of appetizers and called it a night. Without one dark day, the crew never enjoyed a full day off, everyday was a work day.

5th Beatle, Bill Preston, appears on Live From Las Vegas hosted by Tony and Robert

Las Vegas Rocks ®

*1905 – Las Vegas is founded as a city on May 15,
1905, when 110 acres of land, situated between
Stewart Avenue on the north, Garces Avenue to the
south, Main Street to the west, and 5th Street (Las
Vegas Boulevard) to the east, are auctioned off.*

Tony submits a publicity photo when he auditioned for Grease the movie

CHAPTER 8

Finally the eight months were over, the Sacca Twins Revue took their last bows, and the next morning the entire crew boarded a plane headed to Philadelphia. Dana held Tony's hand and promised him they would begin looking for acting jobs. The couple was genuinely happy together; they were in love and shared the same goals and aspirations. Robert and Tony found new apartments close together where they lived with their new loves. It was odd for the boys to return home and not live under their parent's roof, but they each had a wife or fiancé and needed their privacy. As soon as the plane landed Tony called his mom to arrange a meeting. Needless to say after another eight months she was not only anxious to see her sons but their new ladies.

"I insist you come for dinner tomorrow night, and don't forget your fiancé and wife," she laughed. Tony was quick to relay the invite while they gathered a mountain of luggage strewn over the roving carriage. One bag was so large it barely made it through the tunnel. They located two luggage carts, tossed the bags on board a taxi, and exited the airport. The crisp cool air was a refreshing change from the warm tropics: it felt good to be home. The moment Tony and Dana set foot on terra firma they began seeking their dreams in acting. Tony's next call was to their agent, who made an appointment for the following day. Throughout the eight months, Tony had periodically been in contact with Gino making it clear that he and Dana were seeking new career paths and to please find acting jobs in lieu of their current act.

"Not to worry," was always Gino's retort. They hailed two cabs and the foursome met the next morning at Gino's office as they excitedly anticipated their next moves.

"My, my," said Gino, "You're the four most beautiful people in the world." Stretching out his hand he kissed Dana and Susan on the cheek and then brought them back to his cramped office where he had added two additional metal chairs.

"So I heard you had another great eight months and packed them in every night. The entertainment director had nothing but kudos for you. So much so that I had an easy time finding your next engagement, and it's right here in town. The four of you will have your own production, the Sacca Twins," he giddily announced. Tony and Dana's mouths fell open; that was not what they wanted. Shoving the contracts into each of their hands Gino advised them to read through the fine print, and then he walked out of the room to give them some breathing space. Tony looked at Dana who was wearing a scowl while Robert and Susan were already signing away their lives. It suddenly dawned on Tony that he had never mentioned to his brother that he wanted to leave the Revue to pursue his own dreams. Come to think of it, he had never sat down with Robert in the entire eight months to discuss what he wanted out of life, all their free moments were spent tweaking the show, or adding another rehearsal.

Tony and Dana slid the contracts back on the table and sat in silence.

"I don't want to do this anymore," admitted Tony. "I'm sick of the act and I want to do other things. I made a promise to mom that I would stick it out in Puerto Rico, but finally we are home and I'm done. I, rather Dana and I, want to go into acting. We both love it and that is where are ambitions are pointed." Robert angrily stood up, looked into Tony's eyes and began screaming,

"How could you do this to us? You can't leave the act; look how much money we have made and how successful we have become! You just can't leave now, we are just getting started," pronounced Robert. As usual, Gino had been pacing outside the door, and had heard every word uttered inside the room, especially since the conversation had swiftly escalated into a screaming match between the brothers. He knocked on the door and tiptoed back into the room. This time it was Tony who stood up screaming and waving the contract wildly above his head.

"What is this?" asked Tony. "I told you what Dana and I wanted, and you promised us a shot at acting, but instead you offer us the same old routine. I told you, I'm done with the twin act, I want to be my own person." Gino's swollen cheeks and sunken jowls turned bright red, as his blood pressure mounted and his head began to throb; he had been dreading this moment for over two months. He knew what Tony wanted, but he also knew he couldn't deliver what Tony wanted, so he took the easy way out and booked the act where they could all be guaranteed a decent income. Acting was too precarious: a job here or there, it was unpredictable, and so was the agent's fee that went along with it. He knew the twins' act could be a predicable profit maker for many years to come, but right now, he had to convince Tony of that. He plucked the mental crib notes from his head and began to convince his unhappy client of the reasons they should continue the act.

"Tony, Dana, if you read the contract you will see it's quite sound and will provide you with a nice nest egg to begin your lives as newlyweds.

Think of how you will be able to purchase a lovely little home, with plenty of room for the little ones." Tony had not resumed sitting in his seat, he was livid and nothing Gino could say would convince him otherwise.

"I told you what I wanted and you know damn well this contract is not what I wanted. I refuse to sign this." Now Robert stood up, waving the contract in the air,

"Tony, can't you see, this is all we have for now. Take it or leave it."

"Then I guess I will leave it," shouted Tony. "I signed on for eight months, not eighty years and I want out. Dana and I want other things in life."

"Do you want to starve? After all this money we have made together, do you want to just chuck it away and live as paupers? I don't think so. We have all grown too happy with the good life, money in our pockets, the best of everything, and you think you can just walk away from all that? Go ahead, ask Dana if she wants to live in poverty," snarled Robert. Tony turned to Dana, who had remained silent during the confrontation; she was pondering her options and remembering her mother's saying, "A bird in the hand is better than two in the bush." Right now, she had a bird in the hand, a decent contract that could support them while they sought acting jobs. It appeared as though the four were at an impasse, and Gino's encouraging words weren't strong enough to reach an accord.

"Let me make a suggestion. Why don't we all sleep on this tonight and meet tomorrow? You're fresh off the plane and maybe you need a day to get your heads together," suggested a very wise Gino. With that, the four trooped out of the office and slammed the office door shut. They gathered at the sidewalk.

"See you at mom's later," they said together as they simultaneously sped off in the same direction. Gino heard and thought, *Ah ha, they are going to their mom's house.* Acting more as a sleuth than an agent, Gino had spent many hours of conversation with Millie, who had been forthcoming with great insights as to how the boys thought and what they wanted out of life. He picked up the phone and called Millie: the agent explained the scenario and asked her to help smooth over the differences and make Tony see the light, the great light of opportunity, attached with plenty of money. What could be better than their own show and right at home with their family? This was the gig from heaven and here it was sitting right in their laps.

This time, both parents met their sons and their new wife and fiancé, at the front door. Their sister, with her spouse, was busy in the kitchen mixing large stewing pots and opening bottles of wine. Their parents hugged and kissed Dana and Susan, and introduced their daughter and her busy husband.

"This calls for a toast," Joe announced. He rarely, if ever, found anything to celebrate, but tonight, with his three children and their three significant others, there was plenty to celebrate. They raised the crystal flutes, he toasted their health and happiness, and with a few renegade tears, he warmly hugged his three children,

"You make me proud," he said, "every one of you. My daughter, and my two sons, I'm so very proud." As they took their places at the dinner table, Millie joked that it was becoming too small for the burgeoning family.

"We might have to break through a wall in a couple of years for Thanksgiving dinner," she joked. With more time on her hands and the assistance of her husband's excellent meat, their mom's cooking had vastly improved from their childhood. She poured a round Chianti and served the first course: a tomato soup filled with aromatics, cubes of chicken, and tiny grains of orzo. The conversation flowed as easily as the glasses of wine continued to be refilled. Robert seemed to be drinking more than he was eating, trying to drive away his anger from Tony's belligerent reaction to the contract. Dana and Susan cleared away the soup bowls and then set out a tray of grilled veal chops, pasta in an Alfredo sauce, and baby peas with mushrooms.

"This is terrific," said Dana, "Thank you Mrs. Sacca for the wonderful meal."

"Please," she responded, "Call me mom, we are all family now." Susan turned to Robert who had been unusually quiet and watched him drink away his dinner. She knew he was angry, but she certainly didn't want him drunk at his parent's home. Dana noticed that Tony was unusually quiet as well, but she knew he was still seething from the afternoon meeting. The couples both felt as if they had been deceived.

Their mother knew exactly what was going on from her conversation with Gino, but she would suffer through dinner and have a discussion with Tony before dessert. She had to convince him to stay with his brother. After the plates were cleared away, their dad put on a pot of coffee, and Millie led Tony to the basement. She could see how upset he was, and turning the tide to get him back on track would take a lot of conversation.

"Tony," as she spoke, she pointed to the small room in the basement where they practiced, "this is where it all began. Remember all those nights singing and playing your guitar? Remember the angry neighbors banging on our door to shut you guys up? Well they aren't banging anymore. So many memories, and yet the two of you still have so many years ahead to continue."

"Mom, I don't want to do this anymore. I told you before we went back for the second run at the resort that I was through being part of the twins, I just want to act. Dana wants to act too, we both want the same thing."

"Robert tells me you have a contract for the next several months and it's right here in town. How lucky is that? Maybe when you are home and with family and friends you will feel a lot differently. You always loved standing up and singing and playing in front of an audience and this new opportunity will allow you to do that. And if you don't take it what will you do for money? You have a beautiful fiancé and you need to support her. I am begging you, just take this one more contract, put some money aside and then go on your way. Your brother needs you, please just this once, do the show. You'll see, you might even change your mind. Manhattan is a short train ride away. Find another agent and try to get your acting jobs. You usually have one day off a week, use that day to seek out other options, but please just do this engagement." By now tears had flooded her face, all her emotions were spent, she wanted her boys together, at whatever cost.

"Mom, I am sick of being a twin, I want to be on my own, but you are right, I do need to support my fiancé. I will do this last show and then I am done. Please don't ask me to do this again. Dana and I want to have our own lives: we share the same dreams. I really do love her mom, she is more than a lover, she is a friend, she cares for me and we have a great time together." She began to cry even more and took her arms and wrapped them around Tony, who was also crying.

"Son, it's hard to know what to do, but you have made the right decision. Sticking with your brother is the best for everyone. You'll see, you'll all be happy, you'll be making money, and performing and we will all be together. I know tomorrow when you sign that contract you will be a happier person. Please be patient, your time will come and when it does, you will thank me for making you stick with your brother" They hugged, dried their eyes and then ascended the steps to the smell of freshly brewed espresso.

The women had cleaned up the kitchen and reset the table for dessert, while Robert was sulking by himself with another freshly poured glass of wine. He was drunk when Tony and their mother returned from their discussion.

"You don't want to work with me anymore," Robert slurred, "You don't want to be a Sacca Twin? Why don't we settle this right now? Let's go outside and I will whoop your ass." He staggered out of the leather recliner, raised his fists and began pumping the air with his arms. "Let's go brother, or are you too afraid I will show you up in front of our girls?" Susan was disgusted. She had seen Robert drunk, but never like this.

"I think we should go," she said softly, "you really shouldn't cause such a scene in front of your mom and dad." She clutched his arm and pushed Robert toward the front door, but he insisted on duking it out with Tony. He turned back around and walked toward his brother, threatening a fight: this time their dad interceded and turned Robert around again, opened the front door and escorted him to his car. He shoved him into the front seat and warned him never to drink in his presence again.

"Don't ever come to our home and fight with your brother. You're way too old for this juvenile behavior."

"Dad, he wants to leave the act, he wants to leave me out on the street. Can't you see how awful he is? Why does he want to ruin my life?"

"Just go home and I'm sure by tomorrow everything will been fine. Sleep this off and don't drink again," he said tersely, "don't you break your mother's heart." They had lived the lives of entertainers, which was in many ways narcissistic. On the road, constantly travelling from hotel room to hotel room, they were never responsible for things as mundane as bills, or taking care of a car, or paying a mortgage. They were constantly pampered, if it wasn't the consummate crowds and fans, it was the hotels or the limousine drivers. They lived their lives fending off the problems most people face.

"We had a false sense of stability," admitted Tony. "We never thought about the future, about having to save money, or taking care of things or other people: we lived in the moment without answering to anyone. It was an awakening when I returned home from Puerto Rico with a fiancé, and realized that I had to rent my own place, pay the bills, and support my fiancé; I had to learn to grow up."

True to his word, Tony and Dana, walked into Gino's office the next day and signed the contract that would tie him to his brother for the next several months. Gino extended his hand, but Tony refused to shake it as the young couple stormed out of the office outraged. They had been played, lied to, and deceived. Tony knew the agent did what was expedient. The

Sacca twins were his meal ticket, and he wasn't about to give that up. The couple sat in the car in silence, waiting for the other to come up with something that would soothe their disdain, but neither could so Tony turned on the engine and drove home.

"I promise you, we will have a plan, but right now, I'm too exasperated to think," he said. He took her hand and she smiled and kissed his neck.

"We have each other, and our love, and that's enough for me," she said. "Something will turn up. I believe in you and me, and I know we will eventually find something."

Rehearsals began the following day as the band, dancers, and the twins gathered at the showroom at the expansive newly refurbished nightclub. The venue held three hundred people and they were booked five evenings a week, for three months. At least the pay was good; they would be making plenty of money, so they couldn't complain about that. When Robert arrived he was on his best behavior, he hugged his brother and was upbeat about the gig. When they reviewed the new playlist, they were happy to see a lot of top forty hits. The audiences loved to hear the songs that were played on the radio: they would sing along and become completely immersed in the show. The new director thought it would be a novelty if the girls left the stage and danced with some of the men in the audience. Although Tony didn't like the idea, the first night they tried it out everyone had such a good time, they kept it in the act. In the past the men were usually dragged to the shows with their wives, but when one of the beautiful dancers grabbed their hands and got them to their feet dancing the guys loved it.

With fresh new lightweight wool tuxedos, the Sacca Twins entered the stage and the Revue began its successful run. In spite of Tony's anger, when his hands held the microphone, the music had been cued, and he'd opened his mouth to sing, there was no better high. He loved the spotlight, he loved singing, and he loved being on stage. His smile was genuine and his passion for the art was expelled with every note. When he scanned the audience on opening night, he saw old friends and family clapping and supporting their act, and he had a change of heart. Perhaps his mom was right. At that moment, when he and Robert made their final bows on opening night, Tony felt on top of the world. He was home: he was where he was supposed to be. They threw a kiss to his mother and sister, and then the twins walked off stage together, happy and exhilarated.

"Honey, we are going to be late," said Dana as she put on her leggings for morning rehearsal. He didn't answer, so she shrugged her shoulders, walked downstairs to the kitchen, and poured a glass of orange juice. The sun was shining through the windows in the breakfast nook as she surveyed their brand new apartment. A contemporary, spacious two-story apartment, it was more than she had hoped for. There were plenty of bedrooms for children, should they be blessed, a large brick fireplace, a dining room that could comfortably seat the extended family, and a dream kitchen that had every new appliance. She smiled. She was glad they had accepted the contract, it was wonderful waking up each morning in a king bed next to the man she loved: and soon they would be married.

"Hey Tony, it's time to go," she repeated, but there was still no response. She walked upstairs and knocked on the bathroom door, "everything okay sweetie," and then she heard an inexplicable mumble. After knocking again, she barged into the bathroom. Tony was sitting on the floor with his head between his hands and he was trembling. Dana knelt down and took his head in her hands and asked him what was wrong. He pointed to his neck and took her hand: yes she could feel it too, some kind of lump. She began to tremble as well.

"Look, it maybe just nothing," Dana suggested as she ran downstairs and called his mother, who would know just what to do. Next Dana called Robert and told him they would not be at rehearsals, but didn't make an explanation, at that point there was no reason for anyone to become overly concerned.

Dana, Tony, and Millie sat in the waiting room until his named was called. As he was escorted back to the doctor's office, the two women held hands' praying the lump was of no consequence. An hour later, they were escorted back, and took a seat next to Tony.

"First it's benign," advised the doctor, "but the growth must come out and there will be at least a three to four month period where you won't be able to sing." The doctor reassured his patient he would be able to sing and his vocal chords would return to normal, but he had to come to terms that he would be out of commission for at least three months. The doctor picked up the phone and had the nurse schedule the surgery and the three sad people left the office.

The out-patient surgery was scheduled for the day after their last performance. They were frightened, but Tony's mom always saw the glass half full and kept reminding him that it was not cancerous and he would be just fine.

"You always said you wanted some time to look into this acting thing, so now you will have that time. Just please remember it is only for three months and then you will be good as ever," she said. Not wanting to go home and sulk, Tony and Dana walked into the rehearsals and picked up as if nothing was wrong, but after the show that evening, he sat down with Robert and told him about the surgery.

"What about me?" said Robert, "What am I supposed to do while you are sitting around, just sit around too?"

"Listen brother, I'm the one with a problem not you, so why are you turning this on me? I didn't do anything, it just happened, and now I will have to live with this, but I will be better and it's not the end of the world. I thought I could get a little sympathy from you, but you seem just to care about yourself."

"We are part of an act, remember, so if something goes wrong with you, than it goes wrong for me too," responded. "Look, I'm sorry, really sorry." He grabbed his brother and hugged him and swore they would get through this together.

At thirty, with a couple of months of recuperation and plenty of time to think, Tony felt he lacked guidance and he felt trapped. He had always been known as Anthony and his brother Bobby, but on a whim he decided to change his name to Tony and his brother, for different reasons, changed his name to Robert. It was a new person Tony was seeking to find, a new identity and a new spirit. He had always been part of something and somebody else and he wanted to become his own self: changing his name was the beginning of this transformation. With the surgery weighing so heavy on his mind he needed to rethink his life.

True, he didn't go to college, but with a highly functioning brain, he knew what he didn't know, and how to go about discovering it. Creativity weighed heavily on his mind, it was one of the most salient factors insuring his performing art would always be fresh and innovative. He read up on brain physiology, and began exploring how to use his left brain, the more creative side. He pushed himself: he consciously learned how to write left handed, and consequently became ambidextrous, the unusual outcome was that he has the exact same signature regardless of which hand he uses. He used his left hand to brush his teeth, comb his hair, and cook. Forcing the opposite lobe to work harder, he felt more inspired, was able to concentrate more easily, and innovative thoughts were more lucid in a shorter time span: it felt like his brain was on a caffeine high. At least these thoughts kept his mind occupied while the results of the operation weighed heavily.

Luckily he was talented, but what would become of him if the surgery failed and he couldn't sing? It was time to take a long hard introspective look, but where to go for advice he wasn't sure. The one thing he was sure of was that in the long run, Robert wouldn't work out; they simply didn't share the same goals or motivation. Perhaps because he opted out of the college life the time had finally come to insert erudite thinking into his creative brain. While reading, "The New York Times," he stumbled upon an article written about two inspirational books, "Success Through Positive Mental Attitude," and, "Think and Grow Rich." A free introductory seminar was being held in Manhattan and with nothing else on his plate, he hopped the bus and walked into a huge banquet room inside a seedy hotel. The lectern was set up simply: just a podium and a hand held microphone, yet the huge room was filled with two thousand people from every age, ethnic background and walk of life, all sitting pensively waiting for the motivational speaker to commence. The basic concept was simple, everyone in that room was there to improve their lives, to take control of their destiny, and everyone in that room believed the speaker would shed light and lead the way; they would reach their goals, they just had to learn how to follow the template.

"Think and Grow Rich," was inspired from Andrew Carnegie's philosophy to help people succeed in life regardless of their occupation, that they could do and become almost anything they wanted. After he interviewed a large number of people who had achieved success, he created a working theory of how to apply it to the entire populace. Even though these interviews were done over fifty years ago, the concepts remained the same, and are applicable to modern day American Capitalism. Essentially Carnegie believed in hard work, but quality work: show the customers you respect and honor them, in essence become altruistic, treat someone the way you would like to be treated. He postulated taking a personal detailed inventory, and to learn to grow spiritually through self-discipline, 'know thyself.' An innovator, he advised people to seek out new opportunities created by innovation, to make a plan, keep to it, and don't fear failure, or even failing several times. The lecture ended with applause sweeping the banquet room. Tony walked into the street, located a bookstore, and purchased both books. He found a seat on the bus and furiously dug into the first title; a complete guide to self-improvement, which promised to fulfill your dreams, if you thought positively. Almost like self-hypnosis, the goal was to teach yourself motivation, develop self-discipline, and think in an organized manner. Napoleon Hill, the co-writer, began working in a small town newspaper and eventually became a famous motivational author: to this day, both books are among the best selling in American literature. The mind was explained as a secret talisman: one side emblazoned with positive mental thinking, bringing good into your life, and the other with negative thinking which robbed the psyche of all that made life worth living.

As Tony read through the chapters, the concepts began taking hold; it all seemed plausible. It was a set of postulates he could cling to, which could guide him along a positive, successful path. He developed a personal mantra, "I know I have the ability to achieve my goals," and never took no for an answer. He accepted the fact he might fail, but when he did, he dusted himself off and tried again. The basis of his success he holds to the values empowered by those two books. The moment he read them, he began to change his life. Nothing would ever hold him back, and as he experienced life, he lived with those ideals shaping all his decisions. He had to continue to cling to the positive thoughts for the time being, at least until he could finally hear his singing voice ring again.

Tommy DeVito, founding member of the Four Seasons, states, "Tony Sacca you're a great entertainer!"

Tony is presented the key to the city in 2002 from Mayor Oscar Goodman.

Tony singing with Helen Joys Young Entertainers during the White House Holiday celebration.

Tony and Charo stand in front of the Bellagio during her performance.

Tony and Josette opened the Las Vegas Rocks Café in 2010, a restaurant with an entertainment history theme similar to the Hard Rock Café.

Tony Orlando and Tony have been close friends for many years.

"Tony, the city of Las Vegas rightfully bestowed the title ambassador to you, you have been a pillar in the community for introducing some of Las Vegas' greatest entertainers to the world over the past three decades." -Tony Orlando

Tony is pictured with two models when he was voted handsomest man in Philadelphia

Las Vegas Rocks ©

*1909 – The Nevada
Legislature creates Clark
County on July 1, 1909. The
new county was named after
William Clark who brought
the railroad to southern
Nevada. Las Vegas became
the county seat. Prior to the
formation of Clark County,
southern Nevada was part
of Lincoln County.*

Tony and Frankie Avalon, both from the same neighborhood in South Philly, appear on Tony's TV show

CHAPTER 9

His fiancé kissed him gently as the nurses wheeled Tony into surgery. Millie, Dana, Susan, and Robert sat nervously in the waiting room while the fate of their loved one was in the hands of a team of surgeons. Robert and his mom left to grab some coffee and when they were out of sight, Susan began a tirade about her husband's abhorrent behavior.

"He has been drinking a lot lately and he is just not himself. Now with at least three months without any income, I fear we might be losing our home. I couldn't stand the fact that I wouldn't be able to get up every day and see your home across the street from us," admitted Susan. Dana was listening carefully and advised her future sister-in-law to save as much money as she could get her hands on and put it in a secret bank account. Their eyes welled up with tears as they hugged each other; their futures seemed to be precariously perched at the edge of a precipice and at any second, they could all tumble and all that they had would be lost forever.

With steaming cups of coffee, Robert and his mom joined the girls. The pacing continued until the doctor emerged from the operating room with news that the surgery had gone exceedingly well. Tony was in recovery and his voice would be back to normal in another month or two. The four hugged while his mother fondled her rosary, and thanked Jesus for getting her son through the horrible ordeal.

"Look, it's only for a couple of months," said Dana as she prepared to leave for her new job as a lead dancer. "Once you are well, then we will figure out how to get the act back together. I know it's impossible for you to sit around and see me go to work, but if the tables were turned, you would do the same for me." Kissing him, she ran out to the curb and drove off with Susan to Manhattan. Left alone at home, Tony began plotting his next move. Over and over the conversation he had had with Siegfried ran through his mind, Las Vegas, the land of entertainment opportunity. What would capture the attention of the audience? He knew the answer, it was the twins. Alone, he was just another talented singer/showman, but with his brother, now that was an act that would appeal to the casinos. As he lingered around the house, he began researching the possibility of moving to Las Vegas. He called agents, reviewing hotels, casinos, night clubs, and other performers, and he solidified a plan of action. There was no turning back; he had made up his mind. That night when Dana returned, he meticulously laid out his plans. She always trusted him, and from his ardent conversation, she knew he had done his homework. Dana did not want to go to Las Vegas, in the worst way. Although her family lived in California, she loved the life she was living and the abundant opportunities as a dancer in Philadelphia, there was so much more culture and demand, or so she thought, for the type of dancing she performed. She loved Tony and resigned herself to allow him one year in Las Vegas. The next day they notified the landlord and began packing. Tony walked across the street to explain his plans with Robert. It was easy swaying his brother, whose only goal was keeping the act going, so they too notified the landlord and began packing. The four of them met that night, popped open a bottle of champagne and toasted,

"Las Vegas here we come."

Saying good bye to their children was difficult, but Joe and Millie understood how important this move would be for their sons and wife and future wives' careers. Their mom was the most pleased because the boys would remain together: Tony's conversations about going out on his own had ceased for the moment, and the brothers were getting along. That was all a mother could hope for.

Tony turned around and took a final look at his home, the very first home he had lived in. With its colonial style architecture and the sweep of black roofing, it was modest by all standards, yet it represented a bold step, a commitment to his fiancé and the love they so passionately shared. Dana was ready to move on with him, at any costs. They didn't have jobs waiting for them at the end of their long journey; all they had was their talent, opportunity, and blind faith that Las Vegas was all it was touted to be.

The early morning air was damp as gray clouds gathered, promising a rain storm. The cars had been packed for the long drive across the country, but the exodus wouldn't take place without a proper good bye to the twins' family. The two couples caravanned to the home for a tear filled departure. The entire family had assembled, including their sister, her spouse, and their two young children, to wish their brothers well. Overwhelmed by the scene, Tony and Robert stood in silence, this was not the typical gig, this time they were leaving home for good. She handed each son a huge bag of homemade food, and then Millie hugged her sons as if she would never see them again. Then every member of the family followed suit. The parents stood at the doorway and watched the cars drive away. What made it bearable was that their sons were together, their act and there love would continue.

"I told you Tony would see the light. Look how happy they are and think about their future, in the most famous city in the county," she wept.

"You know sweetheart, it is only a plane ride away, and once they are established, we will take a trip," assured Joe. He wrapped his arms around their daughter and grandchildren, "We will all take a trip together. Godspeed."

Tony eased onto the interstate and pushed his foot on the accelerator as the speedometer tipped seventy miles an hour. It wasn't as if he was escaping his past, he just couldn't get to his future quick enough. He smelled the food: the reminders of home were living inside the car. His father, with his stern demeanor, his mother who tempered the household, always seeking a resolution, and his sister, who had learned to love her brothers in spite of the lack of attention, was his heritage. The good with the bad, and that was the mantra he would live with. He no longer felt trapped, he had decided on this move all by himself, he had created the plan, and now the four were driving toward a shared dream. The twin act would be their meal ticket, and then when the timing was right, Tony would strike out on his own. He felt like a pioneer leading the way to a new world. He knew he was responsible for the future of four people, and took this seriously. Dana rubbed his neck assuredly, as if she was reading his mind, twisted the dial on the radio, and began singing along to an upbeat Elvis song. The morning gray clouds had drifted apart as the afternoon sun glared on the windshield.

"I love you, and don't worry, because we are all going to make it. Don't think for a minute that you are responsible for all of our lives. We are all grown-ups and we are all a part of this grand design," said Dana.

"You know, wife to be of mine, I think you should have your own act as a mind reader, because you certainly have my thoughts down pat," laughed Tony. "I think from now on I won't talk, I'll just think about what I am going to say and let you respond." Laughing, his stomach growled, "Now let's dig into that bag of food."

The highway loomed endlessly ahead as the sun sloped deeply to the western sky. The two cars pulled off at the first motel that advertised vacancy. The boys filled up the gas tanks while the girls booked two rooms at the roadside motel. They slept like logs until sunrise the next morning. Since Tony wasn't ready to sing, it had been predetermined that Robert and Susan would move immediately to Las Vegas while Tony and Dana recuperated in California. With sunrise the next morning the cars sped out of the parking lot and forged ahead. The two couples parted ways in the morning, Robert and Susan took the northern route, and Dana and Tony took the southern route. Tony's passion for Elvis was so strong, he wanted to see Graceland, and they drove down to Memphis to get the grand tour of the King's residence. Dana took charge of the wheel as Tony navigated through the heart of the country and then headed directly west. It took another day until they would reach Route 15 and drive onto the renowned Las Vegas strip that split the city between east and west. Within a month's time they would all be together again.

The arid drive to Pomona served as a potent reminder they would be living their lives in the desert, and again, Tony had done his research. He guarded his sacred voice; he had vigilantly abided by every detail of his doctor's edict. He had not sung, or pressed his vocal chords since that last performance in Pennsylvania. He knew his throat was on the mend and he had to protect it at all costs. The climate in Las Vegas was devoid of moisture and they would constantly have to drink water, even on stage, to keep their throats lubricated. In Puerto Rico and the eastern states where the humidity wavered above fifty percent, no one ever worried about dehydration. He had read many articles in Variety Magazine about entertainers like Sammy Davis Jr., or Dean Martin, or even groups like Cornell Gunter's Coasters, who would bring water bottles on the stage and drink them during the performances, sometimes even during a song.

Tony took the wheel and drove the last three hours of Route 15, while Dana barked out directions to her home in Pomona.

"I'm looking forward to meeting your parents, especially after you have been putting up with my smothering family," he said.

"Not to worry," calmed Dana, "My family is nothing like your family. They are quiet, reserved, and have settled into the less frenzied lifestyle of Southern California. Every day the sun shines, you never see a drop of snow, and life seems to meander to a slower beat. We Californians know how to enjoy life and take the time to savor every minute. Yes there are some dark clouds, but on the west coast they aren't as severe and they seem to pass over quickly. Unlike those somber eastern skies that don't seem to be swept away with the winds, the Pacific Ocean has a way of dealing with all of life's troubles."

"You make it all seem so tempting, and that is one of the reasons why I love you. Actually, I must confess, you are a lot like my mom: always seeing the best in people and forever the optimist. If your family is anything like you, than I know it will be a lasting love affair."

She took his hand and pointed,

"Turn here, we are just a couple of miles away." Suddenly, after traveling thousands of miles, Tony couldn't catch his breath, his chest heaved, he was genuinely nervous about meeting her family, and they were planning a wedding. Dana sensed his change in demeanor, she turned to him and promised her parents wouldn't bite, nor would they slice him up and serve him for dinner.

The tall palms danced above their heads as they emerged from the car. The deep purple Bougainvillea laced around the edges of the wide redwood home as they walked onto the flagstone and entered the foyer.

"Dana, is that you?" her mother called out. An attractive thin blonde woman ran to greet her daughter. After she hugged Dana, she wrapped her arms around Tony and greeted him warmly. "So wonderful to finally get to meet. Your dad is still working, but he'll be home later. Come, I'll show you around."

"Mom, I think I know the way," said Dana as she led her future husband through the house and into her childhood bedroom. She looked at the queen size bed, kissed Tony, and promised they would both fit but not until they were married. He would be sleeping in the guest room at the end of the hall until they had exchanged vows. Her parents were old-fashioned.

"It's so beautiful here, I see why your parents love California. It seems as though the sun never stops shining," said Tony. They walked to the spacious backyard filled with low lying deep green shrubs, hollyhock, lilies, begonias, and white daisies under an azure blue sky. There were three glasses of iced-tea on the picnic table for them. The three talked for hours, giving up family secrets, sharing their aspirations, and later that afternoon, the couple drove to the beach and watched the sunset.

"This is going to be a real honeymoon," said Dana as she kissed Tony, "I love you. These short couple weeks in California will make a new man of you, and give you a chance to see an entirely new world. Soon enough we will be joining your brother and the honeymoon will be over. Tomorrow is the big day, the first exercises for your voice, and I want you as relaxed as possible." He returned her kiss as they sat on the beach and held each other until a blanket of stars replaced the setting sun.

I can't talk, I am opening up my mouth and nothing is coming out. I am standing on stage, dressed in a tuxedo, Robert is next to me, and at the edge of the stage I see a man singing into a microphone. He is singing my part. I move my mouth to the words, but he is making all the sounds. I am mute. I can no longer sing. Oh Lord what will I do?

When she heard loud sounds coming from the guest room, Dana darted down the hall and woke Tony up from a nightmare. He was dripping with sweat and trembling.

"It's a bad dream, now go back to sleep." Tony wrapped his arms around her and clung to her until he fell back asleep. This was a wake-up call for Dana: she realized how scared he truly was and how much support he would need in the following weeks. She slipped out of his bed before dawn, but she fretted over her future husband's worries: what if he was unable to sing? How would they make a living? She was just as frightened as he, but she dared not allow her doubts and veil their upcoming nuptials.

That afternoon he opened up his mouth and tentatively began getting his vocal chords back into shape. As she listened from the living room, Dana smiled to herself, and thanked the Lord that his worst fears had been overcome; his sweet voice was back on track.

Meanwhile, Robert had been making some headway in Las Vegas. Armed with videos, and promotional materials, he began knocking on the doors of agents, hotels, and casinos, trying to obtain gigs. Each day the brothers talked on the phone until Tony announced that his voice had thoroughly recovered and he was ready to audition.

The next night Tony let out anther scream, this time due to his future mother-in-law burning a cigarette hole in the center of his wrist. He jolted from the bed and stood in the darkness, befuddled by her behavior. A sliver of moonlight cast a gold shadow across her face as she commenced a thorough explanation of her unhappiness about the wedding.

"You aren't good enough for Dana, you are nothing but an entertainer. I don't want my daughter getting hurt and I believe you will hurt her. You entertainers take advantage of situations. If you're on the road, and she is home, how long will it be before you cheat on her? No, I really do not give my blessing on this marriage, and neither does my husband. Tomorrow we will give you a wedding, but just so you should know, we are not happy to welcome you into our daughter's life," she said. She opened up the door and she twisted her head, "I give it a year."

In the late morning, they dressed and drove down to the wharf in Long Beach, where a 125 foot yacht was anchored and prepared for the wedding guests. The yacht once belonged to General MacArthur, and was now used for wedding ceremonies.

"Maybe her mother plans to throw me overboard," thought a very nervous Tony. The hundred guests gathered at the head of the boat that was threaded with rows of yellow and white daisies. The requisite vows were exchanged in a succinct ceremony and then drinks and dinner were served. It was not a lavish affair, although it certainly rang true of romanticism. The parents felt as if they had done their part, now it was up to the groom to make damn sure he held up his end of the bargain. That night, they slept in Dana's bed. Tony never told his new wife of the night before, he had to think positively. They loved each other and that was all that mattered. In the morning, they gathered their belongings, thanked Dana's parents for their kindness, and drove across the desert to begin their new lives in Las Vegas.

Robert greeted them at a sprawling apartment complex and handed Tony the key to a furnished one bedroom apartment.

"This will do until we establish ourselves," said Dana. "I think we should wait to buy a home until we know exactly what we are going to do. We'll be fine right here for a while." The following morning the twins were scheduled for an audition with MGM, one of the largest hotel and casinos in the city, and they both needed to be at their best. Their New York manager, Hermie Dressel, was friendly with Art Engler, a successful Las Vegas agent. After making a few calls, he and the twins met, and auditions and bookings started coming their way. As luck would have it, there was a musician strike, and the casinos were starved for entertainment. With tracks in hand, the twins could deliver a hell of a show, even without those desperately needed live musicians.

They nervously walked to center stage in matching white tuxedos, the band cued up, and the Sacca twins sang their hearts out. The entertainment director mumbled something to several other people seated in the audience, walked toward the twins and offered them a four week engagement on the spot. They shook hands and were led to a small corporate office where the contract was drawn and signatures notarized. It was the beginning of their Las Vegas career: they were singing in the plush lounge of one of the busiest venues on the strip. The lounges were open twenty-four seven, and so were the accompanying acts. The twins would sing four sets a day, six days a week: a grueling schedule, but the money was excellent, and the exposure was undeniably opportunistic. The only negative was the constant smoke spilling into the air, but the lounge, knowledgeable of the physical needs of the musicians and singers, had installed a sophisticated filtration that eliminated the worst of the smoke. The four week gig kept renewing and rolled into a steady three year run.

"WhenI first arrived in Las Vegas, I realized it was a total town, it was more than just the strip: a town filled with regular people, living regular lives, and having regular jobs. It wasn't just about the excitement and glamour, but about a great way of life. The cost of living was less and the money people made stretched further than in most places. With no state income tax and property taxes incredibly low, owning a home became an easy reality. Besides the school system, everything else in the city was great, from health care, to food, to shopping, and activities. Just show your I.D. and discounts and perks were liberally given to the locals. Wherever I went, people had smiles on their faces, I think they were happy living in such a warm inviting climate."

Both wives obtained jobs as dancers, and with a steady income, they bought homes on a quiet side street a few miles from downtown. Life was ideal, they had pools in their backyards, great jobs, and they were living in a thriving city, with endless opportunities. Which was why Dana was disheartened when Susan approached her that things were not going well in their household.

"He seems to have gotten caught up in the Las Vegas syndrome. Robert has been drinking more and lately he is out gambling after work. He was gone for an entire night, and stumbled into the house dead drunk without a penny in his pockets. I am worried sick about this and I don't know what to do," she cried.

When Tony came home that night, Dana replayed the conversation and he admitted that Robert had not been on the straight and narrow path. He didn't know what to do, so he called his mom the next morning and bitterly complained about Robert's erratic destructive behavior. What advice could she give from three thousand miles away, except to beg Tony to continue supporting his brother?

"He needs you," she repeated over and over again. "Please just support him for now and then later, when things have cooled down, think about alternatives.

To play up the twin concept, the Sacca act always commenced with the song, "It takes Two," as they strolled onto the stage side by side. Tony kept checking his watch every minute, and where the hell was his brother? They were set to go on any second and Robert was nowhere to be seen. The drums rolled and Tony had no choice but to go on by himself. He was livid but there was no way he would display this to the adoring audience, he would think of something. Using the proverbial thought, "the show must go on," he walked out onto the stage by himself and began singing the opening song of their act. Out of the back of the room, Tony heard Robert's voice, but it was slurred as he swayed down the aisle climbing onto the stage and joining his brother in song. His breath wreaked of alcohol, and he could barely stand, but for the benevolence of the Lord above, the two made it through the act. In fact the audience was laughing; they thought Robert's drunken stupor was part of the act. After their final bows they left the stage as quickly as possible. Tony tore off his bow tie and then tore into his brother with vengeance. In the dressing room, the employees could hear the sounds of an angry brother screaming at the top of his lungs.

"How dare you do that to me, to us? Did you hear the audience laughing? They thought we were a comedy act. I can't take this any longer. I want out. This is not how I want my life to go. You are going to ruin us both" He gathered his jacket, stormed out of the theatre, and drove home. He would talk this over with Dana and his mom, and then he would branch out on his own.

Tony was crying when pulled into the driveway. He took a shower and then cried himself to sleep. Maybe in the light of day things would seem better, but when he woke up the next morning and the sun was radiating through the plantation blinds, things were just the same. After a long conversation with Dana, he called his mom, who sounded like a broken record as she encouraged Tony to stay put and support his twin.

"He needs you now more than ever," she pleaded. "You have got to help him, find out what the problem is and help him. If you leave him now, it will crush him."

"But ma, he is crushing me, he is crushing all of us, and I can't go on like this. He made the act a laughing stock, he humiliated me. I can never accept that behavior, nor can I forgive that behavior," ranted Tony. The other phone rang and Dana ran to Tony, pointing to the receiver she said it was very important. "Gotta go, I love you mom."

It was the entertainment director of the casino calling not only to extend the performances but spread the act out to the Reno location.

"Of course we will be there, yes, yes and yes," said Tony as he cradled the receiver. "I guess it's my great luck they are shipping the act up to Reno, but it's only for four weeks and then they promise to return us back to Las Vegas. I need to sit down with my brother." He didn't bother with the phone; he walked the two blocks and banged on Robert's front door. Susan opened the door with a fretful expression and pointed to the kitchen.

"He's in there nursing his hangover. Honestly Tony, he didn't tell me what happened, I can only surmise, but this time he promised me he would sober up and get his head on straight. I know you are upset, but you don't have to live with him. He's making my life hell with the constant drinking and now gambling. I'm begging you to help him. Now I suppose

I am sounding like your mom, but Tony, I believe he will listen to you," cried Susan.

Robert looked up from the steaming black coffee mug, he listlessly stirred in his seat.

"I'm sorry, I don't know what I was thinking last night. You know I've never ever done that to you. Something happened and I just snapped, but I can't answer why. I swear to you that will never happen again. I'll stop drinking. I'll stop today."

Tony sat down and hung his head.

"You won't believe this, but I just got off the phone with the casino's entertainment director and they are booking the act in Reno for four weeks. I told them I would get back to them," he lied. "I can't take you up there and babysit you. I can't watch you every minute to see if you are drinking or gambling your money away. So what's it going to be? If you can't trust yourself to stop, then let's cut the act and go our separate ways." Tony stood up, ready to leave, and then he felt Robert tug on his arm.

"Tony, tell them we will go. I swear I will make this right, you won't have to worry about a thing," he pledged.

"Okay, but this is the last time," warned Tony. "I'll call them back and make the arrangements and get back with you." Robert cried and threw his arms around his brother promising he would never destroy their relationship. "I promise I will never let you down again. I love you."

Tony remembered the only member of his family who could solve problems, his Uncle Nick. He hadn't thought about him in a while and right now he really needed his advice and a shoulder to cry on. He checked his watch, it was too late to call, by now Uncle Nick was fast asleep. Tony kissed his bride good night and tossed and turned, waiting for morning. A free floating anxiety overtook his mind and the reason arrived in the morning: when he dialed his uncle's phone and discovered Uncle Nick had passed away during the night. He placed the phone back into its cradle, slumped back into the bed, and began to cry, he had loved that man so much. An hour later Millie called to tell Tony, but he stopped her in mid-sentence, he already knew. Tony promised to return for the funeral. He called Robert, booked the flight, kissed Dana, and met Robert at the airport. Both somber, they flew home to pay their respects to the leader of the family, and to a relative they dearly loved and honored. Ralph, Uncle Nick's son, threw his arms around his twin cousins as they walked into the funeral home.

"Ralphie, you know how much I loved your dad, my uncle, my advisor, my confidante. If there is anything I can ever do for you just say the word. God, how I loved that man," Tony sobbed.

A day later, Robert and Tony boarded another plane back to Las Vegas, still bathing in a somber feeling. It was scary' Uncle Nick was alive one moment and dead the next, perhaps that was an internal wake-up call.

Tom Jones with the Sacca Twins during an interview promoting his appearance at the original MGM Grand Hotel in Las Vegas

Las Vegas Rocks ®

1911 – Las Vegas is incorporated on March 16, 1911. The
population stands at 800. Clark County has a population
of 3,321. Divorce laws are liberalized in the state of Nevada,
making residency easier to attain. A "quickie" divorce can
be attained after six weeks of residency. These short-term
residents stay at "dude ranches" which are the forerunners of
the sprawling Strip hotels.

Tony and Josette celebrate the making of the PBS TV special hosted by Tony and Charo at an after-party celebration

CHAPTER 10

As things went, Robert was true to his word. The four weeks in Reno were successful. Robert was on time, never had alcohol on his breath, and their performances were perfect. If he was drinking or gambling, he hid it well from the scrupulous eye of his brother. The cool mountain air and backdrop of massive evergreens was a nice change of pace from the heat and sagebrush of Las Vegas, but the crowds were smaller and the venue not as prestigious. Tony kept in touch with Dana every day and Susan called Robert every day. The four weeks flew by quickly and they headed back to Sin City and their wives.

"I got to say Robert, you seemed to have kept your word. I'm glad you did because we are on top of the world. We have a few weeks back at the MGM and then our hungry agent has booked us out for almost two years at every casino on the strip."

With a wild eye expression, Robert was overwhelmed, their fate was sealed. He had concealed his problems and addictions and it had paid off. They were a wanted commodity and he would spend every ounce of his energy making sure of their success. They revamped the act based upon the venues and other competing acts performing within the same casino. Sometimes they sang more standards, while at other times they veered in the direction of top forty hits. They took their four piece band from location to location, and the crew of six solidly bonded. With a simple hand signal or nod of the head, the keyboard player knew exactly what intro was needed for every song. Once in a while, Tony would read the crowd intently offering up an Italian or Spanish song and when he, did the response was always thunderous applause. The itinerary began at one end of the strip, crisscrossed the streets, and then headed back in the opposite direction: The Sahara, The Frontier, The Sands, The Flamingo, MGM Grand, The Mint, and the Golden Nugget were just a few of the mainstay casinos where they logged time.

The Sacca twins became local favorites as they wove their way into the fabric of the community and they became part of an elite group of performers who frequented the town often. They were friendly with many of the world class stars who shared the same marquee on the casino circuit. Singers, dancers, comedians, magicians, and musicians became their fast friends as they trooped in and out of the spotlights. The two year booking turned into three as they rode the tidal wave of fame and success. They added fresh new costumes, dance steps, and songs to ensure people returned time after time to see their act. Tony always held onto the Elvis impersonation, although he changed-up the songs and the costumes, but in Las Vegas, that was a staple, and an anticipated part of their act. They added songs by Michael Jackson, Barry Manilow, Huey Lewis, Madonna, Hall & Oates, and Kool and The Gang, to give the cover songs new flair with their unique arrangements.

As their fame grew, Dana became restless and depressed, she didn't want to remain in the city. Perhaps she felt like she could never compete with the twins, or that time was escaping her, regardless, she began seeking alternative positions. Tony's passion for her never relinquished, even after she announced she had accepted a job on a cruise ship and would be gone for several months. He unabashedly loved her and if she needed time or space, he would suffer the pangs of loneliness if it meant she would stay in their marriage. Dana was beautiful, her thick wavy blonde hair bounced off the corners of her shoulders, her light blue eyes, and bow curved lips made her irresistible. He loved her from the bottom of her toes to the top of her head: and he loved her heart, her soul, and her mind. How he would get through the next several months without her love he didn't know, but he loved her enough to allow her the freedom she desired. He thought about all the times he had wanted to be released from the chains binding himself with Robert, and that trapped feeling. There was no way he wanted his wife to feel that way, so he gave her the freedom she needed and said a prayer every night that she would return to him.

Tony's life went on. By now, he had a large gaggle of friends and spent his free time socializing, networking and immersing himself deeper in the community. He could have cheated, he was constantly accosted by women who were undeterred by a gold band, but he would never give up his scruples, he believed in his marriage vows. If anyone would be doing the cheating in their marriage, it would never be him.

"Sweet heart," she said endearingly, "I'll be back tomorrow night. I know you're working, so let's just meet at home." As happy as Tony was, there was a knot in the middle of his stomach. Was she coming home for good, or a visit, or was she about to call the marriage off? In anticipation of her homecoming, he filled the house with champagne, an assortment of roses, and food in the refrigerator. He flew out of the casino, rushed home, and caught himself as he ran into her arms. He allowed her to make the first move; he didn't know what was in her heart or her mind. She wrapped her arms around his waist in a familiar way, kissed him and they stood holding each other for a moment.

"Let me look at you, so tan and of course in perfect shape. I thought you might fall into the evils of all that luxurious cruise food, but if you did, it sure doesn't show." He twirled her around, kissed her soundly and then took her into the bedroom and turned the last several months of dreams into reality.

With her gone, Tony had to learn how to fend for himself and became an expert omelet maker. He set the table and they sat down in the sun drenched kitchen while he served breakfast. They talked about their lives and their future. She had loved the cruise experience, had made many friends, and loved the people she met along the various ports of call. Her life had turned into one great adventure after another: the places she had seen, the people she had met, and the experiences of living the unusual life on a huge ocean liner. What Dana failed to tell Tony was that she had every intention of returning to the job, the next time she would be sailing around the world. She waited. She had just returned home and it was only fair to give Tony and their marriage sometime to recoup. She had some big decisions to make and after a couple of weeks sleeping with her husband she knew she would see the light: she would leave. Not today, not that morning. She would not ruin the homecoming.

After a very late from a performance, Tony walked into the kitchen and found Dana on the phone.

"Who are you talking to? It's two o'clock in the morning." he asked. "God, I hope you're not complaining to my mother." She sat in an awkward silence as he anticipated the answer to the question.

"No," was all she said and then they walked into the bedroom, closed the lights and pretended to sleep. When he awoke the next morning, the foyer was cluttered with her luggage and a taxi was loudly honking his horn.

"Are you coming back to me? Just give me a yes or a no."

As he clutched her hands, she was undaunted, and she gathered her words carefully. She looked into her husband's eyes: a man who had loved her more than life itself, who had given her his entire heart. She began,

"I have this chance to go around the world. Can you imagine? I will get to see every country on the globe. Please just allow me this last chance." He stood in silence as she wheeled out the luggage. He never allowed himself to cry in her presence. "I'll call you soon dear," she shouted as the taxi sped away. He had been generous, maybe too generous with his heart and his complete commitment, but then, wasn't that was marriage was all about? Perhaps putting trust on the table was an option he would have to face, and for once in his life he knew a call to his mother wasn't going to smooth over the problem. He closed the front door and listened to the silence that cloaked his home. He walked into the bedroom, collapsed on the bed, and began crying. Was it Little Anthony's "Tears On My Pillow", or Patsy Kline's, "I Fall To Pieces," or The Beatle's, "Norwegian Wood," that eventually lulled Tony back to sleep? He would have plenty of time to face reality, but in that very moment, he needed peace.

Rehearsals that afternoon went well, as did the performance that night, and for the next several months. Although he rarely talked to Susan, he knew Robert's marriage wasn't what it should be, and she was miserably unhappy. With Dana gone, Susan never complained to Tony, she knew he had a heavy burden on his heart and she had no right in churning up bad feelings, so she remained silent. Sometimes Tony would envision Dana going around and around, while he just stood in one place. He was horribly lonely, but what scared him the most was how empty he felt inside. He had never been alone. From his mother's stomach, to a lifetime tied to Robert, his bed or bedroom always had the sounds of another life. Now his home and his bedroom were devoid of life. In fact, he couldn't recall the rarity of sleeping alone, from the crib, to touring the road where a hot babe was securely planted next to him, to the army, to the tours and other hot babes, then marriage one and marriage two. *That was it!* he thought, he had a syndrome where he couldn't sleep alone. Nah, his syndrome was being unable to love, especially the one you wanted. All those heartbreaking, heart-wrenching break-up songs constantly filed through his mind like an ongoing movie tag. The problem was, he didn't know when it would end, but he was getting damn sick of waiting, his patience had worn thin.

When the front door burst open six months down the road, it was no surprise when Dana merely pecked him on the cheek. That was his answer: they were done. She never bothered to roll her luggage into the bedroom, rather she took his hand and led him to the kitchen. A confession of her heart revealed she had fallen in love with the cruise director and she planned on returning back to the ship as soon as a few things had been settled at home. The first of those things was a divorce. It was quick, she asked for little except her savings in the bank account. She cared nothing for the home, she didn't and wouldn't need it as long as she had the ocean liner. Tony was taken aback, but not in shock.

"I have been true to you. I would never cheat on you while we were married, but I guess you didn't feel the same," he said. After a brief conversation, she took her belongings and left. That was the last time Tony would allow those sad songs into his psyche. He had wasted almost a year out of his virile life pining over a wife who cheated on him, and he would waste no more time. He thought about all those lovely women clinging to his every note, he would begin dating with a vengeance, never allowing one opportunity to slip out of his fingers. He was strikingly handsome, with a buffed up body: Tony was the most eligible bachelor in the city. He still carried a torch of insecurity and shyness, so it was the women who pursued him. His bed became filled with a bevy of gorgeous women, all wanting a piece of the most comely man that they had ever met, or slept with.

The long strands of shiny black hair covered his chest, he kissed the top of her head, gratified in last night's ardent lovemaking. He had gotten his mojo back, and from that moment on it was all uphill. His mind wondered to the summer of '72 and '73 where he could and did have all the babes he could handle. Right here and right now, they were back in his life and he would rue the day he would give his heart away again. Two marriages had bitten the dust, that was enough heartache for one man. Tonight, and for as long as he had the fortitude to hold out, he would test the waters with new lovers. The excitement would continue on until he found another wife, god forbid, or dropped dead of a heart attack, god forbid. As he scrutinized the perfect warm body underneath his covers he decided on the latter.

It was time to party. He remembered the lavish spreads of the rowdy boisterous family get-togethers, and Tony embarked on making that happen in his own home and in his own way. Monday night football was the commencement of a string of parties that began to make his home the place to be. He spent Sunday afternoons recreating his dad's marinara sauce with roasted sausages and hand rolled meatballs. Monday evening, the guys would cavalcade into his living room and sit around the television, hoisting beers to the players on the turf, while consuming Tony's Italian cuisine. Soon, women wrangled invitations. They nudged some of the men to the floor while they cuddled up next to chef. It was a joyous occasion, and by the time all the beers had been gulped and properly burped, no one really cared who won or lost, but if the Philadelphia team was on the gridiron, they all knew where their host's loyalties lay, and they cheered the team onto victory, or not. Regardless, Tony was having fun, his house was bursting with friends, and love was in the air.

He doggedly set out to expand his circle of friends and acquaintances, and one night he strolled into the Italian American Club, noted for its food, no shocker there, and of course Italians. He didn't have to join the club to eat at the restaurant; he didn't even have to be Italian. He just had to look good and carry a sufficient amount of cash to pay the bill. Tony was always the first person to admit he was shy, but one was hard pressed to believe that as he bellied up to the bar, ordered a Chianti, and began shaking hands and introducing himself to the other men seated on the stools. The consummate performer, before the night had ended, he serenaded the crowd, and was asked back by the happy manager,

"Next time your meal is on the house."

"For that, you know I will return," which he did the next evening and the evening after that, until he had acquired a coterie of Italian friends, who had successfully carved out successful livelihoods in the town. After a short set, Tony reclaimed his stool at the bar, and shook hands with another guy named Tony, who had fallen in love with his voice. He was older, shorter, and had graying hair: the Brooklyn accent gave away his background and they instantly bonded. The two met several times and then one night, when the older Tony was convinced of the singer's ambitions and goals, he took him to the Augustus Society: a small group of elite men who helped local Italians with charity and support. This was not a group looking to sell cookies, but an organization with lofty goals, who were the movers and shakers behind many successful commercial operations in the town.

"I've seen you on television and I quite like your show, and what you do for our town, you make it seem bigger than life, especially with all those fancy headliners you interview," the older Tony complimented.

"I appreciate your thoughts and as long as I can continue to get great sponsors, the shows will go on," his new friend nodded his head and promised that would happen. He had a lot of friends who believed in the city, and supported other people who also believed in the city. He glimpsed his watch and Tony noticed it was getting late: he excused himself, but at the last moment, he turned to his friend and asked if would like to accompany him on the next shoot. A producer from Palm Springs approached Tony about producing a PBS special from the library of the footage he had acquired over the years from his television show, *Entertainment Las Vegas Show*. They advised him that he should have a co-host for the show. They recommended Ann Margaret, Tina Sinatra, and

Sheena Easton, because of their association with Las Vegas, however Tony had a better idea. He recommended Charo who had been on his show many times as a guest, and they readily agreed. Stunning, with thick auburn hair which matched her thick Spanish accent, she was as beautiful as she was talented and humorous. It was a perfect match. Tony and Charo filmed at eleven locations in Las Vegas, featuring some of the hottest attractions: the gondola at the Venetian, the Brooklyn Bridge at New York, New York, the Beach at the Rio, and the Bellagio in front of the dancing waters, in which Charo played her Flamenco guitar.

In the morning when the first cameramen arrived, it came as no surprise when Tony, his friend, showed up. After Tony introduced him around, he handed his friend a pad and paper, and suggested he take notes so he looked like one of the crew. In reality all his friend wanted was to be close to Charo, one of the most gorgeous women he had ever met. Although the shoot was a lot of work, it was fun, entertaining, and truly served the goal the producer was seeking: insight to the stars' intimate lives. The couple introduced a variety of stars: interviewed Billy Ray Cyrus, The Righteous Brothers, The Smothers Brothers, Tony Orlando, Donna Summers, and the cast of Folies Bergere. They used humor and a wide variety of backdrops. The program combined stars with tourism as they showcased the casinos and other eye catching places. At the close of the shoot, his new friend returned the pad and paper and thanked him for an indelible memory, as he glanced over in Charo's direction.

"Tony, I would love you to sing at my New Year's party, and feel free to bring a date, but I promise you won't need one when you see all the drop dead beautiful women I plan to invite. There will be plenty of important people coming, many who can help you with your career. Besides, it will be a lot of fun and you know the food will be delicious!" he proposed. They shook hands and he placed the address in Tony's palm and told him to be there by eight. Tony Smiled. He was thrilled and anxious, and convinced it would be an unforgettable evening.

Worse than a woman, he couldn't figure out what to wear, a tux might be too over-the-top or guests would think he was a waiter, but a sports jacket wasn't dressy enough. He held up a black worsted suit and added a deep purple silk tie. Yes, that was definitely the look he wanted to achieve. He pulled on a pair of patent loafers and tossed a dozen business cards into the interior jacket pocket before he turned over the engine in his car and cruised to the mini mansion burrowed behind a gated community. The valet grabbed the keys and pointed to the front door,

"The party is in there, just walk through the front door." Although it was early, the expansive living room was filled with over a hundred guests drinking, eating, chatting, and dancing. The host spotted Tony in the front foyer, walked over, shook his hand, and then led him to a small area staged for the performance.

"Just an hour, off and on, if that's okay with you?"

He smiled as he set up the music, located the microphone, and then scanned the room for hot babes. There was no doubt about it, there were plenty of gorgeous women interspersed between older men. It would be challenging, but with his voice and face, he was certain he could snag at least one ingénue. He grabbed a champagne flute, circumvented the room, located the bathroom, and was escorted by a stunning young brunette to the backyard where a full bar and buffet was prepared. His eyes dilated as he took in the endless offerings of Italian and seafood dishes, breads, vegetables, and caviar. It was not like the family parties he had back in Philadelphia: no this was how the privileged lived, and this was exactly where he wanted to be. He grabbed a hefty portion of red caviar, downed it and the remains of the champagne flute, and then found his way back to the living room. He shook hands with those he was familiar with, from the Augustus Society and the Italian Club. He felt comfortable, at home, and confident that if he needed support, he had to look no further than the men in this house. One of his new acquaintances suggested a unique waterhole that was known among the entertainers, the Tap Room. It was the place where the locals got together and entertained each other, often trying out new portions of an upcoming act, or just jamming with friends. Tony made a mental note, he wouldn't forget that tip. He glanced at his watch. He was determined not work a moment over the agreed upon hour: there were too many babes to kiss, too many powerful people to mingle with, and way too much delicious food and drink to consume.

Bobby Darin's songs complemented his voice perfectly as he began with, "Mack the Knife," and, "Beyond the Sea," while he demurely scoured the dance floor for eligible women. He spotted a tall blonde in the far corner, her gaze met his when he sang, "she's waiting for me," and the rest of the song belonged to her until he noticed a tuxedoed man take hold of her arm and usher her to the backyard. He tried again, "Dream Lover," that was perfect. Yet again, he opened up his pipes and found a seductive glance from the other side of the room. This time it was a black haired beauty, with exotic eyes, and a curvaceous body that screamed (at least to Tony), *take me now!* The set had finally ended, and rather than chase this beauty, he brushed by her as he walked to the back yard. She tapped him on the shoulder and introduced herself, and with guarded control, he jokingly offered to buy her a drink. They talked and when midnight arrived, they shared a consensual kiss, which endured for the length of Auld Lang Syne. After he made sure this stunner didn't belong to another man, and that she wasn't the niece of his host, they decided to leave the party. She had, quite willingly, lost her ride home, and was all too happy to share the front seat of the singer's car, and shortly after, the other half of his king size bed. When he finally closed his eyes all he could think of was what a night, what a life, he was lucky enough to have embarked upon. His prayers were that it would never end.

The following Monday, Tony showed up at the Terry James Talent Showcase and was pleasantly surprised by the large group of performers who had congregated in the backroom lounge. Although most of the crowd was filled with strangers, he recognized a few, and was determined to become friendly with all of them. Networking was the name of the game. He took a seat at the bar, several musicians from different bands were jamming on the stage. Then one lovely lady, who spent her weekends as a headliner at a top casino, grabbed the mike and began belting out a new song. When she was done, her colleagues yelled out, "right on," just the words she wanted to hear. This small audience was everyone's worst critic, and if it went well with their peers, then for sure the rest of the world would be content. Shy was Tony's middle name and that night, and for the next few Mondays, he sat in the bleachers and made friends until he could get up enough courage to sing before this illustrious crowd. When his turn came, the only musician on the tiny stage was a piano player, but that was all he needed. He decided on a Barry Manilow tune that would be added to his final set and when he was finished, he was thrilled the crowd gave him all the kudos he needed to include it in the act. He continued to go to the Monday night jam sessions, always surprised by the celebrities who would show up: headliners like Wayne Newton, to local comedians would straggle in to meet and greet, and try out new material. Tony tossed a five dollar bill on the bar, thanked his friends, shook many extended hands, left the lounge, and headed home, the next morning he would have to rise before dawn.

Tony convinced the head of K-News Vegas radio station to give him his own talk show that mirrored the televised weekly interview show, *Entertainment Las Vegas Style.* He finally landed the gig, but only if he would do a weekend entertainment report, which translated into an early start on Tuesday mornings. He canvassed the entertainment directors at all of the major casinos and obtained the scheduled headliners. Initially the minute update seemed simple enough, but gathering all the information and then boiling it down to a couple of minutes ended up taking a few hours each week. He had turned himself into his own little networking system, with one media feeding on the other. So he did the minute spots, and then each Saturday afternoon, the hour radio show was aired. The mid-afternoon time slot turned out to have a wider audience than he had anticipated, especially in the summer when tourists lounged by the pool and flipped on the local radio stations while they drifted in and out of their siestas.

He placed the earphones securely over his head, and at the top of the hour, Tony Sacca's Variety Show hit the airwaves. He tossed on a couple of top forties while he impatiently waited for the late arrival of his guests. He filled the hour with happenings around town: who to see, where to see it, and when to see it. On that Saturday, Rich Little was the guest. He brought humor and some of his ingenious voices over the airwaves. On another Saturday, Little Anthony and the Imperials were booked, and they ended up singing live. When the phone lines lit up, the group was only too happy to oblige the listening audience; they sang anther song, one that was in the play list for their evening show. With a few thousand seats to fill, they were thrilled to have the radio time with Tony, as he helped promote their show and sell the few remaining tickets.

Through the ten year run, there were comedians, dancers, and musicians who kept the show vibrant and fresh, but most importantly, insured the sponsors would be happy and supportive. Tony had great flexibility. Although there was a small soundproof room at the back of the radio station, he could grab a couple of microphones and a sound engineer, and off they would go to grab the insights of world famous stars. Because it was radio, and no one cared what they looked like, many of the interviews took place in obscure places: even a bathroom! What did Tony care? He was out for the interview and did whatever it took to make it happen and create interesting stories. Oh the hangovers, the faces patched with plastic surgery, the beauties without make-up, and the men without their wigs, he had been privy to. As long as the stars sold tickets to the shows, and the sponsors sold their products, everyone was happy, especially Tony, who was living out his dreams. Radio was a lot more fun that he thought possible.

Tony's emotional repair was moving along quickly, but Robert had sunk back into his old ways. His gambling and drinking habits, which had remained latent, were coming back to the forefront. One evening as Tony was having a bit of fun at Lady Luck Casino, he received a call from the cops to come bail out his brother Tony.

"Hey wait," he yelled into the phone, "I'm Tony."

"Well responded the clerk, there is a man in jail and he says his name is Tony and to call his brother." Fuming he hopped into his car and drove the two blocks to the precinct, where Robert was sitting in a jail cell charged with drunk driving. When Tony walked in, everyone knew his face and realized they had been duped by his twin. The charges were quickly changed to the proper name, bail paid, and a very glum brother walked out of the holding cell. Tony was beyond livid as he began ranting to his brother.

"How could you? How dare you? Did you think you could give them my name and put the blame on me? I'm not the drunk in this family. You had made a solemn vow to me you would stop, but you lied. You are going to destroy us all. What about your wife? Don't you owe her something? Your drinking is going to ruin your marriage, it's going to ruin our act, and now it's going to ruin our relationship. Will it never end?"

Tony shoved him into the back seat, revved up the engine, and sped to Robert's home. He grabbed his drunk brother out of the car and laid him on the ground in front of the doorsteps. When Susan heard the commotion, she came running out of the house, looked up, and then looked down at her husband sprawled on the grass.

"Tony, I'm fed up with him and from the look on your face, I guess you are too. I really can't take it anymore. I wanted to confide in you, but honestly after Dana left I couldn't bring myself to complain to you. Looking back, maybe I should have said something, and maybe I wouldn't be staring at a drunk on my doorstep," she rambled.

Tony turned to Susan, "It's time I released him to you. I can't take this anymore, he is in self-destruction mode, and I'm putting him into your hands. I'm done being his babysitter"

"I'm done with you brother," screamed Tony. "The act, the Sacca Twins, all gone! You are free to do whatever the hell you want, but it won't be with me." He didn't bother calling his mother, Robert would do that, but he knew this time his mother wouldn't be making her plea from the other side of the country. Tony had been the good brother, had put up with Robert's transgressions for ages and it was time to set him free. Whatever Robert did, he did it to himself and their mother knew at this point it would be unfair to drag Tony down. He didn't deserve it, he had paid his dues and stuck with the act and now she could not fault him for leaving. He was in his thirties; it was time to untie the knot.

Did Tony feel a twinge of guilt? Did he place some of the blame of Robert's demise upon himself? Of course he did: they were identical twins, they had shared a lifetime together, and now one of them was no longer functioning. Tony had struggled through two lost marriages and he wouldn't wish that on his brother, but he knew that Susan would not sit around and watch Robert drink himself to death: she didn't have that kind of strength. Even though Tony was finally cutting the ties, he didn't want this decision to seem as though it were a challenge or even a game to see who would end up on top. Tony just wanted his freedom, and Robert, who had always begged his brother to stay, had opened up a window that would never close.

Again, Tony caved in. The next day his mother called and begged him once again to stay with Robert. She said that he needed Tony even more. Her tirade was relentless until he promised her he would give Robert another chance. Between his own guilty feelings and his mom, he stood with Robert, but he made a solemn promise that this would be the last straw. His brother was in a free fall, and he had no intentions of joining him. Tony knew part of the problem they both shared was a lack of accountability. Even now, as Tony stared down at his brother, had he been a regular guy, he would still be in the county lock up, but as an entertainer and well known celebrity, he was quickly released.

An interesting opportunity was presented to the twins, and to alter the bad blood between them they readily accepted. Comedy was never their front game, but when Frankie Carr approached the duo, they accepted his offer to work as part of his act. The Mint Casino was located at the center of Fremont Street and it was where all the top notch acts were booked. The hotel was so large it had two performing stages, a showroom, and a lounge where live acts came and went seven days a week. Frankie was approaching his late sixties and had been out of show business for a while, but he had stamina and a great act, and he decided to dive back into doing what he loved best. One of the highlights of the act was putting the twins inside an oversized set of overalls with two heads propped at the top. It was hysterically funny, and the twins wowed the audience with their new sense of comedy, while they sang and danced inside the costume. Frankie called this, "The Pete and Repete act," and he made jokes while he gazed at the two heads. The original four week engagement kept extending and ended up being for a full year. Although they later put on their tuxedos and sang well known cover and standards, it was the comedy that attracted the never ending crowds.

"Are you ready?" Frankie asked as he smiled into the eyes of the heads popping up out of the overalls. "I see it's another packed house and I know you guys are going to make them laugh tonight." As he walked out of their dressing room and prepared to enter the stage, Tony had a bad sensation at the base of his neck, and it wasn't from the itchy jean cloth. Frankie walked onto the stage, began his opening and instead of continuing with the next portion of his act, turned and introduced Pete and Repeat, and then lumbered off the stage. Since the brothers were always on top of things, they were dressed and ready to perform, but Tony threw a cautious look to the right of stage and noticed that Frankie had keeled over and was lying on the ground. Without losing a beat, they did their bit, walked off the stage, and signaled the band to play a song or two while they figured out what was going on with Frankie. The stagehand told the guys he had gotten really sick and was rushed to the hospital. They were to try and finish up the performance as best they could. They scrambled back to the dressing room, jumped into their tuxedos, and sang and danced their way through the balance of the night. No one was disappointed.

Immediately after the show they raced to the hospital. Frankie was in the intensive cardiac care ward, with tubes entering every aperture in his body. Things didn't look so good. Three days later he passed away, and a month or so after that, so did the act. *Some things in life you just can't predict, especially when it comes to the fragile health of an aging performer*, thought Tony. The twins had to suck up this loss and forge ahead. Yet another lesson learned in the realm of show business, sometimes the show doesn't always go on. Tony would find another avenue to replace this gig.

Creative in so many ways and enamored with the city, Tony stretched his talent and composed, "Las Vegas, the Greatest Town Around," which he sent to Paul Schaffer, musical conductor for David Letterman's late night talk show. He received an invitation to sing on the show and perform the song he had submitted four years prior. Again, he felt like the little red hen who had done all the work and then the entire roost wanted to enjoy the baked bread: and so it was with Robert. Tony's mom begged and pleaded and insisted he ask Robert to join him in the performance. Again, he placated his mom's wishes. The Letterman show had transported itself for a few days at Bally's Casino, and was surveying the local talent. Tony was the first person he called, and the twins performed the original song to an audience of over five million.

"I was happy he joined me, the song sounded so much better with harmony, but I couldn't believe I had to teach my brother the lyrics." The song had been written by Tony in 1982 and in 1986 the original score was place inside a time capsule near Fremont Street. The city made plans to open the capsule in 50 years, and Tony made plans to be there for it.

Two days later, he opened up an invitation for an outdoor event, and decided to go. It was a charity event and a lot of local entertainers would surely be there, so he found his favorite summer outfit, pulled out a couple of blank checks, and headed to the party. He walked into the crowded room and went directly toward the bar before he began making his rounds, shaking hands with acquaintances and friends. That's when he spotted Darlene. She was standing alone sipping wine and she seemed to be a little lost and sad.

"Hey," said Tony, "How are you?"

"To be honest, my husband Gene and I just separated." Tony was shocked. He had known Gene for years: he was the trumpet player at one of the casinos and had played in the band at several of his shows. Tony took her arm, escorted her outside to the fresh air and found two empty seats at the edge of a long banquet table. Darlene was tall and thin. She had a perfect cream complexion, dark brown eyes, and a head of long, thick, dark brown, bobbing curls: Her slightly curved lips were polished with a lustrous deep plum, and her high cheeks blushed bronze. In every way she was a beautiful woman, and although he had met her several times in the past, he had never looked twice. He always kept to his rule about never dating a married woman, and she was always off limits: but tonight, as he looked into her deep set eyes, her beauty struck him where it always did, in his loins. They spoke for a while, she talked about her life of writing about metaphysics, how she had been handling the divorce, and what her plans were: and then she swung around, looked into his eyes and made him open up.

"Enough about me. Tell me how you are, really truly. You know, with my metaphysical background I can see into your mind."

Without hesitation, he longingly talked about his divorce: how he too had been cheated on, how demeaning and emasculated he felt. As he released pent up emotions he had been storing for months, he felt cleansed, and when he looked into her eyes, she not only showed him she cared, but completely understood how he felt. They had shared the same fate and bonded in a symbiotic relationship.

He took her number and called the next afternoon for a dinner date, this time he was paying the dinner bill. When she appeared at the bistro her face was glowing with all sense of maudlin expressions erased in the brevity of a day. He was nervous; it had been a while since he had been on a grown-up date, rather than one where the only thing on his mind was how fast they could gulp down the rare steaks and jump into bed. Not tonight, this was different. He had known her, had known her ex-husband, and jumping into the sack just seemed inappropriate. This time we would take his time. Down two marriages, he was in no hurry for number three. In spite of his trepidations, dinner conversation flowed seamlessly. They both talked and listened and displayed empathetic retorts, and both hardily agreed that life had sucked with the demise of the marriages. After a dinner of Middle Eastern food, he walked to her car and promised to see her again. As he turned, she grabbed his arm, put her arms gently around his neck and kissed him.

"Are you having a hard time with me because of Gene?" Darlene asked. Shy and at a loss for words, she sensed his dilemma, he felt as if he were in the middle of two friendships and he didn't want to cross the line.

"It's okay, I'm done with Gene and he with me, and as you know, he has moved on to another," she assured him. He wrapped his arms around her, kissed her and thanked her for patience and understanding. It took little time and before two months had passed, he moved in with her and they shared the household bills and a slowly developing love.

The one thing that Tony hadn't counted on was her son, who was in his teenage years and needed a father's guidance. He had never raised a child; most of the time he felt like a teenager himself, and when he vividly remembered those blissful years, the thought terrified him that he would have to help supervise someone like himself. In the one story home, the three moved in separate directions, but they got along and they learned to adjust and accept each other's foibles. After three years, the couple had a small wedding and continued their relationship on an even plateau.

Because the son's father had moved out of state and rarely visited, the foibles became the responsibility handed to Tony. He laid down the law on behaviors that he knew would only lead to despair and harm. At fifteen, the son brought home a classmate and proceeded to take her to his bedroom. Tony grabbed him and told him in no uncertain terms was he to escort her to his bedroom. A huge fight ensued and both teens left the house.

"There is to be no sex with underage girls in this home," Tony demanded. "All that will do is get you into trouble!" And lead to trouble it did, because no matter how loud and hard Tony screamed, the teen became pregnant.

Just weeks later, Tony caught him in the backyard smoking a joint and again he screamed. The boy's biological father was a junkie and Tony hardly wanted that legacy handed down to Darlene's only son. However, the louder he screamed the less the teen obeyed; he never graduated high school, and ended up living with his mom working at a minimum wage job.

Just as Tony was about to let loose another tirade, the teen was saved by the bell. The cell phone read Ralph. When he answered the call, Tony was surprised that his youngest cousin was going to pay a visit. Ralph asked Tony if he could stay at his home for a while. Tony considered the current set of circumstances and was thrilled to have a family member temper the unbalanced household.

Ralph was a handsome, newly single guy, had nothing but time on his hands now that he was in between jobs: he thought a visit out to Las Vegas might be just the place for him to find himself. The youngest of Uncle Nick's brood, he had always been in awe of the twins, and in turn Uncle Nick had been such a huge influence on the twin's lives that welcoming Ralph into his home was the very least Tony could do. Before he could unload his gear into the guestroom, Ralph was off and running with Tony.

"When we went to his office and I saw how archaic all his equipment was I went to work purchasing computers, setting up accounting systems, and finally wearing him down, so I could install a telephone system. Within two months, I had the office humming like a real company." He hired a web designer to make a professional site on the internet, and eventually, he added an internet store that sold unique Las Vegas souvenirs.

During the day, Ralph would follow his cousin around like a puppy: he carried camera equipment to shoots, made notes, screamed out orders to the sound crew, and at night, he would accompany Tony to celebrity shoots or media parties, or performances.

"I couldn't keep up with him, he was always on the go, like a wound up clock, he never stopped moving. I was fifteen years younger and by the end of the first week, I was so tired, I couldn't move. Tony was the most motivated person I ever met. I was wondering how I would have the time to meet the hot chicks, but that came soon enough. As I continued the shoots, I found it very easy to pick up women who were gawking at Tony: since he was married, I became second best. I never lacked a date, and I was having a blast! Las Vegas was all I had hoped it would be and more."

Ralph was incredibly helpful and handy, but he loathed the early morning, especially after a night of drinking, gambling, and dancing. It was that damn juicer that drove him nuts. Unlike his thinner, healthier cousin, he didn't get up at the crack of dawn, exercise, and then make an elixir of vegetables that ended up in liquid form. It was that sound, that inordinate amount of noise coming from that damn healthy machine and interrupting his beauty sleep that drove him to do the unthinkable. One afternoon, when no one was around, he found just the answer inside the garage. He opened up the engine of the juicer and squirted the contents of a tube of gloppy oil into the innards which seized up the motor. The next morning, as he slept in, he smiled to himself as the loud hum of the machine was but an unpleasant memory.

"Hey, Darlene, what the hell happened to my juicer?" Ralph grinned from ear to ear and rolled over in the bed for another couple hours of uninterrupted sleep. Although, he felt a twinge of guilt, he never let on.

Tony wouldn't accept any money from Ralph, but he more than made up for that with his construction background when he built a huge waterfall in the backyard. After several weeks of laying bricks, he had created a six foot wall with a huge stream of water jutting out onto an elaborately designed set of red rocks. It was beautiful and became the center piece of the back yard.

"I was so glad Tony loved the waterfall, it took away my guilt for the juicer and it was my way of saying thank you for all that he had done for me. I stayed for a year before I became homesick. Then I packed my bags and returned back East, but I would never forget that year, nor the kindness he showed me. I never knew a person who was as beloved by so many people as my cousin. Even his first father-in-law became his friend. It seemed like the only people who didn't like my cousin were his ex-wives." Ralph and Tony have always remained friends and when Ralph hit pay dirt, got married, and retired at the ripe old age of thirty-nine, he returned to visit. Flush with money, this time he stayed at a strip hotel and ordered room service for his bride. There were no more noisy juice motors to interfere with his beauty sleep, and no more frenetic racing from location to location.

Darlene's life was dedicated to the metaphysical world; she had published a magazine, "New Dimension," devoted solely to the topic. Tony on the other hand was as pragmatic as one could get, although an artist and a performer, his head was in financial success, and the tangible world.

As time marched on, she became more introspective and Tony, out of the sheer necessity, became more extroverted. They began to grow apart, and as the days evolved into months, it was obvious to the couple this marriage was in a downhill spiral and there was no way up, but out. It didn't help they encountered many fights over her son, who also seemed to share a downward spiral, but that was in the form of drug addiction.

Tony did come to terms with many of the concepts she had purported, acquainting himself with Vision, a series of seminars that drew upon the subliminal mind, turning weaknesses into strengths. At lectures, they were taught intense role playing, which eventually unveiled hidden psychological crutches and taught them how to solve and cope with the revelations.

At the weekly meetings, he developed a kinship among a wide variety of people, all seeking to jump over psychological hurdles that were stunting their ambitions. It was at the last of these seminars that he reached an epiphany and unmasked his deepest unconscious problems. At a three day weekend seminar, the constant uninterrupted session forced him to focus on the problem. An hour here and there was helpful, but with three solid days of introspection, something was bound to happen.

"Your job today," dictated the teacher, "is to write down on a piece of paper what you want to achieve. What is your Achilles heel that is holding you back from attaining your goals and your dreams?"

"I took my pen and scribbled that I needed to develop a new set of balls if I'm to be successful, because I'm so insecure." Everyone took a turn reading their notes and when it came to Tony, he could hear the crowd laughing, but they understood what he was seeking. As he drove home, he felt stronger, and more in charge of his life: he hoped against all hope that he would be able to believe in himself. He fell into a deep sleep and dreamed of a happier life. Suddenly he was awakened in the middle of the night, he felt an itching in his groin. Padding to the bathroom, he turned on the light, sat down on the toilet, and was shocked by what he saw; his manhood, his balls, had shed an entire layer of skin, just like a lizard sheds its skin. He reached down and pulled off a solid mass of skin. He blinked: he thought he was hallucinating, but in his hands he held the metaphor of his worst nightmare. As he flushed the skin down the toilet, he began a new life. The seminar had miraculously worked, it had enabled him to forget about his deep psychological wounds and begin reaching his goals, it had given him permission to move on with his life, and nothing and nobody would ever stand in his way again. He had grown a new set of balls.

Tony continued with the Vision seminars for eight years.

"When you are free flowing with your life, breathing is fun." Surrounded by people of like minds, they fed on each other's positive thinking and brought a perspective of focus into each other's lives. He learned to love life, accept his weaknesses and use his strengths.

Robert hadn't escaped the abuse as he grew up: he was there next to his twin, receiving the same unconscionable beatings, but he chose to bury his problems with alcohol, and later heavy drugs. Tony was too busy trying to save himself, he didn't have the emotional strength nor the knowhow to save his brother. These Vision meetings gave him the ability to deal with his childhood horrors, but Robert chose a much more pernicious path.

"Between the support of the meetings and Darlene's drifting love, I had gathered enough psychological strength, and I moved out becoming single once again. I was having the time of my life and was back dating lots of women. They knew my face from the television shows and the lounge acts and when we were together, fulfilling our greatest fantasies, no one asked me how much money was in my bank account. I lived the façade of a rich man, and to the women who hung out with me that was good enough."

Charo and Tony ride the gondola at the Venetian hotel for the taping of a PBS TV special

Las Vegas Rocks &

*1931 – Beginning in 1931, the construction of Hoover Dam
brings an influx of construction workers which starts a
population boom and gives the Valley's economy, which was
in the grips of the Great Depression, a needed boost. While
gambling took place illegally for many years, it was officially
legalized in March 1931 by the state legislature.*

*Tony talks to Elton John at the media event for Barry
Manilow appearing at the Las Vegas Hilton*

CHAPTER 11

After years of playing the casinos and searching for something new, Tony looked around for other opportunities. He felt like he was drowning and there was no way out. Carrying a constant fear that his brother would appear at one the live performances drunk, he was in a perpetual state of anxiety. He watched television, and the success of the Smothers Brothers, with their humor, singing ability, and gift of gab, and he decided *why not?* Why not star in their own, twin television show? They had the looks, they could sing and dance, they could learn to tell jokes, and they already had ready access to a constant parade of stars coming in and out of the city. Most importantly, if Robert should come to the set drunk, the portions could be edited out, and Tony would be saved humiliation. It was definitely the temporary solution to the problem.

Tony coined the phrase, *Live, From Las Vegas*, a variety show in the heart of the entertainment capital of the world, which began production in 1986. The major problem with such an undertaking was how they would procure the initial production money. Fortunately, Robert stepped up to the plate. After his eventual divorce from his second wife, he began dating an attractive woman, who fell in love with him, and the idea of producing the show. She put up the money and they reserved a time slot on Channel thirteen, the ABC affiliate, for a half hour program. The show was very successful, no one had ever produced a variety show about the city, and the ratings were high, but after a thirty week run, it didn't reach syndication, and Robert's girlfriend closed up the purse strings.

Tony had worked creatively to make the program unique; he designed a stage set where the guests were flanked by either brother,

"I feel like I am at a tennis match," said Frank Sinatra Jr. as he kept turning his head from side to side, conversing with a mirror image. Sometimes they commenced their show with an old scientific phrase, "don't adjust your television set, the images you are about to see are real", as the twins would take their seats on the set. It was comical and filled with their abilities to sing and dance. It was an instant hit. Tony wasn't about to give up after the thirty week run, he loved being in front of the cameras, and they seemed to be forgiving to his brother. The twins purchased all the rights to the show from their original backer: for the total sum of one thousand dollars, they owned all of the assets. Tony set to work finding sponsors and crafting the production to attract the best talent. He began knocking on doors of local merchants and they responded by signing seasonal contracts. With enough money to secure the production needs, the show went on. The guests included out of town talent like Tony Bennett, Red Fox, Billy Preston, as well as some local talents that were housed at major casinos, such as Celine Dion, and the Temptations. With the constant parade of brilliant entertainers, the ratings climbed and the money from the sponsors continued to fill the bank account.

A rare opportunity became available for Tony to arrange interviews with the three top comedians in the country who were all playing at Caesar's Hotel: Danny Thomas, Sid Caesar, and Milton Berle.

"I was set to do the usual format, display portions of the live performance interspersed with private interviews. I had taped the rehearsal with Milton, who had a towel wrapped around his neck. In the middle of the taping he screamed out at me, 'Who the fuck do you think you are: taping without my permission?' Stunned, I explained I had been given permission by his producer to run the tape, but again Milton unleashed a tirade of curse words, and I quickly packed up and left. I was humiliated. The interviews with Danny Thomas and Sid Caesar went off without a hitch and have been archived as part of a sacred history of Las Vegas. Ironically five years later, Milton came out with a magazine, Miltie, and I again interviewed him. This time he was a different man as he reflected on his life and the things he loved. 'When I make people laugh, I get younger.' I could tell he meant every word as a tear fell out of the corner of his eye. He did have a heart, I guess we just got off on the wrong foot.

"One of the most interesting interviews I ever did was with Anthony Quinn. He was endorsing ATM machines, and I was asked to use that as part of the interview, which I agreed to as long as I could be profound and bring an inside look into his life. It is fascinating how people come to be actors, and in Anthony's case it was most unusual. As a young kid, he had accidently cut his tongue causing a speech impediment and instead of going the traditional route and seeing a speech pathologist, he opted for acting lessons. Not only did the lessons cure him, but provided him with the foundation for long successful career.

"Meeting Mickey Rooney at the Desert Inn was another memorable experience. When I walked into the small dressing room with my cameraman, Mickey's son, who was his manager, screamed out, 'five minutes and you're done.' Shaken by memories of Milton, I didn't want to make any enemies, I just wanted to make history. We talked for over an hour as he spilled his guts about Hollywood, the lifestyles, and how the industry had changed. He loved me and just kept talking and talking. I guess with eight wives, he never got a word in edgewise and he felt open and free to speak his mind.

"Then there was the interview with Bobby Berizini, who had a trained orangutan act. I have to admit, it was a lot of fun, but impossible to keep my composure as three animals climbed all over me, pulling my hair, tickling my legs, and running circles around my feet. People love animal acts, and so do I, but they can be very unpredictable. His act continued for many years until he was secretly filmed beating the animals during training sessions. PETA shut down the act, in spite of Bobby's explanation that the animals are five times stronger than humans. This also served to put all the other animal acts in the city on notice, people were watching to make sure there was no cruelty.

"Danny Ganz was one the most historic interviews I did. When he first arrived in the city he did a stint at the Stratosphere. I was very friendly with the entertainment manager, who set up the meeting. Late that Thursday morning, I assembled my small crew and set up in the showroom. It was a great interview, he was a fresh new talent, his shows were sold out, and he was an immediate success. His manager ruled Danny with an iron fist. The very next day his manager called me, ranting that I had hijacked his client, and accused me of taping Danny without his authorization. 'I'll see to it you never ever interview him or anyone else ever again.' Shocked, I didn't know how to answer him so I made a promise I would burn the footage and never air it on my show. As it turned out, Danny and I became friends, our paths were constantly crossing in the small world of performers, and we learned to have each other's backs.

"Seven years later, my show was the number one local show, it clung to high ratings, and everyone knew who I was. I was hosting an awards event with Rita Rudner at the Imperial Palace: a guy came up to me and said, 'Hey I'm Danny Ganz's manager, and I would like you to interview my client, Danny Ganz.' 'Is that so?' I responded. It was quite obvious that his manager never remembered me, but now that I was at the pinnacle, I was good enough to have his client on my show. It was Tuesday night and I gathered my crew together for the interview, which, again, went well as Danny gave a poignant and heartfelt interview. The camera loved his face, and with his talent he was destined for huge success. The next morning I took the tape, placed it at the edge of the bookcase, and held it for the next production. My cell rang, it was Danny's manager who began a tirade, screaming that my cameraman had stolen Danny's credit card and that I was not allowed to air the interview. By now, I had really had it with this guy, he was truly nuts and I wondered if Danny knew how crazy his agent was. Danny and I were friends and the interview would help us both, plus I knew damn well that none of my staff had ever lifted a thing, not even a matchbook. The manager's ranting escalated until he announced that I wasn't allowed to use the interview. After I hung up, I was angry, but not angry enough to burn the video. I turned around, looked at the tape, moved it back into rotation and never gave it another thought. I didn't bother with an explanation to Danny, like water running off the feathers of a bird, I repelled the manager's accusations: they weren't worthy of my time. Two years later when the tragic news of Danny's death made the headlines, I grabbed the tape of the last interview he had given and called the networks. ABC aired the last intimate moments in Danny Ganz's life. I thought back to all the theories of using positive thinking and never allowing negativity into my mind: I was glad I hadn't given in to my anger, that I had saved precious moments of one of the most talented entertainers who played in Las Vegas. His family was also grateful that they had been given some fleeting time with a man who was loved dearly."

They say that necessity is the mother of invention and that old adage became true. When Tony came knocking on the doors of local businesses, everyone recognized that show biz face. They were easily swayed by his smile and buoyant personality and they hopped on board. At the time, he was the only one in town pursuing local television and putting Las Vegas on the network map, and to this day, he is the longest running host in the history of Las Vegas television. Businesses from copy centers, jewelry stores, auto repair shops, to casinos, hotels, pizza parlors, and restaurants handed over money to keep the variety show going. He was obsessed with winning accounts so he did what he did best: sing. Each presentation was tailored for the client.

The clients were seated around an oval table in a small back room: Tony was there to ensure everyone in Las Vegas would know where to get their teeth whitened. The audience of six sat in silence as he introduced himself, and then put on a track and sang an original song for a hypothetical commercial. He walked around the table as he looked into their eyes and sang with all the gusto he used on stage. They loved it so much, the stoic group broke out in applause and nodded their heads in agreement. Yes, this was the guy they wanted handling their business. Tony had an innate understanding of what businesses wanted, before he ever made his presentations. He studied their companies and knew the perfect ploy to not only get their attention and trust, but their support. Within three months he had signed on twenty companies, a feat few, if any, media companies could do. Nobody had his drive or spirit.

He quickly discovered that the clients wanted more; because of his talent they asked him to write and sing jingles, act in the ads, write the scripts, select the music, and film and produce the ads. He obtained a camera and a cameraman and began filming the commercials. When the gems were finished, they played on the local network. The clients were surprised at the success; business was booming and they had Tony to thank. Thinking back to his studies, he realized he could become the, "can do man," he could do anything he set his mind to do, he just had to focus. He called an attorney; papers were drawn and he became a true, full service advertising agency, which meant he could sell media time in all venues including other networks, newspapers, radio, and billboards. As he scanned the balance in his checking account, he knew things were looking up.

It was Saturday morning. He reached across his king size bed to find it empty. *Where had all the babes gone?* He traipsed into the bathroom, gazed at his image in the mirror, and he knew the answer: he didn't have time for the babes. Between producing the show and grinding out the commercials, he was running two full-fledged businesses. He wasn't that teenage heartthrob who sang sensual melodies and walked away every night with the best looking girl in the theatre. He had stepped up to the plate. He had become a grown-up: something he never thought nor desired he would become. What was intensified was the thorn in his side, Robert, who was satisfied to sit on the sidelines doing as little as possible. There were many moments when Tony recalled the Little Red Hen; he had planted the seeds, harvested the grains, baked the bread and now his brother was there to eat the bread: the fruits of all his labor. Promises to his mom had kept him on a steady track with his twin, but as time passed, he was finally ready to say "no" to his mother and brother. He had believed in himself and it had paid off. In every right, he was a complete success. He was driven, and he did whatever he had to do to ensure his dreams survived. The time had come to call it quits and to go out on his own.

It was 1988 and the twins had officially split, ironically they both continued the variety show: Tony took the six o'clock spot and Robert had the next half hour, but the viewing audience never realized that in fact there were two different programs. In less than a year, Robert's show was off the air. He had no funding and he was deeply in debt. He had no choice; he had failed to master how to run the program. On the other hand, Tony's show flourished, he had done his homework, pounded the streets procuring advertisers who remained loyal and happy, and who kept sending in those checks that allowed the show to air.

Thanksgiving had come and gone and the Christmas holiday was looming in the near future. What to do he pondered, and in the middle of another sleepless night, he became inspired to create a Christmas special, "Merry Christmas Las Vegas." The next morning, he called up several sponsors who loved the idea, and promised to send in extra money, but of course there was a catch, Tony had to produce special commercials. He couldn't say no, so he spent the next three weeks in a frenzy, producing the show, creating the sets, and producing a bunch of holiday ads. Sometimes he laughed thinking about how many hours he had been wearing a Santa Claus costume.

To simulate the essence of the holiday, he arranged with a property owner to film the show at the top of Mt. Charleston. He took the band, sound and camera crew, and they set up an outdoor studio centered in the middle of the pine trees with the snowcapped mountain as the backdrop. Tony did the entire show while seated on a stallion, a dream he had kept secret his entire life. He wore an authentic cowboy costume and a black cowboy hat, and sported a freshly grown black beard. He sang a litany of songs, of varying tempos. It was ironic for Las Vegas that the snow on the set was real, and for once it captured the rustic side of life in Sin City. He continued doing the holiday special, and he had no competition; he had the only local variety show that dared to celebrate the Christmas season.

The following year he was bolder and rented out the entire hotel at the mountain. He filled sixty rooms: the program was more elaborate, with several guest singers and acts. The hotel's countrified wooden exterior exuded the perfect place to stage the show; the interior was dark and cozy, with low ceilings a huge fireplace that burned aged wood, and an oak bar with one deer head attached prodigiously to the wall. The tall decorated tree, the cups of frothing eggnog, and the delicious simple meals, all made for a relaxing and memorable experience, but the most important thing was the show's success. The viewers loved the special, and because of that loyalty, Tony used the hotel for several seasons, syndicating the show across the nation.

"That's a wrap," announced Ron as the camera slowly faded. Tony gathered everyone together and thanked them for a great show and then announced cocktails were served and dinner would follow. As he walked toward his room, one of the staff of the hotel found her way to his room as well. She pronounced his accommodations suitable, and Tony seemed to agree, but only after they thoroughly checked the bed for bugs. They enjoyed a pleasurable pre-cocktail time, and later that evening, when the pumpkin pie had been served, she brought an extra can of whipped cream to his room. They shared the rest of the night, squirting and licking the topping from various places not suitable for the dining room. In the crisp cool morning as he gathered his bag, walked to the car, and took a long look around the beauty of the mountain, he realized how happy and content he had become. He had made it on his own, the show was successful, he had his health, and women running to his side, plus a battalion of loyal friends who honestly cared about him. Yes, he was a lucky man, but in his heart, he knew it was because of his dedication to work and faith in himself. He had finally come to the point in his life where he believed in himself, and if he set his mind to something, whatever it was, it became successful. What Tony had finally become was a whole person, not part of a half, or a twin, but a complete person. All the coaching in the self-help books had paid off, he was where and who he wanted to be.

Rita Rudner has appeared multiple times on Tony's TV show during her performances in Las Vegas

*1935 – Hoover Dam is
complete. At 726 feet and
more than 1,200 feet long
when built, it was the tallest
dam in the world. President
Franklin D. Roosevelt spoke
at the dam's dedication.*

Tony Curtis displays the strangle hold on Tony during an interview as he talked about playing the Boston Stranger

CHAPTER 12

It was time to give back. He was financially stable; his enterprises were standing solidly in the black. Tony purchased a home, not luxurious, in an older neighborhood, where he could be near the studio and sense the heartbeat of the town, and a sensible car, not like his first chick magnet: an Alfa Romeo. No, this time his car was used to haul camera equipment, costumes, and of course, wonderful women. One morning he received a knock on his door from a well-known teacher, Helen Joy, who was seeking assistance for young kids who needed money for music lessons and instruments. Her plea took him back to his basement days, when he would practice for hours using a fake microphone, and play inferior instruments: when the neighbors would complain of the noise since he had no other place to practice. Due to of his love for the city, and show business, he formed the Youth Foundation for Performing Arts, a charity to provide kids with money for instruments and lessons. Helen was a singer and a dancer who taught kids how to perform, and when some of her best were unable to afford the lessons, Tony would pick up the tab. Her work was so highly appreciated that she received a medal from the White House.

Tony wanted to escalate the charity and make dreams come true, so he raised enough money from friends and his sponsors to fly eighteen teens to Washington DC over the Christmas holiday and sing at the White House. The two chaperones, Tony and Helen, boarded the plane with an excited group of kids who had never been on a jet, or to Washington DC. When they took off, he watched the look in their eyes as they took in every moment of the experience. His heart swelled, he was proud he could pull this off, because he knew all that was about to take place would forever change the lives of these teens. They would see all they could become, and perhaps one day they would be in the same position to give back. The stately colonial style hotel was located directly across the street from the White House. The teens were handed their room keys and quickly found their beds before they gathered in the lobby. They would be performing that night for the annual lighting of the Christmas tree: a huge honor. The show would be aired live, and the entire country would hear the voices from these underprivileged children from Las Vegas; nothing could have been more thrilling. After a walk around the city, they found a simple café and bought the teens lunch and then prepared for the show. Not surprising, their charges were well behaved and appreciative, they thanked Tony and Helen at every opportunity. As they walked along the wide cement sidewalks, their singing collected smiles from the pedestrians, and they were filled with joy and wonderment.

"Meet us in the lobby in one hour," he announced as the teens scattered to their rooms to change. Alone in the lobby, the head clerk called out, "Antonio Sacca."

"Yes," he quickly responded, thinking the worst.

"We have your presidential suite prepared. Where is your entourage?"

"My what?" After a short discussion, it turned out that the President of El Salvador, who was also booked at Hotel Washington, had the same sounding name, and she mistakenly took Tony for the president. He should have slept in the posh room, and left the imposter to suffer in a queen size bed.

The teens were somberly dressed for the frigid weather as they paraded across the street onto the White House grounds to take their places near the tree. On cue, their voices melted in sync as they sang the Christmas song with unbridled passion. The two chaperones stood in the background and couldn't have been prouder. When the tree was finally lit, and the sound of "ahhs" rang throughout the night air, it was truly breathtaking. Memories, desire, and a belief in the future was the gift from Helen and Tony, and in this case, it was something that only money could buy. Later that year, Tony received a Proclamation from the city of Las Vegas, he had become a man of the town that he loved and had shown the world his love. Unmarried and without children, the foundation became his extended family. He used teachable moments to enlighten the kids about what he had gleaned from the Positive Development Seminars: when you think you can do something for others you will attract them. It's all about creating the persona of how you want other people to see you, not who you really are. This theory was readily applicable in the field of performing arts, it boosted the self-image and vanquished feelings of insecurity.

"I came to believe that when you help others, in the end, you are really helping yourself."

More importantly, Tony used these seminars to enrich his belief in himself and maintain a path of success. In the seminars, mental games were implemented to expand and heighten these concepts; the group leader gave everyone the task of obtaining seventeen hundred dollars, and bringing new students into the classes. It was an impossible task for most, since it involved selling an intangible product. The point of the exercise, besides expanding the teachings, was to learn how to have faith in your ability to sell a product with sincerity: nothing short of acting. He used a strong façade and intense rhetoric, and Tony was the first to come up with the money. For eight years he studied those techniques while developing his businesses. He used the concepts as personal cheerleaders, and he was able to come up with the strength he needed to ask entertainers, and businesses to support his show. He never took no for an answer, sometimes he waited, sometimes he used props, and sometimes he manipulated the situation, but in the end, he always got what he wanted.

No one lives a perfect life. He learned to accept the fact that he grew up in an unbalanced family: his father was overbearing and demanding, and his mother perpetually pleaded for him to stick to his other half. It was all he knew, all he understood. Insecurity was the essence of his personality because he had never envisioned himself as a whole person, but part of another. The seminars brought balance and strength into his life. As with those who sought the same in religion, he found convictions in the positive development seminars, and has been guided by those concepts ever since.

The ramifications of those powerful theories were put to the test as Tony's world crumbled. The split with Robert was final, his second wife said a final good-by, his business was going bankrupt, and his dog died. What had seemed like a perfect life had turned into a hideous nightmare. Sometimes there are circumstances beyond one's control, and you have to find a way out. He woke up in a dark house and turned on the kitchen sink: nothing. He stepped outside and sheltered his eyes from the bright sun: the water company had put a lock on a pipe to stop the flow. He broke off the lock, returned to the kitchen, and waited until a slow trickle began springing from the faucet. He smiled. He had overcome that devastation; he began inching his way out of an overwhelming sad state of affairs. He called a friend who generously lent him enough money to pay the utility bills and the lights were returned, and the water officially on. The goal, his only goal was to keep the thing he loved most, the variety show, the problem was money wasn't hitting the bank as it had once been. The local economy was sluggish, which affected the mom and pop businesses. Somehow, he would find a way to keep his head above water and wait for the tide to turn. He recited his personal mantra out loud: sometimes he screamed it at the top of his lungs.

When he returned from the office, he walked into a stark home. It had been stripped bare, save for the lumpy sofa in the center of the living room. An angry ex-wife had hired a moving van that could get the job done quickly. All that remained were his clothes, a basket of dirty laundry, and a few toiletries on the bathroom shelf. One partial roll of toilet paper remained, the sum total of a marriage gone bad. His head swirled, the air left his lungs as he began hyperventilating, his knees buckled and he felt faint. He lay on the sofa and became lost in a dark place. He envisioned a new life; he would go back to Philadelphia, open up an Italian deli, and place photos on the walls of all of the world famous entertainers he had interviewed on his show. He would nickname each sandwich and it would be known as the Las Vegas deli. When he shook himself out of that daydream, he was sweating. He was where he wanted to be, he was doing what he wanted to do. He recited the mantra several more times. His neighbors could hear him screaming through the walls,

"I'm here to stay, I'm going to get my life back, or die trying!"

And so he began the arduous process of digging himself out of his financial stupor. The local economy had been in the crapper. Tony played the waiting game, and eventually things commenced turning in the upward position. A spirit hit him, along with all his positive thinking, and helped pull him up from financial ruin.

"Life really is one day at a time." When he thought he would be moving out of a home and into a rented apartment, he was devastated. After he considered the money he would spend on rent, he realized that if he purchased a home with a few bedrooms, he would actually be making money instead of flushing it away. With a gift from his mother, and a loan from his cousin Nick, Uncle Nick's oldest son, he purchased a single story home with four bedrooms and before the ink was dry, every bedroom was rented out. Most of the renters were actors, and on the road, so the home rarely felt cramped and everyone was happy knowing their pets had a clean, safe place to live. At night when he closed his eyes, he was secretly happy that he wasn't by himself; he didn't do well alone, not well at all. He could offer what apartments couldn't, privacy, a decent place for a pet, and security.

That worry pushed aside, he took the next step to financial recovery. With forthright courage, he knocked once again on people's doors, and again they responded. Tony had kept the show going and along with that, his local fame and prestige. With a few extra bucks in their bank accounts, a plethora of businesses shelled out money and placed additional ads. The price was right, as spots could be had for as little as five dollars, although that certainly wasn't prime air time. Tony had learned to make the clients feel as comfortable and as important as the celebrity guests on his shows. He deferred to their judgment with a resounding respect, and offered the complete services of his newly formed production company. Although the company was originally set up to produce commercials just for his shows, when he became a full service advertising agency, he fed those same commercials to all the other networks. Tony had created three separate companies which entwined with each other, creating a complementary relationship serving to further promote all of his enterprises. He would procure clients through Sacca Advertising, and then produce the spots through the production company, and later purchase media time on most of the television networks. In turn, the networks were thrilled with the extra money coming their way and when dead air time occurred, they would slot Tony's show for an extra run, thereby expanding his audiences and making his clients extremely satisfied. The happy list of eclectic advertisers included Jim Marsh Automotive, Montesanos Italian Eatery, Smiles Today Dental, Kyocera copy center, Collision Authority, and United Nissan.

Tony still harbored misgivings of being a solo entertainer. Although he was singing on his television show, it had been a while since he had stepped out onto a live stage and performed alone. He had been caught up in gaining back his financial strength, laying aside live performances in lieu of building the various companies. When the local economy became infused with increasing tourism, his production company expanded their business into industrial videos, promotional tapes for other entertainers, and expanded upon the quality and quantity of standard commercials. While he was busy focusing on the pecuniary side of his life, his twin fell in love and married another singer. Together they toured with some success until the marriage went sour.

He was so wrapped up in his live shows, singing, and television production, that Tony had pushed aside his dreams of acting. Sometimes he would reflect on the year he and Robert had spent in New York, seriously studying the art, but those acting jobs were so sporadic, he lost his way. When the phone rang and Marilee Lear, a famous casting director was on the other end, he was quite surprised. She was known for a plethora of blockbusters, and she had called to offer Tony a chance to audition for *Casino*.

He sat impatiently in her busy waiting room and when his name was called, Tony jumped up, grabbed his portfolio, and walked confidently into her well-appointed office. He furtively scanned the walls, and when he saw all the famous movies and actors she had catapulted to fame, he couldn't help but feel he had finally arrived. Marilee held up a script, gave Tony a quick look, and then explained the part: he would play a gambler that cheated, got caught, beaten up, and had both thumbs broken.

"I can do that," smiled Tony, who certainly knew how to gamble, and was comfortable in front of any game table in town. After some small talk, she shook his hand, and he left her office.

A week later, Marilee gave Tony the bad news, that he wasn't given the part, but she asked if would like to be an extra. They needed a pit boss to play opposite Robert De Niro in an intense gambling scene. Before Tony could respond, the agent told him he would be on the set for ten hours and he would only be paid as an extra. Tony turned down the option, not realizing the potential value or future success of the movie. Casino, was a box office smash, and became an American classic film.

There was something Tony could do that would push his singular talent into the public eye, something that had been grating on him for years, his own original song. All the songs he sang were cover songs, there wasn't one song in his decades of performing that he could call his own: one that represented him. Yes, he would always tell himself that he wasn't a recording artist, but now, more than ever he felt compelled to find a tune and make it his own.

"I could have gone to a publisher and found an unrecorded song, but when I read the lyrics, I never found what I was looking for, it had to say exactly what I was feeling."

On an early Saturday morning, when the office was still, and the only sound in the air was the ticking of a clock, he opened up a letter that Eddie, his brother-in-law had mailed. Enclosed was a song, with the sheet music. By noon, the song would become the main release in an album. As he read the lyrics out loud, the melody sprang off the page, as he began humming the tune to, "Listen To My Heart."

"Here we are you and I at last, in the right place at the right time, Every dream I have dreamed has come to pass, Cause you're right here and your all mine, I can't believe the years of holding back are through, I can finally share what's in my heart with you. If you want to know what I'm feeling listen to my heart. All of my life I've been on the road, always searching, never finding, but in my darkest hours somehow the road would lead to you. Sing to my heart. Listen to it sing. Listen to my voice, it wants to tell you everything. I've waited all my life for this moment, I'm not waiting anymore, and you're here and you're listening. Listen to my heart."

As he read and sang the song, he knew it reflected his life, lost loves, and his vision of a new love. Perhaps this tune would predict his own future, there would be that one person he had waited his whole life for, she just hadn't arrived on the scene. Reflective, hopeful, and heartfelt: that was the substance of the song. It wasn't fluff, it was truly a thoughtful song.

When he turned that magic age of fifty, he blocked out time at a local recording studio, requisitioning Gary, his arranger, to draft the sheet music and gather the musicians to record the song. The studio was small, as most in the city were, but they squeezed in the musicians, adjusted the sound, and began rehearsing. Gary lifted his hands in the air and directed while the technician listened acutely to the sounds and adjusted, and readjusted the sound levels. They had reserved the space for a couple of hours, and the clock was ticking away, but the sounds were not perfect. Tony stepped outside the glass enclosed room, and replayed the last take. He heard the problem. After a five minute break, they shuffled back into the room, the technician yelled,

"Make this one to go," and they miraculously came together for a perfect recording. Gary nodded his head and yelled,

"That's a wrap!"

"Thanks for coming guys, it meant a lot to me, and now we have an album that we can really call our own." Tony stayed back and listened to the recording. With the state of the art equipment, they tweaked the sound levels up and down until the right balance between voice and instruments was in harmony. Satisfied, Tony took the master, joined it with several recorded songs, and sent it out to be pressed into his first solo release. The song became the name of his CD: "Listen To My Heart," released in 2002. That song, along with, "Las Vegas, the Greatest Town Around," an original song on the disc, was just enough to make the CD special enough to sell.

When the album was released, he was overjoyed to know there was one ballad that he could call his own. He would make that his theme song forever; it was original, it came from the depths of his soul.

A year had passed and as he reviewed his various bourgeoning bank accounts, he allowed himself the luxury to return to doing what he love best, live performance. With a showmanship background, he needed background singers who could also infuse some dancing into the act, an easy task as he lived and breathed in Las Vegas. With Tony at the helm, he created Passion: three beautiful singer/dancers who could help fill the stage with their voices and endowed bodies. After the last rehearsal and with his confidence fully restored, he knocked on doors and began a one year run at the Boardwalk Casino, which was later replaced by the City Center. Situated in the heart of the southern end of the strip, the lounge was perpetually filled with tourists from around the world. They would take time out from the gaming tables and grab a seat in the relaxed atmosphere of the lounge and listen as the foursome performed an endless playlist of cover songs. At the close of their set, when the managers counted up the drinks, it was always on Tony's watch that the money flowed the richest. He used this as the impetus, and the casino extended his act for several additional months.

In addition to his live lounge gig, Tony continued to keep busy with, *Entertainment Las Vegas Style*. Besides interviewing performers, the show highlighted the attractions within the city, which made it a true travelogue. Tony was a kid at heart, and he spent many days filming at the casinos where there were amusement park rides: the Sahara, a wild roller coaster at New York, New York, the biggest steeple chase in town, and the crème de la crème was located at the Stratosphere, where the scariest, most challenging rides could be found at the highest point in the city. There were swings that lifted off above the ground and then spun over the edge of the building, a roller coaster, and an aerial lift that went up several stories and then splashed down. Tony rode them all live on his show and then touted the exhilarating experience.

"I had a cameraman at the top of the Stratosphere filming me as I rode the one of a kind antigravity lift. As I got in and looked at the top, it seemed simple enough, just up it went and down it went. Well, when the down part came, my stomach felt like it was resting in my throat and when I got off, I was really sick. The cameraman turned to me to tell me he didn't get the shot so I'd better go again. Just as I was ready to punch him in the face, I found the closet garbage pail and threw up. I wiped my face on my shirt and looked around to see the crew laughing at me. They admitted they were kidding. They got the shots, they just wanted to see if I could go on the ride again."

It was the segment of, *Entertainment Las Vegas Style* featuring the Glow Girls which would forever be cemented in Tony's memory. Gorgeous Ladies of Wrestling booked a series of performances in town but instead of using the template of the intimate interview followed by the performance, he decided to become part of their performance. The stage crew set up a mud wrestling ring, Tony removed his shirt to reveal his six pack abs, and several girls joined him in the mud bath, sloshing it out. When he rolled around in the mud with those well-endowed girls, it was not only a highlight of the show, but his life.

"Boy was that fun, as the girls and I crawled all over each other slipping and sliding in the mud. I never played in the mud when I was a kid, and I could have never imagined it being this much fun."

He didn't forget the animals, everyone loves to see animals perform but he never had a large lion or tiger on the show, a lesson well learned from Siegfried and Roy. He kept the animals small, which he believed, was tantamount to keeping things safe. Additionally he showed off the city by visiting various sites: the Titanic Exhibition, the Tournament of Kings, and MGM's Lion Habitat. He displayed the city as a first rate resort town in all its splendor, uniqueness and, quirkiness. There was something for everyone who came to town, and he aired it all on his syndicated program.

The show had a twenty-eight year run, with interviews that spanned all areas of entertainment. Initially it ran on three networks, but finally it culled down to one: local Channel 25, where it aired for years, until it went into syndication as, *Classic Vegas Entertainment Las Vegas Style*" It always had an eclectic blend of stars, so there was something of interest for the viewers. One of the best examples of an earlier production was when he mixed Marcel Marceau with Shaolin, Michael Flatley, and Dorothy Hamill. With bright bulbs, and his back-up band, Tony entered the stage singing his original theme song, and then discussed the line-up. He took the audience to the dressing room of Marcel Marceau, where the guest did one thing no one never saw him do; talk. Without his make-up and costume, he gave a fervent discussion of the art of mime. The camera would flash to his performance, and then back again where Marcel explained to Tony how and why he moved in certain ways and how he gleaned this knowledge in life: the artist was giving up his secrets. When the Paris Hotel opened their doors in Las Vegas, it was Marceau's name on the marquee opening night at the showroom with a one man act, which was unprecedented. Not only did Tony allow us an insight into the man as a performer, but as a humanitarian. Marcel has a foundation both in Paris and New York City where the art of mime is taught: that was the legacy he wanted to leave the world.

The next conversation was with Shaolin: monks who had traveled thousands of miles to show off their unique talents. During the interview, Tony asked the leader, who had a thorough grasp of English, why they had come to Las Vegas, and they responded that it was one of the most diverse cities in the world. Their act relied on tourism, and the monks believed they would be able to fill up all the theatre seats, not only because of their talent, but the fact that people flocked in from all over, including many who from Asia. Tony was so humbled and appeared reverent as the monk described the culture and displayed rare footage of their living quarters and their daily rigorous, Spartan routines. The juxtaposition between their stage performance in the limelight of posh theatres and their austere home was not only interesting, but made for a fascinating short documentary.

Michael Flatley, world famous Irish choreographer, was the next segment of the show. Famous for the production, "Lord of the Dance," he explained the differences between the classic Irish dance and the Las Vegas productions. After he showed a clip of the dance, Michael described the nuances and how he created audience appeal through his innovative style.

The last portion of the half hour program was in the dressing room of Dorothy Hamill, Olympic Ice Skating Champion. They casually chatted, and she admitted that all those revolutions and spins did make her dizzy, although she learned how to shake them off and go directly into the next steps. She explained how she trained for a lift, and then the camera would flash to that portion of the performance demonstrating the lift. It was as if she were critiquing her own act. She loved Las Vegas, and loved performing on some of the best stages in the world. Her interview reflected an intimate view of her unique performance art, and shed light onto how she viewed herself, and the changes she had undergone to get to where she was.

Twenty-eight years was a long time for a show to air on television, and a long time for Tony to continue his reign as the host. The list of performers was a who's who in the world of entertainment: comedian Rita Rudner, Lena Prima, Tony Curtis, comedian Louie Anderson, magician Lance Burton, actor Anthony Quinn, singer Clint Holmes, Lou Rawls, Debbie Reynolds, and Wayne Newton, were just the tip of the iceberg. The popularity of the show, and the ability to see the most cherished moments in the performers' lives, prompted Tony to recreate past productions with a new show title, *Classic Vegas Entertainment*, that now airs locally, regionally, and nationally.

"I'm always reinventing myself, and this new classic show, where some of the entertainers have subsequently died, is part of their legacy to the world. I'm blessed to be a part of that, and to rerun acts that will never be seen again in Las Vegas or the world." (An addendum at the end of this book lists the guests who he interviewed during the three decade run).

"Tony Curtis was one of my favorite interviews, he was sharp, witty, and very funny. The second time I interviewed him was more memorable than the first. I rang the doorbell to his home, and he opened the door. I smiled extended my hand, and then he looked down: he wasn't wearing any pants. The star escorted me into his living, wearing his white Fruit of the Loom underwear, and then said, 'I think I'm going to put on some pants.' A few minutes later, Tony reentered the living room, with a proper pair of shorts, and we continued with the interview."

The blight of 1988 had finally dissipated as he gathered the pieces of his life, recited his daily mantra, and made things go his way. Two years down the road, after he purchased a new home, albeit one he still shared with renters, the rest of his enterprises took a turn for the better.

"With the end of a third marriage, most guys would be sad, but I was happy. I bought a big television, a Mercedes Benz and that was the fresh start of Tony Sacca. I began having fun and enjoying life again. Girls pointed at me, I would bring them over to my home and we would cook in and have fun. I kept thinking and remembering all those positive books I'd read and lectures I had gone to, and they made me continue to believe in myself. I felt like a new man and I was ready to conquer the world." The only vestige of his marriages were Misty, an adorable black cocker spaniel from wife number three and Heidi, a small mixed mutt from marriage number two, who were all too happy to spend their days at the busy, single story home walking in and out as they pleased, and being petted by the most lovely women, who often shared delicious morsels from their plates.

"I guess that was the only thing I could be trusted with in those marriages was the proper care and feeding of the family pets." Tony didn't mind the dogs, in fact he loved having them around, they became part of his exercise program, and with daily walks and runs, they all kept in shape together.

One might have thought that a grown man would have relished the idea of living by himself, but the truth was, Tony did not like living alone. He had never been alone since he was in the womb, having other people around was the only life he ever knew. Growing up, he never slept alone, and then he went into the army, where there are a barracks filled with other men, and shortly afterwards, he got married. Waking up in any empty house was not his style, but he learned to accept it. The fact that he rented out two bedrooms in his home solved two of his pressing problems: it brought in more than enough money to cover the mortgage and utilities, and he didn't have to wake up alone. He liked the soothing sound of the refrigerator door slamming in the middle of the night; he knew others were around, that there was more than just the sound of his own breath in the house. He rented to a young guy who worked on his sound crew, and a woman who had recently left her spouse, the four bedrooms in the home were filled, and he was surrounded by an abundance of life.

Tony and Helen Joy's Young Entertainers singing in the White House during the holiday celebration

Las Vegas Rocks ®

1940s – Las Vegas' population has grown to 8,422. The outbreak of World War II brings the defense industry to the valley. The isolated location along with plentiful water and inexpensive energy makes Las Vegas an ideal site for military defense related industries. The site for the Nellis Air Force Base is located in the northeast, and the Basic Management Complex, providers of raw materials, is located in the southeastern suburb of Henderson. The defense industry continues to employ a significant number of valley residents.

Righteous brother, Bill Medley, celebrates at Tony's 20th anniversary TV celebration

CHAPTER 13

"No one gets to be eighty if they drink all day," Tony lambasted as he smashed the heel of his foot into the wall, "and nobody gets to see eighty when they're bulimic," thrusting the other foot into the wall, "and nobody gets to see eighty if they take hard drugs," butting the wall with both heels. He collapsed into the cocoon of his executive chair, and placed his head between his hands; as tears of regret poured forth, he asked himself for the millionth time,

"Am I my brother's keeper?"

It was Saturday morning: time to review and edit the live show, call on some potential sponsors, line up his date, and pick up the ringing phone.

"Hi Robert, what's going on?"

"Brother can you spare me some money, just so I can hop a plane back to see mom and dad? I'm not feeling so well and I want to see a doctor," asked Robert.

"Why can't you see a doctor here? Why do you have to go all the way home?"

"I just," stammered Robert, "I just need their support. You don't help me at all!"

"Look, if its money you need for the airfare, I'll give it to you. I see you are hurting and I know you have gone through a lot, but I can't keep supporting you. Come over and I'll write you a check." Pensively thumping his fingers over the oak desk, the past few years of his twin's life was in antithesis to his own. He struggled to make a go of his business, the television shows, the live lounge acts, the advertising agency, and the production company, but Tony was a one man business: he was driven and had no patience for his lackadaisical brother. It was no secret that Robert loved to gamble and had a penchant for hard drugs. Tony was not his brother's keeper. When it came to those addicting vices, he hadn't the clout nor the ability to set his brother right. There was too much bad blood between them which left Tony with little, if any, sympathy for Robert.

After the dust had settled between the brothers and Robert finally came to the realization that Tony and the twin act would never again become a reality he was forced to carve out a life of his own. After he married for a third time, Robert and his new wife began performing gigs throughout the city. They scraped through each week and within a couple of years they had a son. However, his new wife also grew tired of his unfocused ways, and felt helpless in fighting his addictions. One morning she packed the baby, set her sights in a different direction, and left him forever. Six weeks later a summons arrived at his front door step, a decree of divorce was tucked inside. He figured, what the hell, she was never coming back so he signed and dated the last page and handed it back to the process server; their marriage was over.

When Robert's third wife abandoned him, he coiled further into despair. Hooked on drugs and gambling, he sought out the only option he thought he had left and became involved with a prostitute, whom he exploited. With cash flowing into his home on a daily basis, he was able to survive, but at a cost too dear to pay. This obscene way of life continued for several months until she too had had enough, and ran out the front door, vowing never to return. Robert called Tony that Sunday lamenting about his finances, how his life had turned into total despair and how a few thousand dollars was all he needed to get back on track. With more gumption that he thought he could muster, Tony simply said no.

"No," responded Robert, "then fuck you, to hell with you! I don't need you!" He slammed down the phone and felt something warm drip down his face: he was bleeding. He rushed to the kitchen, grabbed some paper towels, pressed them against his nose, and then screamed bloody murder. He was in excruciating pain. Hysterical he ransacked the home for anything that would camouflage the pain, but there was nothing. His pockets were empty and there was no money for the solace a line of coke would provide. He collected himself and called his parents to make arrangements to return home until he could get his head set straight. With only a small duffle bag, he clutched the airline ticket Tony had paid for and boarded the plane to Philadelphia, and the safety and security only his parents could provide.

When she met him at the airport, his mom was startled by Robert's condition. His unsteady gait, gray complexion, and sallow cheeks made him appear a decade older than he was. It was painfully clear that her son was sick. She tried to hide the shock on her face as she greeted her son warmly and showered him with kisses and hugs as they walked to the parking lot. He was so weak that she grabbed the duffle bag and placed her arm around his waist for support.

"I don't feel so well," Robert admitted.

"Yes son, I know, I know, and I love you. You did the right thing in coming home. I will take care of you and everything is going to be alright," she promised. They walked at a lethargic pace, and when they finally reached the car, she gently set him in the back seat.

"Mom," said Robert, "I don't feel so good." Shocked that he had repeated himself, she answered the same way she had. At the red traffic light, Millie looked at him in the rear view mirror: she felt a fear she had never felt before. Something was horribly wrong with her son. She opened up the side door to the kitchen and they walked upstairs to his bedroom. She threw back the covers on his bed, helped him out of his clothes, and turned off the lights. Once the door was shut, a flood of tears cascaded down her face, her son was truly ill. She turned up the sound on the television so Robert couldn't eavesdrop, and called Tony. It was three hours earlier, so he would be up and around. It had been almost four years since Joseph had been laid to rest and now this? There was no way she could handle Robert's illness without the strength of her husband.

"I've got to take this call," Tony said as he excused himself from the production meeting.

"Tony, why didn't you tell us what bad shape your brother is in?" she cried. "He could barely walk from the airport to the car. He is upstairs resting. What's wrong with him?"

"Mom I really don't know, but remember I told you he was using a lot of hard drugs, drinking and smoking, maybe it got to him."

"I am taking him to the doctor in the morning and I'll call you. I'm telling you he looks really bad. A mother senses these things. I think it's more than the effects of the drugs."

"I'm sure it's just your imagination, but call me when you find anything out."

The next morning Millie took Robert to the family doctor. His only complaint was pain in his nose. Upon examination, the hole was easily detected, but the reason why it had appeared was not. The doctor took several vials of blood and proceeded with a thorough work up. Before the day had ended, the prognosis was clear, leukemia. He sat Millie and Robert down in his austere office, the facts were harshly put in front of them, there was no sugar coating it, there simply wasn't any time. Robert had been suffering with the disease for years but had ignored the symptoms covering them up with heavy duty drugs. He was so far gone that a bone marrow transplant was his only hope. That night Tony got the call from Robert, pleading with him for help.

"Hey do you remember it was just yesterday that you told me to go to hell and now today you are begging me for help?" Millie could hear the conversation and she grabbed the phone and continued begging for Tony to come back home and save his brother's life. The doctor said he only has two to ten years left to live.

"It hit me like a ton of bricks, the realization that my twin had so little time left. That it was up to me to save his life." Tony immediately plunged into work rearranging his schedule: he placed numerous calls to employees and the next morning he boarded a plane to Philadelphia to do the right thing. He emerged at the foot of the passenger pick up in the cold damp air, which matched his dampened spirit. He waved his hand and smiled widely when he saw his mom's face. It was the first time in his life he could ever remember that she didn't return his smile. He grabbed his bag, tossed it into the back seat, and leaned over to kiss her. The taste of salt rolled off his tongue, tears were rolling down her cheeks as she turned and looked into his eyes.

"Mom, I'll drive," he insisted. He opened up the door and they exchanged positions, "now tell me, what's going on? Did the doctor tell you how serious this is? Ma, I don't think you really know how long this has been going on."

Putting her hand in the air she silenced him, she didn't want to hear it.

"Robert needs you right now and that is all I want to hear. I don't know how he got sick. All I know is that it is not good. The doctor said he is in the final stages and this is the only thing that might save him. I know you are a good son, and good brother and had the tables been reversed, Robert would do the same for you." She laid on the guilt trip in the traditional way only Italian Catholics can. Tony put on a hospital gown and acquiesced to procedure. The family had gathered at the foot of Robert's bed when the doctor walked in with the results.

"Tony will not do, his match isn't going to help his brother, it's too close. Is there anyone else?" Tony was beside himself and followed the doctor out of the room, he needed answers. Tears spilled down his cheekbones as he tried to get the words out. The doctor asked him to come into his office for a discussion, he didn't have the time, but he was going to make the time. Seated in the tiny physician's office, tears still flooding his vision, Tony looked up at the doctor and tried to say what was on his mind, but the words still wouldn't come.

"I know what you are going to ask me, I see it in your eyes," said the doctor. "Why? I'm not going to give you an answer, because I don't have one. I know you are worried about your own health, and as an identical twin, I would be worried too, but you are completely healthy."

"Okay," he sobbed, "I don't do drugs, alcohol in excess, and I'm sure not bulimic. Was it his immune system that got shot to hell?" The doctor stroked his chin, looked into Tony's eyes and shook his head,

"Tony, if I could answer that question, then perhaps I could have cured your brother, but sometimes our lives belong to God: I wish there was more I could do, but our options have run out." He stood up, shook Tony's hand, opened the door, and Tony watched him shuffle out of the office. There was nothing more either one of them could say, the illness had gotten the best of Robert.

"Yes," responded Millie, "the sister." The next afternoon Marie arrived and when tested, it was a perfect match. Frightened, she bravely succumbed to the procedure all the while praying it would save her brother's life. Robert stayed in Philadelphia convalescing at his parent's home, trying to recover. When he found the strength, he drove to Atlantic City and gambled away his disability check. When that was gone, he took markers from several of the casinos. His parents picked up the tab and bailed him out of a guaranteed horror story.

"How can it be that Robert is so ill, and I am so healthy? Am I am going to end up like him? Will leukemia to be my end reward? Will I die before I reach sixty? Maybe I'm dying right now, maybe I'm sick." With death weighing heavy on his mind, Tony did what any sane person would do: when he returned to Las Vegas, he visited his doctor. He insisted on a battery of tests that would uncover any illness. He put his arm out for ten vials of blood. Later that week when his doctor called reporting that he was in perfect shape and the only disease he suffered from was hypochondria, he could finally breathe. It was more than simple biology that explained the well and the sick brother, it was the complete lifestyle. Tony ate well, exercised, never took heavy drugs, smoked cigarettes, or drank in excess. All good things in moderation and an inner strength that provided focus and a balance: therein lay the difference. It was too late to turn back the clock, to undo the harm Robert had invoked upon his body. The inner siege was on and all the hoping, wishing, and regrets couldn't reverse the affect.

When he picked up the office phone, Tony could hear her uneasy, heavy breath. It was one more call, one more request from his mom. Remission had broken and Robert was going downhill. There was a last option, taking Tony's bone marrow, but this time the procedure was a lot more elaborate and risky to Tony. Unable to say no, he hopped on the next plane home. He relived the same routine as before, only this time things were much graver.

"Tony, I will let the doctor explain the procedure. It's not as simple as last time and it could badly affect you." Millie cried and screamed that she didn't want to lose both of her boys. He couldn't say no, and when he saw his brother with a mask over his face feeding oxygen into his lungs, the guilt was too strong. They wheeled Tony into the operating room, and then the surgeons spent six hours taking what they needed and infusing the blood and marrow into Robert's weak body.

The Italian community was keenly aware of Robert's plight. They were constantly calling and lending emotional support, but what the Sacca family needed was cash. The hospital bills were mounting up and there was no way they could pay for everything. John, Tony's best friend, began making inquiries, and helped to bring several bands together for a benefit concert. Tony would be the headliner, back home to ask friends and family to support his brother. The Holy Ghost Hall donated the space for the evening, several bands donated their time, and their sister helped publicized the event. The hall was filled with well-wishers, as donations were dropped in the pot at the entrance foyer.

John announced the line-up and brought out Tony, whose eyes were filled with tears as he thanked everyone for supporting his brother. His legs were shaky, and his hands trembled as they caressed the microphone. Slicing his fingers through his hair, he suddenly felt alone. Home in South Philadelphia, he was on stage, but his twin wasn't at his side. A cold sense of emptiness took over his mood, as the realty of Robert's death swung like a heavy pendulum in his mind.

"Could this be the end? Just look at the big crowd of people, they aren't here for me, they are here for my brother." Like a true showman, he banished the maudlin thoughts, broke out in song, and entertained the crowd without missing a beat for the full set.

Unlike all other shows there was no cause for celebration as Tony's mom greeted him backstage. There were no pats on the back, or outpourings of praise, rather, they were engulfed in a feeling of utter sadness. As hard as it was for Tony to sing, it was just as hard for them to accept charity. The money would be put to good use, trying to save Robert's life, and if money was all that was needed to save Robert's life, then Tony would have toiled his life away. Arm in arm the Millie and Tony walked to the car as Tony turned over the engine and drove the old van home. Millie opened up the cupboard, placed two glasses to the kitchen table, and filled them with grappa. "Salute," she quietly said as they sat in silence sipping, hoping the alcohol would be strong enough to induce sleep.

Dropping his bag at the edge of the door, he walked into the hospital room and looked into Robert's eyes. The oxygen mask had covered up most of his comatose face as he lay listlessly on the bed. The silence was broken as Robert's eyes blinked open sensing Tony's presence. He threw off the mask gasping for air unable to speak as he searched the room for his twin. Tony went over to his side, put his arm around his shoulder and propped him up. Two images stared back at them from across the room. They were looking into a mirror, and on one side was death and the other life.

"I love you brother, I love you with all my heart and soul." Side by side they remained until Robert was unable to sit up. Tony placed his hand on his twin's heart, eased him back down on the bed and kissed him a final good bye. A sudden chill cloaked the room as Tony shuddered and his heart raced. Outside, black clouds had gathered, splattering the window pane with a harsh cold rain, thunder erupted, and then suddenly, the sun burst through the center of the storm clouds. Was heaven opening up to retrieve his brother's soul? He prayed it was, and that he would the find peace and solace he deserved.

Hundreds swelled the cemetery as they laid Robert to rest.

"It was as if I were at my own funeral. People weren't sure which one of us had died. I shook their hands to receive their condolences, and people would utter how sorry they were about Anthony. I quickly responded, it was Robert who had passed, and then I would receive another sorrowful look, or a pat on the shoulder. Robert's life had ended, and as they lowered the casket into the ground the finality of it splashed onto my face like ice-cold water. I promised myself to remember the good times, the happy times, and all that was right with Robert. From that moment on, I ceased dwelling on his destructive ways, from that moment on when I thought of my brother he would always be wearing a smile."

Las Vegas Rocks ®

*1945 – Following World War II lavishly
decorated resort hotels and gambling
casinos offering top-name entertaining
come into existence. Tourism and
entertainment took over as the largest
employer in the valley.*

Don Rickles interviews with Tony during the 45th anniversary of the Stardust Hotel

CHAPTER 14

Marion had been on his mind for months. He had been introduced to her at a media party, and her provocative smile was filled with possibilities. She had been the one who initiated the first flirt, the first flip of the hair, the first deep stare, but he had never forgotten that face. They met before the end of his third marriage, and though they enjoyed a fleeting friendship, cheating went against his grain. After the divorce, he ran into her while he was performing his one man show at the Rivera. It was not accidental, she had been watching and waiting for just the right moment to pick up where they left off, and now that he was divorced their friendship could be a lot more intriguing. She learned as much as she could about the local star, she knew he never had a penchant for cheating and so she patiently waited, scouring the newspapers and the county records for the decree of divorce. When it finally arrived, she found an empty seat near the front of the lounge, dressed in the most stylish cocktail dress hanging in her closet, strapped on her sexiest stilettos, doused her neck with Chanel, and she was ready for the roundup.

He was intoxicating as he emerged from behind the black curtain singing a version of, "My Way." On the video screen, pictures flashed of his twin brother Robert, his family and his home in Philadelphia. He was dressed in a sculptured black Versace tuxedo, and black patent shoes. He was more handsome than the first time she had laid eyes upon him at the media event. He seemed bigger than life as he surveyed the audience, made jokes, and filled the air with his Italian crooner voice. The tracks played out for an hour and a half, as he sang and danced his way into her heart. So filled with sincere passion, he was a highly polished entertainer, he knew how to hold your attention, and he knew how to assuage an audience. When he took his final bow, she stood up, applauded, and invited him for a drink. He barely finished a glass of Chianti, before he collected his wallet from the dressing room and they returned to his home for a euphoric night of lovemaking. She fell madly in love with him and they routinely met each Saturday evening and stayed together for the remainder of the weekend. She always went to his place. During the week if either had time, they would see each other, but it was always at his home. He was happy and satisfied, and never questioned why her home seemed to be off limits. Marion harbored a secret in the form of a lover, who, without discretion, would pop over to her home at unexpected moments. He was paying her rent, so she couldn't very well have another warm body in her king size bed sharing the satin sheets. Months later, Tony found out about her situation, not only was she cheating on him, but she was having an affair with a married man.

"I was in the mood to see you last night, but you never picked up your phone. Where were you?" he angrily asked. He knew the answer and wanted to test the waters for the truth. She became quiet and listless, she knew that he knew exactly where she had been and that her closely held secret had been found out. The one thing she was sure of was that she loved Tony but the only thing Tony could see was a deceptive woman.

"You have led me into your web of deceit, giving me your heart, but it was all just talk. I can't even look at you, so cunning betraying our love, my love for you. Everything we had was just one big deception. All this time your love had been pledged to another guy. I want to be the one and only, I don't want to stand in line for second place. I am finished playing this game!"

Tears welled up in her eyes as she reached out to take his hand,

"It's you I love, it's you I want. I swear to you, I will leave the other guy," she pleaded.

"What, and make me be your sugar daddy: pay your rent, buy you clothing and jewelry? I don't want that, I want to share my life with someone, not to support someone. You have been lying to me for months, I can't trust you, and I will never trust you. We're done!" He stormed out of the room, grabbed a garbage bag, and loaded it with her clothing. He threw open the closet, packed up her shoes, and dresses, walked her out the front door, and tossed it all haphazardly into the trunk of her car. She stood in the driveway, tears continued to stream down her face as she begged him to allow her to stay. He never looked back; he never wanted to see her lying, cheating face again. He turned around, slammed the front door, and reminded himself to change the locks. This love game was overwhelming, another one bit the dust. He wondered what song in his repertoire would fit this scenario and it had to be, Little Anthony's, "It Hurts So Bad." Maybe he would sing that at the next shooting.

He filled his hours with work, and the occasional black jack game at the casino tables, it didn't take but a fleeting moment, and he bounced back into new relationships experimenting with a series of eight young women.

"I was having a great time meeting new women, gambling, performing at the casinos, and running my businesses. The lounges were always filled with exciting women who would sit and watch me sing. After an hour of performing, I would take a break and there were always a few lovely ladies who approached me and offered to buy me a drink, followed by an offer of sex, which, upon many occasions, I accepted.

"One night I was singing at a local casino and an exotic svelte woman sat quietly in the front row and watched me perform. I couldn't take my eyes off of her, she was alluring, with Asian features that were strikingly beautiful. It was she who approached me after the show and offered me a drink. We sat for a while, began talking, and I took her out for a late night meal and then we returned to my home. In every way she was as lovely as she was beguiling. She took her time and introduced me to the Kama Sutra, sex yoga style, which took my senses to a place I had never been before. She used the art of massage and the unique techniques, each meeting had a happy ending as my mind and body soared to places I couldn't ever imagine. We saw each other for months as she cooked and cleaned her way into my heart but she was a jealous woman. One day she saw me hug a dear friend of mine and she became outraged. Unable to listen to reason, her jealousy predicated our relationship until I asked her to leave." As he prepared himself for yet another relationship gone sour, he sat her down and explained that they were not going to continue. There was no doubt he would miss the sex, but there had to be a balance, and sex wasn't the only reason they should stay together. He needed someone to support him emotionally as well as physically, and he knew if he continued looking, that woman was on the horizon.

The two things that Tony was expert at were meeting people, and knowing just the right places to meet those people. He would always be the first to admit he was shy, but just at the right time the show business personality kicked in and allowed him to become the extrovert the world had come to know. It was a Monday night, and by most standards, nightlife had cooled down from the weekend, but not so in Las Vegas. After a day of working on productions, planning shows, and drafting scripts, he wanted to be a single man on the town. That evening he turned up at the best address in town, The Stirling Club at Turnberry Towers. It was classy in every way; unless you were a member, or had an invitation, the doorman wouldn't allow entrance. It was a true private club, reserved for the members of Turnberry. They knew Tony, and sometimes he performed, so getting past security was a simple matter. Atop the thirty story building, the view was breathtaking, and so were many of the women who frequented the bar. Tony ordered a dry martini and gazed around the floor connecting with familiar faces, but that night the only one he recognized was Paul Stubblefield's, the crooner who had just taken a five minute break. Paul was talking to a stunning blonde woman; Tony walked over and said hello and turned his head toward the blonde woman. Paul introduced the two, and returned to finish out his last set of the night. He didn't want to step on another man's woman, so Tony asked Josette if she was free for a drink. She nodded her head yes, they walked her over to a small cocktail table, ordered a couple more martinis, and spent the next half hour in pleasant conversation, all the while he kept noticing her striking beauty.

The next morning Tony woke up with a smile on his face and the scent of her perfume clinging to his memory. Josette, so beautiful, so lovely, and damned if he didn't forget her number, but he would never forget her face, that smile, and her bubbly French accent. *Why oh why didn't I get her number?*

Her blonde hair was filled with perspiration as she unloaded a catered dinner for one hundred and fifty people. She was used to hard work, but this was a charity donation and she had expected at least a couple of useful hands to carry the food to its final destination. She located an empty pallet, dragged it through the glass doors, opened the trunk of the van, and thrust the trays of food onto the base of the pallet. Her palled filled with warmed dishes precariously balanced on top of each other, Josette grabbed a uniformed hotel clerk, and with her sweet French accent, cajoled him into helping her into the banquet room by promising to pay him with a plate of food. As they wheeled the cart to the back room, she was taken aback by the attendees at the charitable event; they were all dressed as impersonators. There were numerous Elvis', Cher, Liberace, Gladys Knight and the Pips, Flamenco dancers, strippers, lion tamers, all there for a good time, great food, and to raise money for a good cause.

When the last dinner plate had been filled, the chef let out a sigh of relief, and then began circumnavigating the room. After all, everyone at the event had tasted her food, she did have a lovely restaurant not too far down the road, and she wanted to make sure this event would bring back happy diners. She laughed at the costumes, and some of the drunk party goers: when she spotted a man meticulously dressed in an Italian worsted suit, who was holding a microphone, staring into a camera, interviewing the guests at the event. Filled with inquisitiveness, she waited until the man was alone and she walked over and introduced herself.

"Hi," she said, "My name is Josette, and I am the person who catered the dinner tonight. Did you eat the food? Did you like my cooking?"

Tony was in shock, this was the same women he had met at Turnberry two weeks prior. Had she forgotten him? Between the noisy crowd and her French accent he could barely understand the beautiful blond as he simply smiled and nodded. In spite of her mussed blonde coiffure, she had a softness and a femininity about her, perhaps it was the imported perfume, or the slender neck, or her genuine smile, but in an instant, he decided to put her on camera.

"Can I interview you for the news?" he questioned. "I'm sure the city would love to know where to go to get a great French meal prepared by someone as beautiful as you." A flush ran to her cream colored complexion, as she boldly answered Tony's questions. When the short interview was over, they stood looking into each other's eyes, but Tony was torn away, another person was waiting to be interviewed. Josette caught his sleeve, pulled a business card out of her pocket and pressed it into his palm.

"There, if you want another great meal, please come and see me." Still smiling, he carefully tucked the card into his pocket, and then turned to the cameras for another set of interviews. Two weeks later he had made a dinner date with a few friends, one of whom insisted on eating at a different place. Tony agreed, out of habit, his group of cronies found themselves at the same spot week after week. It was then he remembered Josette and the business card. He called the bistro on Flamingo Road, booked a reservation for six hungry people, and when they arrived, he was pleasantly surprised to see the chef greeting the customers and serving the food. She placed a plate of beef Bourgogne in front of Tony and flirtatiously asked if he needed anything else. As a gentleman's gentleman, he simply answered no, but found he couldn't take his eyes off of her the rest of the evening. He plunged his fork into the plateful of food: every taste bud lit up, this was the best food, at least the best French food, he had ever eaten. The six friends at the table wholeheartedly agreed, it was the finest French dinner any of them had been served in Las Vegas. They ordered a couple more bottles of red wine, drowned their entrees, and for the first time, Tony insisted they order dessert. Josette came back to the table after the busboy had completed his tasks and asked if anyone would like dessert. Tony, who had no sweet tooth at all, suggested she bring her favorites to the table and that they would share.

"You know," she said, "I'm well known for my baking and I promise not to disappoint." With that, she brought out a tray of decorously decorated pastries, cakes, cookies and mousse. The six dug into the desserts with such gusto it was as if their stomachs hadn't remembered they had just finished off appetizers, a main course, and several glasses of wine. The glorious delicacies were greedily savored and when the check finally arrived, no one winced. Everyone agreed that Tony had made a wonderful decision and he was the hero of the night. As the table filed out, he lingered back and thanked the chef for a sublime meal.

"I shall return," he said. His stomach was so full he was barely able to walk to his car. He couldn't remember when he had stuffed himself as much as he had that night. His face always in the camera, or one stage, or out in public, he vigilantly watched his physique. Tonight, it had all gone awry, he had lost total control over his stomach.

He slept like a log, his dreams were filled with the tastes and smells of the food, but yet all he pictured was Josette's face: the lovely woman with sparkling eyes, translucent skin, and a thin sexual body. So he went back. And he went back again, and again, and again. Sometimes he was alone, sometimes he brought friends, but Josette became his kitchen, his friend, and hopefully something more. Each night she was would see his glowing face, his delicious smile, and would select just the perfect table. If he was alone, it was always the small table near the kitchen where she could talk with him as she herded out the entrees, and if he brought friends, it was always the table in the center of the restaurant. Josette had done a little investigation of her own and discovered her return diner was not only handsome, but a famous entertainer in the city, and he was single. Since she couldn't get out to see his performances, she would make him tell her every detail. Of course there were some nights when the diner made no appearance, he had his performances and television show to attend to and sometimes he was on the road.

They say that the true road to a man's heart is through his stomach and if ever an old proverb could be true, Josette made it so. One evening, as Tony sat alone, watching the chef flit from table to table, he stayed until the very last customer had left and then asked Josette to join him. After a week of serving this handsome man, she knew his favorite wine. She poured two glasses and brought them to his table to toast her loyal customer.

"Salute," he said, "One thing for sure, I know you are the best cook in the city." He patted his stomach. He felt his perfect physique would rue the day he and Josette met. "You must be from France. I can hear it in every word you say. You intrigue me and I would love to hear your story."

"You know Tony, I have owned this bistro for seven years and have never seen your face, but meeting you at the charity event, well, it was like all good things come in due time. Like a good aged red wine, it had to be fermented for many years before either one of us could drink it." And Josette began her story, but left Tony with enough intrigue that he would return the next night to find out what happened.

She was born in Everux, Normandie, on the outskirts of Paris's countryside. True to the photos, her family lived a bucolic life that reflected the landscape. Her father was a butcher, but their store was not how an American would imagine a butcher shop, it was filled with raw butchered meats as well as cases upon cases of cured meats, charcuterie, and delicacies.

"What a coincidence," interrupted Tony, "My dad was also a butcher, but all he sold was fresh meat that he had butchered early in the morning."

"Ahh, well in France, it has a completely different meaning. My family lived above the store. There was my mother, my sister and my two older brothers. We all worked in the family business. It was convenient living above the store considering the amount of hours we put in, and at the end of the day we were happy to walk up a flight of steps and be home. The store was always open, seven days a week twelve hours a day, except Sundays when we would close at 2:00pm. We were Catholic, and we rarely ever got to church because there was so much to do, so many things to prepare. You would think we would be fat, but we were all thin; there wasn't time to eat." Josette glanced down at her watch, and Tony took this a sign he should leave.

"I want to hear all of your story."

"The next time you come back, I shall tell you more." He took her hand and kissed her cheek, dropped some bills onto the empty tablecloth and slowly left the restaurant. As he turned he could hear Josette calling out orders to the few staff left in the kitchen.

He returned the next night, and took the same place at the small table.

He suggested Josette bring out her favorite dishes, but only if she promised to complete her story. By then she too was quite smitten and was very agreeable to the idea that she finish her story, but first she had to prepare a sumptuous dish for her customer. Except tonight he would not be paying, tonight was her treat. She poured a substantial glass of red Bordeaux, and brought over an appetizer of duck confit with a baguette, followed by snapper, in a shallot white wine sauce, and of course dessert, pot du chocolate. When Tony had inhaled the last drop of dessert, and the restaurant was almost empty, the chef brought over two glasses of port and asked her patron if he wished to hear more. He instantly took her hand, and playfully mocked the French accent,

"But of course."

"I finished my formal education at fourteen and then began a three year apprenticeship under the tutelage of my father. He taught me everything I know when it comes to cooking, and my mother taught me how to bake, so between the two, I learned the art of French cooking. Everything we made was fresh, all the ingredients were came from local farms and our backyard. Oh, the cheeses, the fine wines, and the herbs, all came from the local townspeople. If you can imagine waking up at dawn, many hours before the sun rose, running down to the store, twisting the closed sign to read open and then waiting for the first customer to walk through the door and then twisting back the sign twelve hours later to finally read closed, well that was my life. I worked every day from morning until night, but I loved it, it was the only life I knew. I loved my parents and my brothers and sister, and for me it was a good life, even though it was a hard life. All I knew was working and creating and then watching the happy faces of our customers as they returned day after day, and year after year."

After three years of apprenticeship, she became the head of the store, and she managed and ran the business. Not only gifted in cooking, but with a head for numbers, she knew how to turn a profit, and turn a profit she did. On her eighteenth birthday, her family held a surprise party and asked everyone from the store to join them. It was during the celebration that Michel Leblond, one of the chefs, proposed to the ingénue. Startled that he had asked for her hand in marriage, they began a short courtship and were married at the local Catholic Church on a warm spring Sunday afternoon. There was no time for a honeymoon; they had all of Sunday evening to consummate the marriage. Michel was Josette's first boyfriend; she had never dated, had never seen the world, and had never travelled outside the country. All she knew was her family, the store, and now a husband. The art of love was as foreign to her as Chinese food, and love was slow to take hold, but after five years of marriage, she gave birth to a son, Anthony, born on February 17th.

"Hey," interrupted Tony, "You named your son Anthony, that is my given name and I know you won't believe me, but my birthday is also February 17th. My brother's name is Robert and so is your father's. It's like we were destined to meet, but how it took me seven years to find your restaurant I can't answer."

"So," she continued, "when I became the boss, I eventually bought my parent's store and made them retire. When they moved away, I purchased the home above the restaurant and lived as they did their entire lives. You see, that was all I knew. I hadn't seen the world, had never ventured anyplace and my husband was just as tied to the business as I. Another five years passed as our son began to grow and then our marriage was not what it was, it simply fell apart. I didn't want Michel in my bed, nor did I want to see him every single day at my business, so I bought him out and he left silently." The hour was late as the chef checked her watch, that was enough for tonight. Tony scanned the empty restaurant, searched Josette's eyes, and realized it was probably time to leave.

"Again, I'm your last customer, and I guess I should be leaving. May I please ask you for the check for this fine meal," he said. Shaking her head, she kissed him on the cheek and told him that tonight she was treating him.

"I will return and you must promise me you'll finish the story." Josette was not about to finish the story, she would change the subject, talk about other things, but to finish the story would mean an end to his presence. She would continue the story until, well, until she really didn't have the answer just yet. What she did know was that this beautiful man was sitting in her restaurant watching her every move and she had to reach deep within her mind to keep him returning.

He hadn't said a word and was absent from the restaurant for almost a week. Glum, she presumed his love affair with her food had vanished, but then he walked in late on a Monday night, and took his usual spot. Instead of taking his order, she pulled out the empty seat next to his and sat waiting for his explanation. He had been travelling, performing at various casinos out of state. They felt like they were boxers in a match as each waited for the other to respond to the first punch. She sat patiently waiting for his next move as he reached across the table and took her hand.

"It's been almost a year," Tony said, "And I have yet to hear the end of your story. I have been thinking a lot about you and you know what I am thinking? That you should have your own food show, right here in this city. I could produce it and I promise you would be a hit. Nobody in this city cooks like you, and with your beautiful face and French accent, everyone would watch the show."

"Okay," she smiled as she continued with her story. After her divorce, and purchasing the family business she felt it was time to take a real vacation. She booked two weeks at the Club Med in Martinique, where many French speaking people stayed. Her first time on a plane, she held little Anthony tightly as they flew over the vast ocean landing in a small warm tropical island. Everything was foreign to both mother and child as they drove through the small Caribbean towns: the people, the palm trees, the flowers, and the different foods. Once they arrived at the resort it was all fun and games as they basked in the sun, made new acquaintances, ate new foods and played water sports. Every hour was filled with fun, adventure, and learning about other people and other cultures. Josette was in heaven, so much so, that she became employed by the hotel for the balance of the summer as an au pair. She was able to watch little Anthony and at the same time obtain a salary for watching other young visitors to the resort. It wasn't in her plan, nor was it in her original intention, but she extended her visa and booked a flight and the two landed in America on July 4, 1985, just in time to catch the fireworks. She had brazenly taken a vacation out of her tiny French village, had tasted the delight of the islands, and since they were so close to a country she had only read about, she seized the opportunity to visit the United States. She had no friends, nor did she speak English, but something drew her to America. With luggage in hand, she purchased round trip tickets to Los Angeles, because her cousin had a cousin who worked as a chef on the Queen Mary. She held Anthony's hand tightly as they lifted off over the ocean of the Caribbean Sea and landed over the Pacific Ocean. They rented a car and the two eventually found their way to the Queen Mary and finally met up with Jean Pierre. They stayed with him for a couple of days while they travelled through the city, the beaches and of course, to Disney Land. There was a party that evening for the executive chef from the Queen Mary, and Jean Pierre insisted that Josette come. By now, she had picked up enough English to understand basic conversation and when the chef met the party crasher, he was instantly impressed with her credentials. No one on the ship had had her impressive background, and he hired her on the spot as a garde man ger, the chef in charge of appetizers and desserts. She took her first position in America at $3.25 per hour. Initially it was just for two weeks, but when the food emerged from their kitchens and the customers went wild, her visa was extended and she began the process of becoming an American citizen.

"They didn't let me go, they did everything they could to keep me in their employ as they extended my visa and showed me how to obtain a green card. I loved the job and began to love America," she said. She stayed at the position for almost a year, cooking and learning English. She had made up her mind, she intended to stay in the country: she would never go back to France to live. Everywhere she looked, she saw opportunities: with her talents and vast knowledge of the culinary arts she knew she could sustain a professional career, but she worried about Anthony, she wanted him to be happy too.

Josette was too ambitious to remain at the position, especially when so many people approached her to open up her own restaurant. Although she had the cooking talent, and the ability to manage money, she felt her language skills would limit her ability with the English speaking customers, so she decided she would open a wholesale business producing the fine charcuterie that she had perfected growing up in Normandie.

"What do you think?" she asked Anthony as she surveyed the massive one story building situated in downtown Los Angeles? "We don't have to live above the kitchen, we will have our own place," she joked. Although she was thrilled, she could sense her son was not all that happy, the new culture was hard for him to adjust to. She would often take his hand, offer an intense hug and remind him it would take time to learn English, and how lucky was he to know two languages.

Within a short period of time, Josette was churning out Pate Inc's first deliveries of world class pates and charcuterie, the likes of which Americans had never tasted. It attracted all the high end food distributors, and her delicacies ended up at every party in town. Her reputation spread faster than lightning, in the world of foodies. The success of her business continued for many years as she expanded the production to new products. However, Anthony was still unhappy, and as his twelfth birthday approached Josette asked her son what he would like as a present,

"I want to visit my family in France," was his startling answer. At the end of the school year, she purchased her son a round trip ticket to Paris, notified her family, and kissed him good bye. As soon as he was out of sight, tears dripped down her cheeks, she had a haunting sensation that he would not be returning. No matter what she did, he never embraced the American culture as she did, perhaps it was because she was working most of the time. It was as the plane was lifting off that she began to feel the guilty pangs of motherhood. All she knew was work. Both her parents worked every single day, and so did she, it was the only way of life she had ever known and now, as she took a hard introspective look, she knew she had not given her son the time he needed. She had never compared her life to others, she lived her life to achieve success, and for that no one, especially in the capitalist democracy of the American fabric, could fault her. She turned on the ignition of her new car, drove to the shop, and spent the day immersed in the life of pates.

Each night when she returned home she raced to gather the mail in hopes there would be a letter from Anthony, and finally she received word from her son. In the letter he described how happy he was to be surrounded by the rest of his family, and he said that he was apprenticing with his uncle to become a baker. As she read the letter, she envisioned his smile, his face splattered with white flour, and his hands crafting the perfect pastry dough for an airy croissant, or a pie crust. The more she thought about Anthony's skills, she realized how she could get him back. The next day, she began the process of splitting the warehouse into two parts, one half would become an authentic French bakery and the other would remain as Pate, Inc. She excitedly wrote her son and told him of the transition and begged him to return to her. He would have his own business: he would be the head baker and she would hand over the business to him. He would be doing everything he loved, and they would be together.

She worked around the clock to prepare the bakery: she sent pictures of the construction to her son to entice him. However, with each letter, he never mentioned the new business, nor returning to America. There was a ribbon cutting ceremony as Normandie Country Bakery opened its doors, but her son was missing. The employees smiled as they rushed behind the counters to wait on the throng of customers, while Josette held back the tears and her disappointment. She waited, and she still waits for Anthony to come and take his place next to her side.

"After that," Josette added, "I expanded and opened up five locations throughout the Los Angeles area. Everyone loved my French pastries and one day, a customer suggested that I look into Las Vegas. I took a ride to the city, and my, my how exciting! So much to see and do and I noticed all of the casinos with their fancy restaurants and knew right away they would love my pastries. So I opened a bakery not too far from the strip, hired pastry chefs, and began distributing my products to all of the casinos, hotels, and restaurants. I just kept coming back, I fell in love with the city, and its great energy. I noticed there were hardly any French restaurants, other than a few within the hotels, so I decided to open up Josette's Bistro, and viola, here you sit today, Tony. Eating my French heritage and listening to my long tale of making food." He handed her his CD, "Listen To My Heart," he hoped she would begin to care for him. The lyrics, "I can show you my love, my voice wants to tell you everything," was the only way he knew he could truly tell her how he felt.

"I would drive by and watch her working in her restaurant. She had live entertainment and probably thought I was just another singer who wanted a gig."

He gathered a modicum of courage, pulled the car over, and walked into the bustling bistro. When her eyes met his, she held a fleeting smile and then came over to greet him. Seated in the corner he was forced to listen to the annoying sounds of a crooner wannabe.

"How about I sing for a glass of wine tonight?"

"Okay," she agreed, "You can start tomorrow." The next day, when he walked in, after a long day of shooting commercials, preparing the television show, and selling production, she didn't have a clue about his life as an entertainer. All she knew is that he was handsome as he was talented, and when he arrived, her heart felt a little lighter. As he prepared the sheet music, Josette brought over a large glass of the best red wine in the house and set it down on the barstool. He beamed, took a sip, and then proceeded to serenade the crowd with romantic tunes from the seventies. As she scribbled orders, served up meals, and gathered empty plates, his eyes never left her, he was singing for her, not for the hungry crowd. He became a welcome regular, performing, bringing in new customers and draining the inventory of her finest cabernets.

It was Saturday night and the last of the weekend dates had left the place. Tony asked her to join him for sushi late Sunday morning, thinking she had probably never sampled the stuff. She happily accepted and they began making that a weekend tradition. They talked for hours; she complained about the kitchen staff, or her love for a certain wine, or the customers, but there was always plenty for her to say. He revealed little about himself, but savored their private time together. The more she talked the more he realized this was the woman for him.

Tony pulled up to the guard at the classiest address a block off the strip, and told him who he was visiting.

"No problem Mr. Sacca," he responded, "And it's always a pleasure to see you. I caught your show last week and my wife and I really loved you." He unlatched the elaborate white metal gate and the doors slid open as he patiently waited in the elaborately mirrored lobby for Josette to arrive. She smelt of Chanel, and he was aroused when she glanced up at his face: the last thing on his mind was another plate of sushi, but he held back. He didn't want to blow this, whatever it was. He drove around the curved entranceway, pulled out of the high rises, and made a left onto the empty street.

"Bye, Mr. Sacca," shouted the guard.

"He seems to know you," noticed Josette.

"Well yes, in a way he knows me," he discretely responded.

"I never really thought of myself as a star, and I never portrayed myself to her in that way, but the time came when I wanted her to understand who I was. I wasn't singing in her restaurant for lack of other things to do, I was there to be near her, to watch her and get to know her. When I dropped her off, I invited her to see my show the following Friday and I was really happy to see her sitting in the audience, in the front row. It was her turn to see the real me." Later that Friday night he arrived at her restaurant, her smile was broad as she made an unusual effort to greet him. He reached into his soul, pulled out the most romantic tunes in his repertoire, and spent the night pouring out his heart. He loved her no doubt, but it was the kind that simmered, it needed time and a lot of nurturing if it was to ever come to fruition. So he waited and he waited, while he sang, and drank delicious wine.

After the last empty dish had been sent to the kitchen, she brought over two wine glasses, a chilled bottle of her secret stash, and a small plate of cheeses. They toasted his music and she pecked him on the cheek,

"Your show was terrific, you are terrific. I adore your music, your show and," she caught herself, she simply couldn't get the words out. Maybe it was because she was French, and had to maintain a clandestine secrecy when it came to proclaiming love, or maybe she didn't trust him, or perhaps she didn't trust any man. Regardless, the words of love were not forthcoming.

"How about coming on an interview with me? There is a big media party, and I will be speaking with a chef, I would love for you to come: but please, this may sound very odd, don't hold me or touch me. If you do people will think we are sleeping together and I don't want to ruin your reputation." Taken aback, she acquiesced to his weird invitation and showed up in a spectacular black chemise, adorned with freshwater pearls, and black silk pumps. With her mane of blonde hair, she was strikingly beautiful as she walked confidently into the gathering. Tony's eyes bulged out when he saw her at the entrance foyer, He took her hand he began introducing her to his friends and colleagues. She pulled away. She remembered his warning and kept her distance while they flitted from one person to another. When the time came to meet the chef, she was quite at home as they two conversed in French at a rapid pace. After the interview was completed, the chef kissed Josette and then Tony asked her what the hell he said,

"Don't worry, it's all up here," she responded as she pointed to her head. I will give you all the information you need."

For years, actually decades, his dates were much younger than he, so much so that many of his colleagues joked he was robbing the cradle, but none of those women gave him the feelings he felt when he was by Josette's side. It was more than her distinctive beauty, it was her ability to genuinely care about him, that drew his passion. When they were together, she took pains to make sure he was comfortable and his needs met. The younger women were hedonistic, they wanted sex, money and a piece of his fame, but all Josette wanted was for him to be happy. Even after she was privy to his fame, she never changed her disposition. She asked for nothing more than his company and companionship, she never took a moment of his time for granted, and initially he felt the same, but that would change as their relationship drew closer. It could have been best described as a complete meeting of the minds. They completely understood each other, their values, their goals, and how they wanted to live their lives; they were compatible in every sense of the word. As Tony matured, he valued that more than a roll in the hay with a one night fling.

True to his word, Tony produced a weekly show called, "La Cuisine," starring the one and only Josette, who taught the fine art of basic bistro cooking. Unaccustomed to appearing on television, he methodically taught her how to look into the camera, how to smile, and how to project her personality. Whenever the two were together they were happy, but for some reason, they hadn't progressed in their physical ties. They loved each other as friends, but Tony, remained too much of a gentleman. By now the two had shared so many things, perhaps he feared rocking the boat. It was New Year's Eve and Josette's sister had called from France to wish her a good year and then inquired about her love life and said that it was high time she began dating and having some fun.

"What about this Tony you talk about?" she asked, "He sounds like a great man, why not go after him?" Josette pondered this. It was New Year's Eve, and although he had a performance and she worked, they planned to see each other later that evening. When she hung up the phone, she decided it was time for a change in their platonic relationship. As she prepared for their date, she splashed on extra perfume, slipped into a deep purple silk sheath, plucked a bottle of red wine from the cabinet, and drove to his home. When he opened the door, he gave her a perfunctory kiss on the cheek, threw some CDs on, opened up the wine, and toasted the New Year. After the bottle had been drained she threw all caution to the wind, leaned over, and kissed him on his delicious lips. It was as if she had opened Pandora's Box, and the electricity pent up for a year had been unbridled. He returned her kisses, supplying a multitude of his own and that night, they consummated a passion that had been stirring for months. A deeper love than Tony had never known, it was more than physical, they had a meeting of the minds, and he dubbed Josette his soul mate and partner in life. It wasn't as if Josette had led the life of a nun for the past two decades, but she had never found anyone she could truly connect with. If their relationship could pinpoint one commonality, it was a passion for their life's work; Josette's ingrained since eight years old in the culinary arts, and Tony's at the same age, began the life of a performer.

"Let's go to Paris to celebrate. We could kill two birds with one stone: a honeymoon, and I could produce a couple of your cooking shows right in the heart of where you grew up." That didn't take much prodding as Josette was already dreaming of seeing her family, especially her son and sister. They booked flights on Air France. They were ushered across the Atlantic in refined style and landed safely in Paris.

"It was absolutely the most beautiful town I had ever seen. Although my brother and I travelled extensively, we were never booked in Europe, and this trip was a real eye opener." With no knowledge of the language, he clung to Josette, feeling a bit helpless. They followed the crowd, gathered their luggage, hailed a cab, and spent a couple of nights in heaven at a Paris Hotel. It seemed as though the entire city was dedicated to love and romance: flowers bloomed everywhere, the women were beautiful and all wore scents that left a lingering smell in the air. The restaurants were cozy, the food outrageously delicious, and the streets pristine.

"It's time," announced Josette, as they departed the hotel and headed to the southeast of France to meet her father, her hero. He drove the compact car while she navigated, but the scenery was so spectacular that Tony was hard pressed to watch the road. The rolling hills were vibrantly green and lush, the air smelled refreshingly clean, and that day the sky was cloudless. Hours later they arrived at a small brick home where her father had lived for decades. He pulled the car up to the front of the house, killed the engine, and they saw the front door fly open. Her dad threw his hands in the air and hugged his daughter, smothering kisses on her cheeks.

"Dad, meet Tony," she said proudly. As he shook her father's hand, Tony couldn't understand one word of her dad's warm demeanor.

Before he left the states, he had downloaded an interpreting app on his phone. When he really needed help, this would prove the perfect solution. That evening at dinner, he would wow his father-in-law with his adeptness of the language: at least that was what he thought. After a stroll around the property, and a tour of the house, they toasted with flutes of quality champagne: more bubbles than he had ever drank in one glass. The secret was the quality of the wine, made in Champagne; the grapes were perfection, releasing millions of bubbles when the cork was popped. Soft pink in color, one sip and the effect went right to his head, truly a taste of heaven.

"It has been five years since I have seen my Josette," her dad said as he turned to Tony, "please make sure it isn't another five years until you return her to me." Which such a forthright statement, Tony decided he would answer the comment in French. Playing back the response, his recording device translated it to say, "Please don't come back for at least five years."

Josette was laughing hysterically, "I think you better trust me to do the talking."

They spent the night in the tiny guest bedroom, they picked up early the next morning driving to central France visiting her sister and her son, who were steeped in the world of baking and charcuterie. White flour dusted throughout her hair, her sister rushed out of the kitchen and wrapped her arms around Josette as tears sprang from both sets of eyes. The scene was repeated when her son grabbed his mom and they exchanged a series of kisses. Stiff from the long ride, Josette made her son give Tony a tour of the land and their operation while they stretched out their legs. Impressed with the beauty of the property, he was more impressed with the decades old architecture, and how highly maintained the property appeared. The huge farm kitchen had been renovated with state of the art equipment which sped up the once all hand done production, and allowed them to make more product in less time and with less manual labor. Many things never changed, like the pounding of the dough to coax the mixture into a perfectly light and airy baguette. As she extracted one from the oven, Josette slathered soft butter on top and put it into Tony's mouth,

"The best thing I've ever eaten, bon, bon!" Which was the full extent of his French vocabulary.

They spent the next few nights at the farmhouse, squeezed in a twin bed. There was no need for an alarm clock, the crows of the roosters and the sounds of her sister padding through the oak floors was enough to jar them out of a deep sleep , it was five thirty and time to bake the bread. Still dark, Tony would wait for the next round of crowing before rising from underneath the warm covers. They filled the days exploring cheese factories, oyster farms (where oysters are grown and cultivated), mushroom farms, wineries, and touring the Calvados apple brandy factory. Josette gathered as many nonperishable products as possible in preparation for the taping of the television shows. It was painful saying good bye to her family, but time was limited and they had two shows to produce. The drive to the coast was magnificent, filled with more greenery, pastoral lands and endless vineyards until they finally arrived in Nice. Josette had reserved a space at a well-known bistro, whose owner allowed them to film in the kitchen as long as they mentioned the name of the restaurant and allowed him to be a part of the video. Everyone was in agreement, it would add to the authenticity: both chefs would wear the revered white jackets and the slightly tilted white hats.

"Don't forget, this is for an American audience, please speak English." The owner just waved his hands in the air, but with her smile, Josette prevailed upon him to just follow along, they would wing it. Two hours later the local cameraman handed over the tapes and called it a wrap. She kissed her fellow chef, and they departed the bistro and turned onto the two lane road heading for Cannes: home of the world famous film festival.

This time, Josette had found a location with a backdrop of the ocean, on top of a hill. The view was spectacular from the patio of the bistro, but she would have limited access to the kitchen, which was why she had plucked many fine cheeses from the farms, she would make a cold summer aperitif platter. Of course the star of the dish was all the wonderful mousses, sausages, and breads from her family's farm. She kidded Tony,

"Like you say, killing three birds with one stone." How wonderful to promote the products she put her life into during her childhood. Her only regret was that those two episodes would probably never make it to the French television networks. She arranged the products on top of a picnic table spread with a handmade cloth. She looked into the camera and saw

Tony's eyes directed on her. It hit her at that moment how much she really loved him and how much he must love her. He literally went to the ends of the earth to make her happy, to share a tiny bed, to try to learn the language, and to let her have her way. In all ways a gentleman, kind, caring thoughtful and tender, she was in love as she could be. She watched him ordering around the two cameramen; not knowing a word of the language was challenging to say the least, but with his persistence, she plodded through the demonstration, all the while pointing out the beauty of her homeland. In her heart she knew this wonderful meal could never be duplicated in America, especially the cheeses, but for foodies, it was entertaining to see her deftly assemble the entrée. They spent their last night at a boutique hotel with a tiny balcony that opened up to a spectacular view of the ocean. They allowed the cool evening breezes into the small bedroom, the slight taste of salt filled the air and they caught the romantic fever swirling around. There was nothing like France.

With two hours to kill before take-off, Josette had plenty of time to shop at the numerous boutiques in the long corridors of the huge airport. She found just the right silk tie, had it wrapped as a gift, and slipped it into her purse. When they got home, it would serve as a reminder of their trip, and perhaps a hint of more trips to come.

Business class seats were roomy, comfortable, and clean. The plane had settled into its cruising altitude and the crew had served the first round of drinks, it was time for Tony to broach the subject stewing in his mind. His father had died four years prior to his brother's death in 1999, his brother was gone, his sister had moved away, and his mom was living by herself. She was lonely and Tony felt compelled to change that situation, he would ask his mom to move in with him, but Josette was living under his roof and she would have to agree.

"Sweetheart, I see how hard it is for you to leave your family, they are all so far away, and I promise we will return. I look at my mother who is all alone and I feel horrible for her. Do you mind if I ask her out for a short visit just to see if she might like living in a warmer climate? She is desperately lonely and I worry about her." Josette just smiled and kissed him, if that would make him happy, then so be it. It was only for a short while and then she would go back home. She was absolutely sure the two of them would get along in the one story home just splendidly. After the second glass of champagne the idea didn't seem too bad and after the third glass, and kisses smothered on her lips, the idea seemed just right.

When Josette returned home from work, she could hear Tony yelling at his mom to stop cleaning the kitchen, it was clean enough. She walked in with a big smile and warmly hugged Millie.

"I was just doing a little light cleaning, but I can see that my son thinks the oven is clean enough," she said stripping the yellow rubber gloves off her hands. "An oven can never be too clean, don't you agree?"

Josette would have no part of this war, so she said nothing, but she privately admitted it was nice having someone else scrub the kitchen. After decades of running bakeries, and restaurants, it was quite a change to have someone voluntarily do the grunge work.

"I think we should all go out tonight, relax and get to know each other, what do you think Tony?" Which translated into, we are all going out tonight. As they dressed for dinner, Josette never uttered a word about his mom, she had just arrived and they needed time to get to know each other. He picked a simple place that served simple food and large glasses of beer and wine. He didn't know how that first evening would go, so long as they had access to those ample glasses of liquid courage, he felt confident the three would make it through the meal.

Dressed in a black skirt and flowered top, Millie's face reflected a long hard life, her once thick black hair was replaced with silver curls, her face was covered with a myriad of tiny lines, her eyes drawn deeper, and her skin drier: she was growing older. That night as her face caught the last glare of the evening sun was it was clear to Tony how much she had aged.

Inviting her to stay with him was the right thing to do, perhaps he could make her happy, he would try.

"Too much salt," Millie critiqued, because she really could NOT be complaining. She raised her eyes to Josette for compliance, but none was offered because Josette didn't think the food had too much salt, nor as Millie would later comment, did the food have too many onions, or too much butter, or too small portions. In fact, according to the chef, the food was quite right, especially for the price. This was only the first night, and Millie was probably exhausted from the long flight and the fact it was three hours later. After two hours of combative conversation and three substantial glasses of red wine, Tony practically tripped the waiter grabbing his attention and asking him to bring over the check. Tony stood up, and extracted the keys from his coat pocket. He was a sober as a church mouse, the wine did little to soothe his split nerves as Millie took them from one uncomfortable topic to another.

As he lay in bed with his honey, he pondered the nature of the situation, it's only the first night kept repeating in his brain like a broken record. Things would get better, it's only the first night.

"For me it was a love, resentment situation. Ma always favored Robert because she saw him as the weaker kid, like the runt of the litter. His wants and needs often fell before mine: from her perspective, he needed a little extra attention and as the years progressed and he became ill, he became her sole focus. Maybe I wanted to prove to my mom I could take Robert's place, or show her how successful my life had become and that she should be proud of my accomplishments. It was one thing to tell her about my life, but quite another for her to see my life." As he fell asleep he hoped that day was an aberration and not a premonition of what was to come.

It was nice to awaken to the smell of freshly brewed coffee. Josette was always out the door early, and he hated making coffee. After decades on the road where he was waited on hand and foot, coffee was something he loathed to bother with.

"How did you sleep ma?"

"Well, after I changed the sheets and dusted the room for cobwebs, I slept very well thank you. Tonight, I promise you a wonderful home cooked meal." She grabbed his cheeks with her thumb and index finger and pinched him lightly, "just like I used to make for you kids." She handed him the grocery list and he ran to the store, purchased all of the items, dropped them off on the kitchen counter, and then ran out the door. He felt like he was back in high school running errands, except now he had to be bothered with running errands, and a blossoming business.

The dinner would be worth it, his mom was quite the cook. He called Josette after lunch to make sure she would arrive back at the house in time for the auspicious meal, which she was happy to do, regardless of her busy schedule. Since the day she met Tony, his family was always the center of his thoughts and heart, she would do whatever it took to make him happy, he was too good of a man to lose. Promptly at six they gathered around the dinner table while Josette selected the proper wine for Tony to open. She was quite sure he would need some before the night ended. They raised their glasses and he auspiciously toasted his mother and welcomed her to his home,

"Ma, stay as long as you want, my home is your home." Josette's heart began to race, was Millie to become a permanent fixture, or was this just a vacation until she sorted out her life? Perhaps she was the one who would need three glasses of wine tonight. Millie returned to the kitchen and brought out a huge antipasto salad laden with cheeses, meats, olives, and marinated eggplant: simply delicious, but for Josette's tiny appetite this was all the food she needed. She placed a warm garlic bread at the edge of the table and brought out a savory Italian stew, with a side of homemade orzo, to soak up all that garlic drenched gravy. Tony was too busy eating to worry about conversation. Josette timidly dug in, there was no doubt about it,

"Millie your food is absolutely wonderful so rich and flavorful, C'est magnifique!" Her meager appetite became ravenous, and she ate more at that one sitting than she did in an entire week. When they were sufficiently stuffed, Josette pulled her seat back to clear the table, but Millie would have none of that,

"No, you have worked hard all day, I will do this but don't leave, I made dessert." Josette was bursting, she could not eat another bite, that was, until Millie place a panforte at the table, a rich delectable end to the meal. She sliced large pieces and handed out fresh forks as they dug into the last course. Tony and Josette could barely move as they shoved in their chairs, thanked the cook and then, slower than sloths, walked down the hallway to their room.

"If this keeps up, we are going to have to purchase a California King bed. I hope this was just a one night stand. Mon dieu! I surely hope this is not going to happen every night, I will become a fat cow in a month and you will have to wheel me to my store." Tony turned on the hot water and just before entering the shower, he glimpsed in the mirror, oh my God, she's right! His stomach was protruding as if he had swallowed a water buffalo. Oh hell, he would work it off in the in the morning, a few extra push-up. Eat and repent through exercise, that was his motto, at least for the next morning.

Millie nested into her room at the end of the hall and in no time she had the house in ship shape. In fact it was sterile. Even Josette couldn't believe how clean Millie made the place. She left no spot untouched by her voracious habitual cleaning. Any tiny animal crawling about had no chance when Millie was in charge, the few ants occasionally carried into the house on the paws of the dog had vanished, and the house was immaculate. Once she had conquered the major rooms, she opened her son's closet and began mending and cleaning his suits and shoes, and pressing his jeans.

When Tony arrived home that evening he found his mom snoring on the sofa and the smell of a roasted chicken in the oven. Not wanting to wake her, he tip-toed around the house, playing with the dogs and catching up on his emails. A timer went off on the kitchen stove and Millie's eyes blinked open.

"Tony, you're home. I think you will like what I cooked for dinner. When is your sweetie coming?" she asked. After a week of heavy eating, Josette returned to her bakery in Los Angeles, she needed to spend time at her business and time away from the all the food Millie was setting on the table each night. She had to admit, Millie's dishes were delicious, just much heavier fare and more abundant than she was used to eating. A break was definitely in order.

"I guess I fell asleep. I set the timer on the stove so I would be awake when you got home."

"Ma, I brought you here so you could take a rest, relax, and be on vacation. I didn't invite you out to clean, cook, and be our live in housekeeper! You have got to stop all of this. Besides we are all going to weigh two hundred pounds if you keep this up. You need to take it easy, you are wearing yourself out and that's crazy." She set the food on the table as he explained that Josette would be in Los Angeles for a few days, and with just the two of them, she needn't fuss, he would take her out.

"If that's what you want, I guess I have to listen to you now that I am living in your home," was her Italian guilt ridden response.

"Ma, don't make me feel guilty for telling you not to work so hard, but all this cleaning and cooking has got to stop, or, ah, slow down. If you keep this up, you will exhaust yourself. I found you napping in the late afternoon, you never did that, you are working yourself up. Please try and take it easy." They spent the evening in quiet conversation, later he flipped on the television to listen to the latest news while they critiqued the political scene. The next night, he took her to a movie, and the night after that to a casino, and the night after that to a lounge show. She took her son's advice and slowed down the cleaning, because there really wasn't much left to clean, especially with Josette away. She spent her days reading, enjoying the delicious clean air, swimming in the heated pool, and reading her favorite novels. All was well, quiet and copasetic.

When Josette returned she was five pounds thinner, determined not to allow Millie's cooking to get the best of her. She walked into the home, and was pleasantly surprised to see Millie sitting in the backyard reading a thick detective novel. Now that was how things should be, nice and peaceful. With a peck on the cheek, Millie smiled and welcomed Josette home.

"Tonight, I keep it very simple, just pizza, and a salad." When they sat down to dinner in fact it was pizza and a salad, but there were two huge pizzas on the table, made from scratch, and a salad so large that it was incorporated into an unfamiliar bowl.

"You know Tony's serving pieces are so small, not big enough to feed two people, so I found a couple of very inexpensive serving pieces." Between the pizzas and the salad there was barely room for the tableware. All Josette could think about was Tony purchasing a bigger dining table to hold his mom's dinosaur portions.

The three shared the household as Millie took them through her journey of pasta, meats, vegetables, salads, and desserts. It was the meatballs that undid the semblance of order and caused the destruction of the family. Tony was surrounded by two strong controlling women, which in most instances would have played out perfectly fine, but in this instance it was control over the kitchen: the ultimate battle between the French Chef and the Italian mama. It was innocent as it began

Josette strolled into the kitchen, sniffed around like bloodhound and immediately sensed a dearth of fresh onions in the chopped meat. She grabbed an onion, handed it delicately to Millie, and suggested it be added to the mixture.

"Na, I don't put that into my meatballs, I put that into the sauce, that way there is a nice blend of the garlic and the onions." Josette was persistent and commenced chopping away at that innocent little onion and when

Millie turned her head, she flung the pieces into the mixture. Aghast, Millie was appalled, nobody but nobody touched her meatballs. It was as if the devil himself became cradled into her right palm, because she found herself flinging the mixture into Josette's face, screaming not to touch her meatballs. And in turn, the devil retaliated, as the chef grabbed a small handful flinging it back at Millie's face and then the pent up yelling began. When Tony pulled up in the car, the screaming from the kitchen caught his attention as he burst open the side door and found the two women in his life covered with meat, and no, it wasn't blood, but layers of tomato sauce.

"Fresh tomatoes,"

"No canned is better." His face became the color of the sauce as he tried to calm them down and make peace.

"This isn't going to work," said Millie as she stormed out of the kitchen to take a shower. It took a lot of strength for Tony not to break out in laughter as he gazed at the mess on Josette's face and clothing.

"Go take a shower, and tonight, I'll clean up." He tossed off his jacket, got out the mop, and began scrubbing away. Perplexed as to how the entire event occurred, it appeared as if he could never keep all the important women in his life happy. The writing was on the wall, albeit one that had been freshly scrubbed, that Millie's time was quickly coming to an end. No one sat at the dinner table that night, it seemed as though no one was hungry, but later that evening, after the Agatha Christie movie, Millie met Tony in the living room and announced she was going back home.

"I miss my friends and my family, what remains of them. I don't mind living by myself, I might even go to the pound and get an old dog, that would be nice, save its life. I miss watching the leaves turning, I miss the climate changes, and I miss the memories that were made in my home. I love you son, and I know you tried your hardest, but it's not your responsibility to care for me. I'll be fine, I promise." She kissed him on the cheek and hugged him, and he said he would book her flight home. That was how the meatballs unglued the Sacca household.

As time went on Tony began taking over more of Josette's life. She closed the bistro and together they opened a monstrous restaurant, Las Vegas Rocks Café at the heart of downtown Fremont Street. A twenty thousand square foot structure, it had its ups and downs in the area but the two planned to make this a successful venture. The front portion was an expansive restaurant, while the back room was set up as a full stage and they planned on having live performances nightly. An ambitious venture, it was on the track to success when the entire air-conditioning system failed. No matter what expert was brought into fix the problem, it became unfixable and they closed the white elephant.

Las Vegas Rocks Café, for all its faltering moments, held one stellar memory. A pilot for television, *Resurrection*, written by Jeff Ross, and Victoria Claibourn, was filmed inside the restaurant. Frank Vincent, of the famed Sopranos, starred in the new Mafia show. The camera crew had set up across the floor of the eating area, and spilled into the theater. Tony's job was to sing, "Fly Me to the Moon" in the background, while the characters plotted their next moves. Later in the scene, Tony was to walk off stage, and approach Frank to welcome him to the bistro.

"I remember trying so hard to act like a tough guy, and then Frank turned to me, and said, 'Just act like yourself, no tough stuff, that's not who you are.' I listened to his advice, and for the rest of the shooting, I was just me." As things go, this project never got off the ground, yet another disappointment attributed to this white elephant.

Josette, who had flourishing bakeries in Los Angeles, decided to keep her energies on that business, and expand upon a tried and true product. She split her time between Los Angeles and Las Vegas, as did Tony. Since neither one could ever be satisfied with the status quo, they began working on the next big project: a cookbook that would include a disk inserted into the back of the book. What made this a unique cookbook, other than the fact that Josette's French food was famous, was the video showing how to prepare each recipe as she would explain how to alter the recipes based upon personal preferences.

The love the couple had for each other was so entwined between the passion they had for their professions and the love they had for each other it was impossible to separate the two.

"In so many ways, Josette was like my father. Neither had finished a formal education, but instead went to the school of hard knocks. Work was all they knew or understood, and from morning until night they fought to make a living supporting their families. She is an independent, self-made woman, brilliant, stubborn, balanced, and focused. She told me that I am the second man in her entire life." Married so young at seventeen, she waited decades to find the right man; she trusted no one, but she finally began to trust Tony and let down her stalwart guard.

Tony and Jossette

Johnny Carson's sidekick, Ed McMahon, is interviewed by Tony when promoting his new book at Caesars Palace

Las Vegas Rocks ®

*1951 – The first atomic bomb is
detonated at the Nevada Test Site
north of Las Vegas. People flocked
to watch the tests until the limited
Test Ban Treaty of 1963 required that
nuclear tests be moved underground.*

Tony joins the male review Thunder From Down Under
during his 50th anniversary of being in show business - he
trained and dieted for 90 days to join the cast

CHAPTER 15

"Diet and exercise has always been on my mind and has allowed me to live well and remain healthy. I travelled around the world, locked in hotel rooms, but I needed to stay in shape and I developed an exercise routine that would keep me in shape within the confines of a small space. Even if a hotel had a gym, there was no privacy, and I would be pestered for autographs and girls so I gave up and kept to my room. As the years went by and saw my brother destroy his body through drugs, bulimia, and smoking, it served as a further warning what can happen if you don't treat your body well. I keep a photo of his headstone in my cell phone so I never forget."

Tony has gone through phases, plucking philosophies from different sources, and although he has exercised and eaten in a balanced fashion, Stanly Burrough's, "Master Cleanse" caught his attention and he began to implement the program which can be loosely defined as the, "Lemonade Diet." A type of ten day fast, it purports rapid weight loss along with detoxification of the body. The diet is exceedingly simple, select the amount of days you want to fast and consume the following concoction: mix 2 tablespoons of freshly squeezed lemon juice, 2 tablespoons of organic maple syrup, and a pinch of cayenne pepper into a glass of filtered water and drink. That's it, there is no food or additional supplements. The pounds fall off at a rapid weight and according to Tony, he never felt hungry. This worked well for Tony, but upon scanning the research, it is not a highly touted weight loss system. Every three to four months, he reverted to this diet, which has stabilized his weight, giving him the six pack abs he owned as a teen.

On one of his Friday afternoons filming of the variety show, he had the courage to stand beside, "Thunder Down Under," a famous male stripper group, with no tee-shirt on. He flexed his muscles on live television, and his physique held up with the best of them.

"Exercise is not an option. I have exercised my entire life, and I believe that has been what has kept me healthy and able to do the things I love doing. Exercise and good eating habits are the keys to a long healthy life." His daily regimen of exercise consists of a combination of weight training, stretching, and cardio. He built a complete gym in his home, so he would have no excuses. Seven days a week, an hour and a half a day, he works different parts of his body to keep in top condition. The camera doesn't lie, looking physically good is part and parcel of show business and it is the one thing he can control. Stamina is also a big part of his job, spending most of his time standing, singing, and walking around the stage requires a body in great condition. He can't afford to be sick, or take time off to relax, he is simply too driven to excellence. To comply with the rigorous schedule or running three businesses, his body demanded to be able to withstand a dozen hours at a time toiling on different projects. Being in physical shape is a big secret to Tony's sustained success.

"I stopped eating red meat over a decade ago. The thought of killing an animal, ripping it apart and devouring its muscle doesn't seem appetizing to me. When you pick an apple from the tree and eat it, you are eating the original life source, but not so for a pig or a cow. A fish, caught from the ocean, a natural phenomena, is part of the biological structure of our earth and it seems only natural to consume it. You don't have to put a gun to its head to capture and eat it, it's there for the taking. Truly, what are you getting from meat that you could not get from other foods, foods that don't require slaughtering and the injection of hormones. I eat nuts, edamame, tons of vegetables, fruits, and I drink at least a quart of water a day. I know this may sound strange coming from a family whose dad was a butcher and Josette, who is world famous for her charcuterie, but it is how I live my life.

"After years of travelling, I had discovered that a good night's sleep is the cure for many aliments: allowing my mind to rest so I can handle all the problems facing me the next day." Rounding out his philosophy of healthy living he believes in the power of positive thinking, surrounding himself with people who share those same thoughts.

"We don't have the luxury of negative thinking, I avoid it, ignore it, pass on it, or pretend it doesn't exist. The people who surround me make a difference, and I don't like negative people, they spoil all the goodness that comes with each day. When someone makes me angry I found that the best way to fight back was to ignore them, and let whatever harm they throw my way get out of my train of thinking. There are times when I can't avoid a confrontation and I have to defend myself, but they are rare."

When Tony wasn't reading up on the latest diet or exercise program, he spent a great deal of time and effort on charitable organizations.

"I feel like I owe people back for putting me, and keeping me in the limelight for so many years." The Youth Foundation for Performing Arts, now twenty-five years strong, continues to be his favorite and most successful charity. It still provides funds to independent music teachers and purchases instruments, and now third generation performers are emerging into the show business spotlight. Twice a year, he gives the students a chance to perform live at the Christmas and Patriotic July Fourth specials. Taking them backstage, he explains the workings of live television, while the cameramen, stage crew, musical director, and lighting specialist describe their jobs. The kids put on costumes, sing and dance before a live audience, and watch the video feed directly after the show. Tony gives them something money can't buy, his talent, interest, and knowledge of the profession.

"I was in Los Angeles at a nightclub and I heard this cute blonde girl yell out, 'Tony Sacca it's you.' She introduced herself as Chelsa and told me she had been a part of the youth group when she was eight years old. She was so inspired that she continued, and was getting numerous roles. She had just landed the lead in Disney's, 'Barbie,' and would be travelling the world. She hugged and kissed me and thanked me for helping her get her career off the ground. In recent years, Mikalah Gordon, was another success story, coming in the top ten on American Idol. I get a thrill out of knowing I have impacted so many kids who have gone on to have success in show business. I think there is no better way to give back than to pay it forward."

So immersed within the entertainment community, he took over the presidency of the Show Business Society for Las Vegas, a philanthropic organization whose mission is to recognize and award outstanding entertainers, and provide financial aid for emergencies. The organization assists local charities by producing events, holding fund raisers, and supporting community outreach and mentoring programs. Donating their time, they give concerts raising money for groups or individuals who are in dire need. Additionally, Tony records public service and radio announcements, and hosts and performs at an endless list of charitable functions throughout the year. Giving back is a part of who he is, rooted in church when the plate was passed, his mother taught him it was better to give than to receive.

*Tony performers as a Thunder From
Down Under male review*

1957 – Topless Showgirls
debut on the Strip with
"Minsky's Follies."

Legendary comedian, David Brenner, appears on the Tony's TV show. They grew up in the same neighborhood in south Philadelphia

CHAPTER 16

Although it was the end of Thanksgiving weekend, and a big football game was scheduled that Sunday afternoon, Tony, along with almost fifty members of the Show Business Society, gave a two hour benefit for a stricken colleague. Tony acted as host and singer and worked the stage through the entire benefit: introducing acts, performing, and thanking the artists, including the huge band, who all came to give their time and talents to raise money. A packed house, most of the attendees were well known performers, a true who's who in the Las Vegas large repertoire of famous entertainers. To open up the show, Tony sang, "Dancing In the Streets," and the Scintas, one of the longest running groups in the city, closed the show with a beautiful Christmas song. A true star studded event: several of the local news channels were there to record the show and interview the performers.

"Giving back is what it is all about," said Tony.

For all that he has given back to the city, it has not gone unnoticed. His office walls are covered with declarations, tributes, commendations from the city and state, and a myriad of nonprofit organizations that have benefited from Tony's talent, time, money, and energy. Using his public persona, he has been able to bring to light organizations and people who are in need, by offering a public platform. Free publicity is a rare commodity, he uses it wisely, honestly, and humanely.

Tony will never take all the credit for his success, especially given his generous nature. Savvy, he surrounds himself with talented people who know how to make the right moves to obtain the next rung on his ladder of success. Building a Las Vegas based business; his tentacles reach out to hundreds of people affecting their lives helping to create a constantly fomenting and evolving, bourgeoning economic base. Jackie Brett, an entertainment columnist for several newspapers and online websites, took on an additional job as Tony's publicist. Her job was enviable as she covered all the entertainment venues in the city. Up until 1983, the vast majority of shows were performed in the cozier more personalized lounges of the casinos, but there were often two or three shows a day to accommodate the hordes of tourists. The dawn of the mega casinos, also heralded a new era of larger showrooms and arenas. Although the intimacy was replaced by largesse, it opened the door for different types of entertainment and headliners. In came the Cirque de Soleil, and magicians, and world famous headliners, all of which she covered in her columns. Jackie not only could assist Tony with public relations, but help him land some of the interviews for his show, *Entertainment Las Vegas Style*. Her career has lasted thirty-nine years, and she is still at it, there was always a new star entering the city's arena, a new lounge opening up, or a new show, it is a city with an insatiable appetite for fresh, cutting-edge talent. With every new casino cropping up across the states, it only served to reinforce why Las Vegas is the greatest city in the country, and why more people than ever flock to the town. The city was built on gambling, but that is not what has sustained and developed the town, it's the world class entertainment, restaurants, shopping, resorts, and the idyllic weather. It has been and remains to be, the number one adult tourist town in the country, and one of the top in the world. Jackie's press releases reflect all that is happening in the town, and luckily, her enviable job will always have a bottomless well of exciting and anticipated information.

In the early 1990s, with decades of writing under her belt, and the ear of the media, she was able to jump start Tony's solo Las Vegas career, helping to fill the audiences with her sharp, well-written critiques. She gained his trust and respect and the two became fast friends, but it was always about business, even when they shared a cocktail or dinner. Poor Tony with his notorious reputation as a Don Juan, Jackie's husband was often circumspect, but as the months and years passed, he too understood their close relationship was based solely upon business.

"When I first interviewed the Sacca Twins, it was Tony who did all the talking. He was bubbling with energy and loved performing; in fact, he even sang a song for me. We have remained close friends for years and I have watched him suffer through his brother and mother's passing. He hid his emotions well when it came to his family, he never wore his heart on his sleeve.

"When he returned home from his mother's funeral, we invited him to spend that Sunday at Lake Mead on our boat, reminding him that it was casual, no need to get dressed up. In spite of the season, the sun had kept the temperatures mild and the water brisk, but not frigid. We were preparing the boat when we see Tony walking up to the edge of the wharf toting a suitcase filled with clothes. Laughing hysterically, his Italian lust for always looking great, regardless of the situation, struck us as quite funny. He had to look great, even if we were his only audience. He was joking around and having a good time and I kept warning him that the hurting would hit him, the thoughts of the funeral would come crashing down. It could have been the combination of the two beers, with the swaying of the motorboat that caused him to heave, but I knew better. Cleaning up the mess, I encouraged him to jump into the lake with my husband, who was skinny dipping off the forward deck. Tony never even bothered to say don't peek, he stripped off his filthy clothes and dove into the water stark naked. Perhaps that was a purifying moment for him because when they both climbed back into the boat, he was wearing a smile. Letting go of his inhibitions, at least when it came to clothing, it helped him begin the long process of grieving. To this day, I still have a picture I snapped as he dove into the water, one that I eventually handed over when he fell in love with Josette, I thought she deserved to share the memories. When Monday rolled around, he was back at his desk and his job, toiling away, and keeping me busy."

Behind the scenes people who are loyal, hard-working and trustworthy were hard to come by, and Tony found that perfect person in Mike Lawson.

The evening show was over. Tony was hungry and ended up at the local Smith's grocery store where a bachelor could find plenty of fresh vegetables, fruits and, nuts. Unlike most bachelors, he was an avid fan of healthy eating, and didn't mind spending the time preparing a decent meal. With Josette busy in Los Angeles a microwave was as much work as he wanted to do in his kitchen while he concentrated on the rest of his life. Walking into the empty store, he was singing one of his favorite Manilow tunes with gusto, raising his arms out as if he had an audience,

"I can't smile without you, can't laugh without you."

Hearing the song, the evening manager curiously approached him, gave him a round of applause and asked if he could assist the tired hungry performer.

"Hi, I'm Mike Lawson, aren't you Tony Sacca? Can I help you with something?" Aware his customer was tired, he offered his services and escorted him around the store, making selections that were ready to eat and satisfy his need for wholesome healthy fare. It was near one in the morning when Mike dropped the last bag in the trunk of the performer's car and thanked him for shopping at Smith's and for the song.

"I'll be back," Tony promised. And he did return. He and Mike struck up a conversation and then he asked Mike if he would like to accompany him on an interview. In the grocery store business for over thirty years, Mike could never remember meeting a star, let alone one who would actually speak to him, and so he jumped at the chance to see a real live television interview. Meeting Tony at the casino, they walked to the back of the theatre into a dimly lit dressing room where Louie Anderson was preparing for his show.

"Wow, what an opportunity! I can't believe I get to see such a famous star and watch Tony do a one on one! It was fascinating to observe the cameraman and the crew preparing the area, placing microphones, setting up lights and rearranging the backdrop. The taping lasted an hour, although it would be edited down to thirty minutes, but boy was Louie funny, yet when asked tough questions, he quickly changed his tone and answered with a deep authenticity. I felt like Tony had a real gift for bringing out the best in everyone. After that interview, he asked me to tag along to meet Charo for another television special, but that time I actually helped lug some of the equipment and set up the lighting. I was handy, and I didn't mind. Meeting these world famous stars and getting to see them perform live and in person was payback enough for me. That Charo was one of the most beautiful women I have ever met, she was funny, talented, and what a body!

"Tony is a personable guy, he is easy to like, and I have to admit I was star struck not only by him, but all the famous talent that surrounds him. I began tagging along on all of his interviews and eventually, I became his stage and production manager. Although I had no formal training as a stage manager, I did have thirty years under my belt as a store manager and I knew how to get things done and how to talk to people. When it came time for the Feast of San Gennaro, he entrusted the entire production in my hands and with that success, I have continued working steadily with him."

"Do you think you could help me remodel the kitchen? I love my house, but it needs a lot of repair and you are the only man I trust."

"So I couldn't very well turn down that offer. I picked up a bunch of supplies and drove to his home which is on a decent spread of property in a quiet part of town. Yep, walking around the first floor, it sang out, "renovation time," but I was prepared. Carrying bags of tools and supplies, I began the process, sweating as I pulled down walls, and laid down fresh floors. Maybe Tony felt guilty, or the need to show me he had other talents, but he grabbed the edge of a large board and I just missed pounding his thumb into the wall. Tell you what Tony, you stick to singing and I'll stick to hammering and that was the way it went until I finished the project. When I left he had all his fingers intact."

Tony had the knack and the luck for attracting just the right people to get the job done and another such talented individual was Ron Garrett, a former entertainment director at the Sahara Hotel and Casino booked Tony at the Sahara Hotel. In fact Ron booked Tony to ring in the New Year for two consecutive years. Ron is currently the floor director and voice of the *Las Vegas Rocks Variety Show*. Their twenty year relationship began as a friendship, and Ron eventually became part of the production on the live shows. With so many traits in common, it was bound to happen.

Making cold calls, Tony landed an appointment with United Nissan, one of the biggest car dealers in the city. Thrilled, he went to great pains putting together a pitch that he hoped would land him the account. Dressing in his best suit, crisp white shirt, and shiny uncomfortable shoes, he was escorted into a large conference room. As he pulled out a brochure, complete with sketches and photos, a young man barged into the room flanked with a camera crew, sound equipment and microphones.

"Who the hell is this guy stealing my thunder?" Ron angrily thought to himself. "This man, yes he was very handsome, and from the cut of his Italian worsted suit, knew how to dress, and then he started talking. He seemed so bloody aloof, like he held the world on a string. Hell, I'll never look that good. I might as well pack it all in." That was Ron's first meeting with Tony.

Through luck, and years of hard work, Ron became the executive director of marketing at a large casino. One day his phone jingled and Tony was at the other end trying to sell spots on his variety show.

"Ah ha," thought Ron, "now I will get back at him for stealing an account from underneath my nose. But the guy who showed up at my office, was not the haughty person I had first met, he was really nice, and he really cared about what he did. Astounded, I actually liked the guy before he left my office. As we continued to do business together I found him to be the nicest, sweetest, most sincere man I had ever met. He didn't have a mean bone in his body. Through the years, I watched him work hard, harder than any person I knew, and I grew to admire him. We saw each other around town for years and when I moved to the Sahara Casino, I found a place for Tony to perform and we continued to support each other both professionally and in business ventures.

"He had fifty ideas a second, some were stupid and some were brilliant, but he was always thinking and innovating. He was the consummate salesperson and never antagonized others or created confrontations; he knew how to solve problems amicably and epitomized the essence of a perfect negotiator. What I saw in Tony was a great performing artist, who became better at his craft as he put years into his television productions. His singing and stage presence became more polished as he attracted the biggest and most famous celebrities to share his stage."

After Ron retired from the Sahara Casino, he took a bigger part in Tony's labyrinth of businesses and began announcing the live variety shows. Using his wit and their intimate friendship, they bantered on and off camera creating a sub-comedy act supplanting the final edited show.

"The future couldn't look brighter. The variety show has been picked up across the country and over half the households will have the ability to turn on the only show that highlights Las Vegas. The reason for the success, other than Tony's talent, is that he is a self-contained entity. Not only does he act as host and performing artist, but he owns the production company which produces the show and the advertising agency which assembles the sponsors to sustain and fund the show. People are seeking anything and everything Las Vegas, and as the show goes national, he will be a major talking point that draws more attention to the city. With every new casino that pops up across the country, Sin City becomes a more sought after destination; competition only serves to illuminate the wealth and depth of the town."

Never bothering to knock, Ron barged into the office with a long list of ideas for the bourgeoning company. Filling the silent air with one line jokes, Tony looked up from the computer, and began laughing hysterically.

"I think I will use that one when comedian leaves the stage."

"Like I said Tony, you got to practice those jokes and don't rush them. You can be real funny," advised Ron.

"How about, if you can think you can do it or if you think you can't do it, then you are probably right."

"Frankly, I think that will go way above the heads of our audience. Keep the jokes simple." Changing the subject, they reviewed the calendar, rehearsals for the variety show, meeting with a potential sponsor, and an appearance at a press party for the opening of a headliner show.

"Ugh, I will hardly have time to breathe today."

Because gathering sponsors was paramount, insuring the security and future of the show, Tony took chances on innovative products, and produced the very first ad for, "The Vapor Dome" a revolutionary change to traditional microwave cooking. Endorsed by Chef Josette, the inventor Georges Pralus, a world famous French chef, who doesn't speak a word of

English, Tony produced and directed the info-commercial. The patented design, picked up on the concept of the microwave by using a dome covered container, the food is cooked using water vapors. Josette demonstrated how canned products, once a big no-no can, be cooked safely, cheaply, and quickly, using the new dome. The only way one could appreciate the art of producing a commercial was to bear witness to the shooting; the key character spoke no English, the product so unique that every detail had to be deliberately demonstrated, and the banter between the two chefs made filming a very lengthy and exhausting process. Each scene was taped time and time again, with dialogue reformatted to fit each portion of the demonstration. When the editing was finally completed, they had created a masterpiece, bringing into American homes a new product that would revolutionize the concept of microwave cooking, quite a nice legacy to add to Tony's advertising company's resume.

Exhausted, Tony dropped Georges off at the airport, praying he would have a safe return home and then he and Josette drove across the desert to their retreat in Los Angeles.

"I have made plans for dinner tonight sweetheart," cooed Josette. "I'm sorry the filming was so difficult, you know I'm not a television person." Kissing him on the neck she promised him a weekend of solitude to recover from the rantings of two stubborn chefs. The afternoon sun glared directly into his line of vision as he pulled into the familiar road winding up to the top of the hill. Neither one would ever tire of the panoramic view of the ocean, the morning cloak of marine clouds, or the brilliantly lit orange and rose colored sunsets. Easing the car to a stop, she clicked open the garage door, gathered their two puppies, and swung open the plantation shutters, just as the sun was dipping into the Pacific Ocean. Flipping on a jazz CD, Tony kissed the back of her neck and held her as they watched the last glimmer of daylight sink into the horizon.

"Ah no time for that, we have a dinner date at my favorite Bistro, and Tony, if you think about it, can you toss your guitar into the car, you know how my friends can get," she said. Yes, Tony knew about her friends and he also knew about his own friends. When people found out he was an entertainer, they wanted him to entertain them, but that was impossible since he didn't carry around a full orchestra, or a director, so he learned to improvise creating what he called a performance within a performance.

"Look, guys, I can hardly perform as you can see I don't have band." From the corner, he would grab his guitar, and sing a few bars of a song, or tell cryptic jokes so they could have a tiny slice of his act.

"That was always just enough. I would leave everyone entertained, without realizing they had just seen a performance," he joked. There probably isn't a place that Tony wouldn't sing or perform; it is his passion and his lifelong profession. Give him an audience and he will be there, singing his heart out. For him it's more than performing, it's what he can share with others, and how he is able to bring happiness into people's lives. Whatever he gives to his audience, he gets back in the form of love, loyalty, and the knowledge he has made them happy. For a short while, he transports people to a higher plateau, brushing away their problems, their sicknesses, their fights, and their anger. Life becomes sweet and pleasurable as his voice resonates a genuine passion for music, the sounds of his soul.

In the morning he begins again with a regimen of exercise, juicing, plotting and planning, his mind never stops working, but from the sharp growls of the two dogs, he has forgotten their breakfast. Freshening up their water dishes, he extracts a roasted chicken from the refrigerator, slicing off several tiny bits and dropping them into an empty bowl. Standing on hind legs, they jump up and down, gobbling up the food in record time. While Josette runs off to the downtown bakery, he is left alone with his computer and cell phone: all the tools he needed to conduct business.

That morning he had one thing on his mind, an upcoming convention, one that had given him the opportunity to perform, "Las Vegas The Show," at the largest venue in the city. He had spent years putting the production together, creating the music, the video shots, the script, and the stage set. He had competed with hundreds of other acts and it was selected to give the main presentation at the upcoming convention. The media production end of his multifaceted company allowed him entrée into the yearly convention of NAPTA, an association of media producers who mix, mingle and network to get the maximum exposure for whatever new concept they are trying to promote. Along with producers is a long, "A" list of stars who frequent the show, which that year, just happened to be in Las Vegas. Tony was thrilled at winning the opportunity to sell his show to producers from across the country. Picking up the cell phone, he checked in with the office staff, jotted down messages, and checked with the cameramen making sure there were plenty of fresh batteries for their next location shoot. His next call was to Robin Leach, a longtime friend he had met through the association. When he told Robin his show had been selected to be showcased at the convention, it was no surprise to his dear friend.

"Robin had been a great influence on how I conducted myself, I loved his interviews, and the way he spoke to people was filled with genuine honesty. His show, 'Life Styles of the Rich and Famous,' added a lot of class to prime time television and was one of the true reality programs offered at that time. In several ways I emulated many of his techniques."

The next morning he kissed Josette, picked up the younger of the pups and raced across the desert to put the finishing touches on the production. An hour and a half long, every moment was filled with song, dance, humor, and history, incorporating a wide variety of media and everything had to work together perfectly, this was live theatre. He only got one chance and it had to be perfect. The concept of the production was a history of Las Vegas using song, dance, humor, rare film footage and photos. From the first bang on the drum, until a quick bow at the end, the audience was riveted to their seats as they watched the story unfold. It was a hit with the conventioneers, as it had been with the tourists who had seen the show in a much smaller venue. Later, Robin came backstage and told Tony how much he had loved the show and how impressed he was with the concept of the presentation.

"For me, that was one of the greatest compliments I could've received. A man whose work I had admired for years was telling me how much he had admired my work."

Writing with David Brenner, the two created a unique historical view of Sin City, highlighting each decade with its particular scenarios that helped frame the place, Las Vegas would take on the American landscape of tourism. Commencing in 1829, each period was introduced by a celebrity and portrayed through a variety of genres: from the initial downtown hot springs discovered by an Indian tribe, by 1905 the town was simply a short train stop to pick up provisions on the way to California. In the 1930s the city and state drastically changed several laws allowing gambling, building of the massive Hoover dam, and quickie divorces. It was those three changes, plus the invention of air-conditioning, that allowed the city to explode into a tourist destination, and has remained so ever since.

Tony had woken up at an unusually early hour, and drove over to the office. It was quiet, the sun was slowly ascending up the horizon. He sat fretting over the next show, the song list, and who the next new sponsor would be: when the phone rang. It was barely six, who would be calling at this hour?

"Is this Tony Sacca?" asked a strange voice.

"Why yes."

After introducing herself, she explained that his high school was honoring him and she extended an invitation for him to come home to Philadelphia and receive the award for High Achievement. The air fare would be taken care of and the ceremony would be held at the auditorium.

Providing the date and time, he checked his calendar, blocked out the time and accepted the invitation. Going home to South Philadelphia just to be honored by his classmates and the city meant a great deal to him. He felt like the local boy, making good and returning to his roots. Rearranging his hectic schedule, his office assistant made the necessary changes to allow him the opportunity to leave the business for a couple of days.

Stepping outside the busy airport, he caught a breath of that familiar eastern air filled with a cool dampness, he was home, but on a good note. Spending the night in his old bedroom, he and Millie prepared for the big day. Driving the family car, which had become a true relic, they made it safely to the school, parking at the edge of the curb. A space had been reserved in his name.

"See that mom, I guess they all think I'm pretty special." Proudly walking up the steps, he was greeted by the principal, and a gaggle of friends and classmates, as they guided him into the auditorium. As he looked around, he was amazed how every seat was filled, and the applause he received as he walked onto the stage to receive the award. Immaculately groomed and dressed, he was the epitome of success, he was the person everyone wanted to become: famous, successful, and happy. After presenting the plaque, several classmates reminisced, drawing laughter, and tears as they remembered Robert as well. The orchestra had practiced two songs and was anxiously anticipating accompanying the star. They handed over the microphone, and Tony turned to the kids and asked if they were ready, raised his hands, and began singing. Up on their feet, the audience gave him a well-deserved standing ovation.

"I was truly humbled by the experience and surprised at how many of my classmates showed up. It was fun to see how everyone had changed, especially all my old girlfriends." Carrying the award in his hand, he escorted his mom back to the car.

"I'm so proud of you. I love you so much and I am so happy that you received this award, you deserve it son. Just look at all of your accomplishments."

"Mom, stop, you make this sound more like a eulogy. I'm happy, I love my profession, and I know I'm lucky to be doing what I love, I only wish Robert were here to accept his half of the award." He opened up the car window, thrust the award in his left hand raised it toward the sky,

"This one is for you brother. I wish you could've been there with me today. Oh, by the way, I caught a look at one of your old girlfriends and she got real fat."

Louie Anderson with Tony on the set of the
first of many interviews with Tony in 1988

Las Vegas Rocks ®

1959 – "Welcome to Fabulous Las Vegas" sign is created by Betty Willis. The Nevada State Legislature creates the Nevada Gaming Commission.

Tony spoke with George Burns, 95, when he appeared at Caesars Palace

CHAPTER 17

He would make one more trip back to South Philly, the inevitable happened and Millie, Tony's beloved mother, passed away. He had been a good son, doting, caring, loving and if and when she needed something he was there for her. She lived into her mid-eighties until her body and mind were ready to go. He packed his bag, and clung to the cell phone, giving an array of orders to his trusty secretary. He would be gone for a few days, there was so much to do, but he had Marie, his sister to lean on and assist with the arrangements. She would share in all that had to be done; he could count on her for that. His cluttered schedule rarely left time for him to take a breath, let alone a week off, but for this, he would put his entire life and business on hold while he attended to family matters. When the plane door slammed shut, his eyes welled up with tears, it was final, he would never take this trip home again, never see his mom smile while stirring a pot of soup, never feel her comforting arms wrapped around his back, never get another kiss on the cheek, or another birthday present. He was going to miss her, and the unconditional love she had showered upon him since the day he was born. Always the first to brag about his achievements, she ignored his failures and mistakes. She wasn't perfect, but then neither was he. He closed his eyes and forced himself to remember the happy times: the summers at the beach, the family dinners, Christmas holidays, and the pride in her face when he and Robert would perform on stage.

As he waited in line for a taxi, he shivered. November in Philadelphia was usually gray, damp and rainy, and that evening was no different. He dropped a few bills in the front seat of the cab, grabbed his one bag, loosened the handle, and dragged it up the front porch. After decades, his key still worked as he slipped it into the familiar brass lock. There wasn't a sound, it was pitch dark, and a stale smell permeated the air. He draped his top coat on the lounge chair, flicked on a couple of lights, went into the kitchen, grabbed a glass, and poured himself some red wine. He had so much do to, yet he was in no condition mentally to do anything. How was he supposed to wrap up his mother's life in a few days? He answered his cell phone and was relieved to hear his sister's voice. She would be arriving shortly and then they would take care of things together; neither would be alone in this arduous and somber process. As he sipped on the wine, he found his way to his childhood room, stretched out on the bed, and starred up at the ceiling. It would be the last time he would sleep there. He guarded every sacred memory: it would be all he would have to cling onto until he joined his brother. Maudlin thoughts rarely, if ever, entered his head, but he had to accept the finality of the situation and allow himself to grieve.

The priest was called and the siblings made all the proper arrangements, but even in death things didn't go as planned. A large crowd had gathered at the local Catholic Church for morning mass, and prayers, and then they took their places in the funeral procession and began the forty minute drive to the gravesite outside of the city. The limo procession was long, a tribute to the multitude of friends and the rich life Millie had lead. Seated in the third car, Tony and Marie reminisced while they anticipated the eulogies they were about to make, and wondered how the priest would handle the ceremony. Oblivious to their surroundings, the limo had come to a full stop and for a few minutes they didn't notice anything unusual, but the waiting continued.

"I rolled down the window and saw several policemen had stopped the procession, we looked at each other shrugging our shoulders, as this should never happen. A few minutes later the reason for this was explained as we saw the presidential seal and the American Flag on a limousine pass by, it was President Obama. Of all days and times for this to happen, I saw this as a fitting tribute to our mom, a final salute from the country she loved."

Reported by Vegas Media, Jackie Brett's column began:

"Mama Sacca Receives A Presidential Drive By. Local entertainer Tony Sacca was in Philadelphia, PA this week to bury his mother Carmella 'Millie" Sacca, who passed away Friday, Nov. 4, 2011. On Tuesday, Nov. 8, 2011, when the funeral procession was going from the church to Holy Cross Cemetery in Yeadon, Pa. around 11:00 am, the procession was stopped by the police, which never happens. Everything came to a complete halt and Sacca could see helicopters hovering above and police everywhere. For a minute he thought they might be under attack or something, however it turned out President Obama was traveling with all his security to the Head Start School in Yeadon. Pa. Sacca said he could see the president's vehicle with the American flags on it as it passed in front of his mother's vehicle. The funeral procession was then made to take a detour that resulted with the funeral party being 20 minutes late to the cemetery. The real topper from this adventure was that the priest didn't even wait, which resulted with a relative singing a song and the family saying their good-byes to their dearly departed. What are the odds? It turns out the school was practically next to the cemetery."

When they walked up to the gravesite, the priest had vanished, too impatient to wait for the casket.

"I can't believe I have to wing my own mother's burial." Luckily the funeral director had seen this occur before and knew exactly what to do. A couple of cousins sang psalms, the funeral director said a couple requisite prayers and they all piled backed into the procession heading to a reserved hall for the memorial. Almost a two hundred people were gathered and milling around in hushed voices as Tony and Marie walked in. They embraced old friends and family members, and they were handed plates of food and glasses of wine as they circumnavigated through the crowd. Older cousins gave their own eulogies in the form of raising their glasses and toasting her life,

"To Millie, a woman so filled with life and love!"

"To Millie who had to put up with a house filled with noisy kids!"

"To Millie who never learned how to make a marinara sauce!"

"To Millie who was so proud of her kids!"

"To Millie who loved her children unconditionally!" By the time the crowd had finished toasting, they were all a bit tipsy, an awful lot to celebrate for a woman who was loved by so many people. As the crowd dwindled and dispersed into the damp afternoon air, Marie took Tony's hand, it was time to go home for the last time.

As they sat in the living room of their home, brother and sister reflected on the day, Millie's life and, the reality that it was just the two of them.

"I will make you a promise, Marie, I will see to it you have this home, it should stay in our family, forever. I'm sad so sad about mom, but thank God I feel this way because when dad died although I cried, I didn't feel the same. I could never accept his cruelty and the way he beat Robert and me, it was pointless and senseless. We feared him, we didn't understand him until much later when I did forgive him and I came to realize that I loved him very much. I don't think that's what a parent should be. He was laid to rest knowing that his dream had come true, that Robert and I had become successful professional entertainers: but what we never told him was the split, it was enough that mom knew. I relinquished my deeply held grudge, but I just promised myself I would never be like our dad. I get that dad was raised in a completely different time where punishments were corporal, and I also get that a third grade education has little leeway into the understanding of how to reason. He used his brawn and not his brain." Marie had a sympathetic ear, although her dad was cruel, she was never subject to the beatings her brothers received, and in turn she never laid a hand on her own kids.

The doorbell rang, it was the next door neighbors bringing condolences, as well as a hefty casserole of baked ziti. They stood in the doorway for a few moments, offered their prayers, hugged and kissed the siblings, and quickly left.

"I don't think I could eat another thing," Marie said as she sat the food on the kitchen counter, "but let's have some wine." She pulled out two glasses. The doorbell rang again, and again, until the house was packed with well-wishers and a dining table filled with meat sauce, pasta, cakes and bottles of wine. Insisting their friends and cousins remain to help eat the generous amount of home cooked food, the memorial to Millie went on until after midnight. Stuffed and drunk, the siblings made it to their rooms, collapsed onto their respective twin beds, and snoozed off the remnants of the very long day. The next day they would have to deal with harsh matters of disposing of Millie's possessions.

On the long, sad plane ride home, Tony put to good use his philosophy of positive thinking, and remembered only the happy times with his mother and the love she had given him throughout his life. She was always there for him, always loved him, and never gave up her job as the doting mother. He would miss her so, but he was grateful for all that she had given him, her legacy was showing him how to love, and for that he would always be indebted.

When Veteran's Day approached in 2013, Tony honored his parents in a unique way. After his mother had passed away, he and Marie had divided the family photos, but there was one that had stuck out in his mind, a picture of his parents kissing good-bye as Joseph boarded a train heading off to war, while Millie remained at home. At the time, kissing in public was a taboo, but a reporter was at the scene and clicked his camera at the right moment, photographing a rare and poignant memory. The press release read,

"With Veteran's Day approaching on Monday, Nov. 11, entertainer and television host Tony Sacca reflects on a particular family photo of his father, Joseph Sacca a Word War II Veteran Soldier, making national news when Associated Press in 1943 captured his farewell kiss to his then sweetheart, and future wife Millie D'Angelo. Sacca's mother explained that during those days single women did not kiss men out in the open and that her father, was very upset about his daughter being recognized while kissing out in public."

As much as Tony loved performing, producing, and directing, he was always the first one to respond when called to do charity functions. The walls of his office reflect so many of those experiences: besides the Youth Foundation Awards, he received a Certificate of Recognition from the office of the governor and a congressional certificate from the United States House of Representatives for producing, "Entertainment Las Vegas," a certificate for recognition designing and manufacturing the number one souvenir, "Las Vegas Musical Clock", and a certificate of commendation for twenty years of production of, "Merry Christmas Las Vegas," signed by US Senator, Harry Reid. Of all those awards, and more, the one that stood out was his star on the, "Walk of Stars" etched into the cement on Las Vegas Boulevard, February 17, 2008. Congresswomen Shelly Berkley raised a flag for twenty-four hours at the Capital Building in which she gifted the flag to Tony with a certificate of recognition. There are other cities that have a walk of stars, most notably, Los Angeles, but to be recognized in Las Vegas, where entertainers come in from all around the globe, makes the award that much more meaningful.

"I'm not Frank Sinatra, but Governor Gibbons, and the board of directors believed I deserved the recognition. I remember when Bobby Darin's celebration took place at the Hilton Hotel and he asked me to sing his signature song, 'Mack the Knife' at his ceremony. This award is a big deal, and I was humbled by the experience."

The process commences when the foundation meets, nominates, and selects the recipients, who are then notified in writing of the award. A ceremony takes place, for Tony, he decided on Josette's Bistro, where friends, several members of the board, and city officials came together and honored him. There were the requisite short speeches, fraught with endearments and accolades, followed by food and drink and the next morning, cement was torn up and the star permanently embedded into the sidewalk. The stars are lined up from Tropicana north to Sahara, on both the east and west sides of the street, with the availability of installing up to three thousand. Tony is the twenty-third star, and as his name was laid into the sidewalk, his contribution to the city will be immortalized forever. It is quite the adulation.

Tony with his star that was placed on the Las Vegas Boulevard sidewalk

Las Vegas Rocks ®

1960s – During the 1960s a phenomenon, led by Howard Hughes, occurs in Las Vegas. Corporations are building and/or buying hotel/casino properties. They have the capital necessary and the profitability makes entrance into the casino industry extremely attractive. Gambling becomes "gaming" and starts the transition into legitimate business.

Tony performing at his annual "Merry Christmas Las Vegas" TV holiday special

CHAPTER 18

The Live Shows: Life Behind and In Front of the Cameras

Crack open the local paper each Friday and find the Neon, an entertainment magazine burrowed in between two sections of the newspaper that reports all the entertainment in town for the weekend. From headliners at the major casinos, to a single jazz singer at a local pub, everything and everybody is included. The vast array of entertainment genres leaves no one wanting: comedy, singing, dancing, live theatre, concerts from the classic to rock, art shows, cirque, dueling pianos, karaoke, dinner shows, impersonators, magicians, transvestites, ballet, to bull riding, it's all listed with times and locations. The movie section is so small, many theatres stopped advertising. Out-of-towners come for the experiences they can't enjoy at home, they are seeking the unusual and the memorable, which is how Tony fills up the Friday afternoon taping of the live television variety shows. There are a tiny handful of places people can go to experience being part of a live audience during the taping of a nationally televised show. Not only is it fun, but for many, it is an interesting learning experience. The Boulder Station Casino, just a couple of miles east of the strip, provided the ideal place to set up shop. Free, as advertised in the Neon, people come from around the world to take part in the live performance.

To say Tony was a busy performer is an understatement. On the first Saturday in September he performed a one man show, in midweek he began a string of nightly performances at the Feast of San Gennaro, followed by a Friday afternoon taping of his live television show. In 1981, the Las Vegas version of The Feast of San Gennaro was created by Vincent J. Palmisano, who brought a Las Vegas twist to the Italian tradition by adding professional entertainment, amusement rides, fireworks, arts and crafts, and a huge bounty of over 100 food booths. The festival is still around. It runs for four days and attracts thousands of locals and tourists. Upon Palmisano's passing, his nephew, Anthony Palmisano, began carrying on the tradition. After entertaining every night, Tony was exhausted by the time the Sunday night fireworks pronounced the end of the festival.

Not only does an entertainer have to have unprecedented talent, but the stamina to make each performance as exhilarating as the last. The, Las Vegas Rocks Variety Show is produced completely by Tony. He does all the writing, obtains all the sponsors, directs, selects the wardrobes, hires the guests, and creates the stage set. All this and it's an hour show. At the beginning of each week, which for him commences on a Saturday morning, his film editor begins piecing together the live show from the day before. In a quiet dark room, the editor works his magic, splicing the segments of the show into one complete flawless presentation which will be aired the following week: because of the space in time between the live and the broadcast presentation, Tony is careful not to make any jokes or allowances that specify the day. One such faux pas was Friday the thirteenth when he began cracking jokes and then realized the show wouldn't air on that date. The audience was privy to an entirely new set of jokes as the cameramen reshot the opening monologue.

No locally owned and produced show using local crew has ever been aired on nationally syndicated television. Without a doubt there are thousands of shows but none that are a weekly variety originating on a real time basis. Thanks to deregulation instead of four television channels, there are hundreds to select from, and now with the internet, even more to stream. The market for original, innovative programming has become an insatiable serpent that cries out to be fed, but with something exclusive. It hails from Las Vegas, the most sought after adult vacation destination, the name is magic, but so is the host, Tony Sacca, who has put in thirty years hosting, *Entertainment Las Vegas Style.*

Networks are hungry for programming, especially one of a kind, authentic material. There are hundreds of cable and broadcast access stations that are constantly combing the country seeking something new, exciting, and charismatic, and they apparently had found that niche in, Las Vegas Rocks Variety Show. Any guest staying in a hotel can view the program, streamed into their room at two o'clock in the morning, and so it must have been for visiting chiefs of several national broadcast companies when they arrived for a yearly conference. They fell in love with the format, the host, and the eclectic range of talent, they made a call to Tony, offering him air time on over a hundred stations throughout the country, his show could be viewed in half of the population, over fifty million households. To see the stars perform and give intimate details about their talent, piques the interest of tourists and potential tourists. Although this type of show had been tried in the past, others didn't have the savvy, the talent, or the connections to keep a running parade of talented artists taking the stage. Tony's show is based on the local talent, highlighting the personalities never promoted. Once they perform, he has a short interview where the audience is privy to their backgrounds, but the emphasis is on their performing art. The show is a reflection of where television is going: reality. After scoping the local talent, Tony highlighted them in a way no one else has ever done. It is a one of a kind, Las Vegas based, reality show, where the world captures a glimpse at the vast array of talent and entertainment the city has to offer and serves as a vehicle for budding stars. After the performer is finished, Tony takes the artist aside and talks about their background, how they came to the city and how their talent was nurtured.

The initial concept germinated at the Las Vegas Hilton Christmas Show. The live telecast on the local network was a huge hit,

"No one had ever done Christmas in Las Vegas." Thrilled with the size of the crowd, they remained there for two weeks, later migrating to the East Side Cannery, until the production found a permanent home at Boulder Station.

"The hardest part of producing television was finding sponsors; I've been on television so long that I didn't realize my credibility. I have the longest running show in the city and I am the longest running host on any production in town. When I picked up the phone, people responded. The financial back bone was set in place, and the show could go on."

Drafting the productions, he provides the stage direction and the lighting specialist the scenes within the show and how he wants each one to be treated, down to the last note at the closing song. Through almost three decades of practice, he knows exactly what he wants and needs, and the crew, who has been at his side for years, has an understanding of his wishes. The opening scene is filled with bright colors and laser beams bouncing into the starlit night, as the camera pans the Las Vegas skyline. The viewer is immediately immersed into the theme of the show, Las Vegas: the excitement, the entertainment, and the extravagant casinos built for gambling and having a great time.

Scripting comes next, as he, along with a joke writer, create just the right wording to complement the guests, as well as current happenings in the city. Scouring the paper, researching city calendars, talking to media, he has a handle on the heartbeat of the city and its happenings, and he brings this to the show. Sometimes it's not a guest, but an event which he promotes, regardless, the show is all about the city, its personalities, and the effervescent lifestyle.

At the edge of his desk sits piles of CDs, head shots and promotional materials for hopeful talent who want a chance at being seen on his show. Selecting the guests, he picked up the phone calling agents, or the agents called him, booking engagements. Creating a balance between permanent and artists passing through, he creates the line-up, and it is always varied. With an hour slot, which boils down to forty-five minutes of air time, he mixes all genres of performance art so there is no conflict or competition between the guests. He then makes his selections of songs to open and close the show, and sometimes he interacts with performers. He isn't afraid to laugh at himself at the expense of his guests, he just seeks a great show each and every week.

Selecting his wardrobe and the costuming, he designs the sets, hiring staff handymen to craft the props. Working with Michael T, the musical director, they pull charts, writing and rewriting the songs and background music. Keys, rhythms, harmonies and beats are altered based upon the singer's needs and voice. To be able to pick up a new song, writing all the parts for the six piece band within a day or two notice, takes years of expertise, and the talent of great musicians.

The Santa Fe Station Casinos' marque, standing over fifty feet tall, announced Tony Sacca's, headliner show. As the audience walked into the crowded Chrome showroom, they sat quietly, as a video of many of the performer's interviews with world class stars was played. This was a warm-up introduction to the artist. Displaying cryptic interviews with The Temptations, Lou Rawls, Gladys Knight, David Brenner, Rita Rudner,

Anthony Quinn, Celine Dion, Robin Williams, and Mel Brooks the fans were treated to the celebrity aura surrounding Tony Sacca: no one in Las Vegas had been privy to as many interviews with international stars, as the star of the show himself. The eight piece band warmed up, and from the dark curtains sprang Tony, clad in an Italian black tuxedo, he boasted a wide smile as he surveyed the packed house. He grabbed the microphone and began with, "For Once In My Life," followed by songs from several decades and genres. A melody of Frankie Valli's greatest hits, with the four women singing and dancing in perfect unison, would have made Valli proud. Interspersed with his solo numbers were the Saccettes: three, gorgeous svelte singers and dancers who added a Las Vegas review style to the performance. The hour and a half show was filled with costume changes, and such an abundance of variety of songs and dances that it left the audience fiercely entertained. As he took his final bows to a standing ovation, he darted back stage for a brief moment and then mingled with the crowd. He thanked people for coming, shook their hands, kissed his friends, and beamed with delight for the kudos warmly expressed.

What is the barometer by which true talent is measured? It rarely comes in a package like Tony. He bubbled over with genuine talent: a great singer, joke teller, and audience appeaser, his passion emulated from the bottom of his feet to the top of his head. As loved ones surrounded him, his eyes cast to others in the audience, people he didn't know, people who had gone to see an international talent. He excused himself, briefly broke away from the tight circle, extended his hand to strangers, and humbly thanked them for attending the show. Tony loved his audiences as much as he loved his music. The last song of the evening is a reflection of his heart and soul: "What a Wonderful World."

At 1:30 pm on Friday the 13th, the croupiers annoyingly turned to see the gamblers fleeing their tables jockeying in line to get into the, *Tony Sacca's, Las Vegas Rocks Variety*, live television show. Left alone with just their dice, and chips, they watched the long human chain stream into the Railhead Theatre. Mostly seniors and vacationers, when the glass doors opened the next two hours would prove lonely for the usually busy table game activity; everyone was there to see and be a part of a live television show to be broadcast across the country. One vacationer in his late fifties, standing next to his wife, had brought a pink talking stuffed animal he had purchased from the online store. Holding it into the air, he made it talk and squeak, he was proud of his souvenir and brought it with him whenever he returned to Las Vegas. Confessing it was his good luck charm, he was convinced it had paid off in spades at the roulette wheel.

The medium sized theatre was truly a venue to experience. With its highly polished dark oak floors, gray walls, contemporary glass, chrome bar, circular cocktail tables, and plush black chairs it was not only pleasing but comfortable for the audience. The lighting and sound systems were state of the art, as well as the stage equipment, and the crew running the production.

Cameras in hand, cell phones turned off, the audience grabbed seats at the front of the theatre and sat quietly waiting for the performance. There were six cameramen primed, standing at the ready to tape the live show. Ron Garrett, the master of ceremonies and well known comedian/deejay, warmed up the audience prior to the actual performance. Once he got everyone laughing, he then gave a short lesson in how to respond during the course of the show. Explaining the audience became part of the live show, everyone responded diligently to his simple directions. It was fun, exciting and it was easy to see why there were so many return participants. Ron counted down, "five, four, three, two, one" and the audience exploded into clamorous applause as the blue velvet curtains separated revealing the eight piece Michael T. Band, and the star, Tony Sacca. Microphone in hand, and his two back-up singers at his side, the brass began wailing to the Pointer Sisters', "I'm So Excited." Watching the show from home it's impossible to glean the energy bouncing off the performers and musicians as they play the upbeat tempo classic song. The experience was rejuvenating and exhilarating as the audience ingested the high spirit permeating the theatre.

The first show of the season Tony pulled in world famous stars to share the stage, making for an unforgettable experience. Lena Prima was the first outstanding guest of the night as she sang, "Jump and Jive" a song made famous by her dad, Louis, the king of swing. Her voice along with the eight piece band was reminiscent of the era, giving an authenticity to her impeccable performance. The entire audience shared the effervescence of the music as they clapped and swayed to the music. Bringing the audience back to reality, there was a break, while the broadcast stations advertised a myriad of products. To keep things going during commercial breaks Tony told a series of Friday the 13th jokes written by Cliff Lawrence, best known as the joke writer to Jay Leno's Tonight Show. At once Tony stopped in the middle of a one-liner, the live show would not be broadcast for two weeks, when Friday the 13th had long disappeared.

"Cut the jokes," he yelled to the cameraman. Things would have been fine for everyone in the audience except for one individual, Cliff, who had spent the day before creating twenty jokes commemorating the ominous day. Miffed, he swore off Friday 13th jokes forever.

"Hey," said Tony to the man in the front row, "It's okay to blow your nose, we are still at commercial break. Laughing he took Tony at his word and loudly blew into a handful of tissues. Again, Ron began the countdown and the audience became hushed as they received their cue to applaud. Introducing the next act, Terry Forsythe's Tribute Band to the Temptations, five men bounced onto the stage, and began singing the songs of the Temptations. Not only were they dressed and groomed like the originals, but the choreography, and the voices, were as identical as it gets when imitating a group. Wearing black sequin jackets, black tuxedo pants, pristine white shirts with red bow ties, their energetic singing was electrifying. Everyone was having the time of their lives listening and clapping to the tunes the Temptations made famous. When they finished with, "Ain't Too Proud To Beg," and, "My Girl," it was as if the audience was privy to the original music. The falsetto and the harmonies were right on the mark.

As with all live shows, not all things go as planned. Louie Anderson, a world famous comedian, who has made his home in Las Vegas, didn't appear, "He called in fat." In reality, Louie was out of town and rescheduled for the following week, a longtime friend, he always kept his promises. Not a worry for a professional like Tony who filled the spot singing an extra duet with one of the guests. He brought out an old friend from Philadelphia, Philly Cuzz (Philip Battaglia), who just happened to be vacationing in town. The two had been friends since childhood, "and they didn't get any more loyal than Philly." As a kid he would join Tony and Robert in the basement of their home while they practiced music. Initially, they had met at a summer swim club, each with their own bands, Philly was playing with the Emanos and Tony was with the twins. They never lost touch, but after high school graduation, Philly went to Temple University to study music, and Tony continued touring. When he called and said he was coming out for a visit, Tony insisted he stay at his home, which, upon retrospect turned out for the best. Tony got his missing act, and Philly got a rare opportunity to perform.

A couple of years later, always looking for gigs, Philly had a friend, John, who asked him to play keyboards and sing at some of the local coffee houses in Philadelphia, not a high point in his career. At the time, Philly was in no position to turn down the offer, but he had another buddy who mentioned the Sacca Twins were looking for a keyboard player. When he made the phone call, they remembered meeting at the swim club, and immediately offered him the position. Better money, better act, and much better women, he happily took the job, especially since they were booked at the 500 Club, a well- known night club.

That Memorial Day weekend the band brought their instruments to the beach town, stored them at the 500 Club, and put a deposit on a summer rental. They were set for the tourist season. Cruising around the city, they heard an announcement on the radio, "The 500 Club had burnt to the ground." They were in shock, not only had they lost their gig, but all of their instruments. To make matters worse for Philly, a month or so later, he turned on the late night television and who did he see? His friend John who took Darryl Oates as his partner, was becoming one of the most famous duos in pop music; Hall & Oates. The balance of the summer became pretty much a wash. They ended up playing some short gigs in Wildwood, and in the fall, Philly returned to college while the twins forged ahead with their touring.

Time travel three decades or so later and the two are still bosom buddies. Philly, tall and blessed with a thick head of light brown hair and arrestingly handsome looks, sang a new song he had both written and recorded. How fortuitous, visiting his old buddy and ending up on the show, a perfect platform for a wide audience to hear his original song. The tune was a throwback to the melodies of the early sixties, romantic and catchy. Since Philly was a perfectionist, and the band didn't know the score, the stage crew popped in the background track and he sang live while the band pretended to play their instruments. Sitting in the audience, it was fun watching the musicians smile while they pretended to play the music. There is nothing like live entertainment.

The show closed with Tony, The Saccettes, and Philly singing, "Together," before they left the stage to a standing ovation, while Tony thanked, and re-thanked his guests for appearing. There is no doubt why this show has seen continued success, Tony is genuine, giving, and the passion for his music shines through every moment on the live show. His love for the city, for music, and zest for life exudes an energy few performers ever have or can sustain. He thanked the audience again, and reminded them to keep Las Vegas green,

"Gamble!" he said.

Giving back to the community has been a part of his regiment for decades. The city has done a lot to maintain and sustain Tony's career and in turn Tony has done a lot for Las Vegas helping to put it on the map as the entertainment capital of the world. Performing at the Feast of San Gennaro is one of his favorite charities. Beginning on Tuesday afternoon through Sunday evening, when the fireworks mark the end of the festival, he performs for a vast audience. Bringing his band and back-up singers, they put on a professional show. Not only does Tony provide entertainment, he procures all of the talent for five hours of nightly music for the entire festival. Always crowded, the festival is one of the biggest happenings off the strip. Originally the festival was located in empty, dust laden lots but as it grew, it finally found a permanent home at the edge of a mall where the parking was ample and the space vast enough to hold the entire carnival experience. The one variable the festival could always count on was dry warm weather, perfect for trekking out as dusk arrived around 6:00 pm. Even as people parked their car blocks away, the smells from the Italian kitchens filled the air, adding an excitement and anticipation to the experience. Paying a nominal fee, the main entrance was lined with rows upon rows of local concession stands making homemade Italian foods. Meatballs and sausages and pepper heroes, pizza of every size shape and flavor, pasta with a variety of sauces, and of course funnel cakes or fried dough sprinkled with powdered sugar. Although there were several small booths interspersed between the carts selling beer and hard liquor, very few were imbibing. People came to eat, having a beer that was something they could do at home. Beyond the seemingly endless line of food lies the midway, teeming with rides. Brightly lit, the Ferris wheels, and twenty other assorted rides decorated the night skies with hundreds of twinkling lights. At seven o'clock the live entertainment commenced. A full band filled most of the stage, instantly becoming alive with singers, comedians, and musicians, with performances lasting until midnight. Unlike other cities, because of the abundance of local talent, when going to these events the local talent is international talent.

For the privilege of living in Las Vegas, Tony has abundantly given back to its citizenry. The time consuming festival rakes in tons of money for local charities and thanks to his devotion, it is not only a successful undertaking, but it draws people into the town from all over. Even at Manhattan's lower east side, the festival, although some would say the pizza is better, is not as large or fraught with as much entertainment as Sin City. The shining star of the Italian community, this twice yearly event raises enough money to sustain most of the financial needs of a wide array of charities.

It would be hard to fathom Tony was able to meet the next live Friday afternoon show with the same gusto and impact as the last, but in fact it each show had a life of its own. The following Friday the line waiting to grab a seat at the Railhead Theatre inside Boulder Station was just as long, but the audience was new save for Tony's cronies who would follow him to the ends of the earth. Once he had befriended a person, they became a part of his extended family.

With Ron Garret at the helm, he again took over the reins of announcing and cuing the audience as to their parts in the live television show. Today he gave a practice lesson on laughing, but when the comedians arrived for their portion of the show, the practice had been unnecessary. As the band played the opening them song, and the announcer said,

"From the Entertainment Capital of the World," the curtains parted and out strutted the star singing, "Somewhere Beyond the Sea," made popular by Bobby Darin. Wearing a gray silk suit with matching shirt and tie, he appeared alight with energy as he proudly announced the list of performers. Tony portrayed the impression that he was not only excited to have the lineup, but thrilled they had acquiesced to come on his humble show, (which isn't so humble at all).

"Las Vegas is the greatest town around for three reasons," he commented, "Number one, it has gambling, number two, quickie divorces: just live here six weeks and the divorce is final. Number three, the building of Hoover Dam." To add to the fact the city truly is the entertainment capital of America, Tony has done a lot to spread the idea that Las Vegas was/is the most wonderful town in the USA.

The stage crew, who always stood in the background, took their jobs seriously and was there not only to professionally film the production but to assist the performers in whatever was needed to expedite a perfect presentation. The six cameramen stood at their cameras, never leaving them unattended for a moment. At the first commercial break, a technician rushed to help the left cameraman fix a tiny problem, and it was on with the show.

The opening guest was Rich Natole, a young comedian and impressionist who immediately inspired laughter, with his jokes and hilarious impersonations. After his act, the host graciously thanked him and plugged Rich's act at the Plaza Hotel and Casino, where he was a warm up act for Louie Anderson. Rich first turned to Tony and then the cameras, and publicly thanked Tony for the opportunities he gave to all of the Las Vegas entertainers to be seen and heard on syndicated television: a genuine and endearing gesture. As the applause rang out the next act was introduced, the famous comedian, Louie Anderson, who made his permanent home in Las Vegas. They kissed each other, and Tony escorted Louie to center stage while he recited just a few of Louie's accomplishments. Best known for his standup comedy, he had the audience in stitches with his newest clot of jokes, all related to losing weight.

"I live to eat," he admitted as he continued with the fat jokes. Arsenio Hall had just opened his latest evening talk show and Louie was set to appear. He used the Las Vegas Rocks Show, to test out the jokes and from the rave reaction, he was sure to proceed with the fat material. Louie who topped the scales at well over four hundred pounds, had done a short series television show, "Splash," which had performers diving off a ten meter board into an Olympic swimming pool. The show sought humor as well as a diversity of celebrities, so Louie took the job and told the audience it became his inspiration to losing weight. There was a standing ovation at the end of his act, as Tony reentered the stage, clapped and laughed, and then kissed his guest and escorted him off the stage. The respect, warmth and love those two men shared for each other was obvious, and the audience soaked it all in, how rare to see men show such genuine emotion. To the audience witnessing the action live, the raw emotions and the underlying nuances are seen, heard, and felt. There is something lost in translation when the show airs on TV: nothing is more exciting than watching it unfold before your eyes.

Next, a local group, The Phat Pack, who had assembled from three diverse points on the globe, sang two classical songs in an operatic style. The notes the three men hit were not only extraordinary in pitch, but volume. Their voices filled the theatre and bounced off the ceiling, the floors, and into the audience's ears. The song they sang, "Night of a Thousand Nights Leading to Heaven's Door," succinctly described the quality of their voices, utterly heavenly. When the three men departed the stage, a subtle fog, coming from the roof of the stage slowly immersed the entire theatre creating an ambiance of a small kitschy nightclub. Tony closed the show with Frankie Valli's, "Can't Take My Eyes off of You," gazing directly at Josette, the love of his life.

The following Friday was an eclectic commemorative show, highlighting Tony's fifty years in the business. Joe Krathwohl, known as, "The Birdman," who had been preforming on the strip for years, held an emerald green parrot on his left arm, it began to squawk and then said,

"Hello, pretty girl," followed by simple sayings of, "peek a boo," and the sounds of kissing. Since the parrot was in an unusual environment with brilliant colored lights flickering on and off, it lost its cues and began reciting the beginning of the act. The audience was roaring with laughter. Live, things didn't always go as planned, but the act was absurdly entertaining, no one would ever forget that parrot. As Joe tried to collect the faltering bird, he finally got the parrot to sing, "Happy Birthday," and, "Old McDonald's Farm." Sweat pouring from his face, Joe put the misbehaved parrot into his cage and brought out a twenty three year old Condor who's only job was to sit graciously on the trainer's arm while he explained the species and the fact the breed was almost extinct. Joe explained that condors are vultures and the band best behave because the bird had his eye on the drummer. With a roaring applause, the bird flew off backstage as the host returned to center stage thanking Joe for his presentation. The problem arose when the condor began screeching loudly in an unusual harsh chirp and overtaking the conversation between its trainer and the host. Finally Tony yelled out, "That bird sounds like my ex-wives," which put the final stamp of the act as nothing short of hilarious. From there the production went straight to commercial while Ron Garrett, the MC, screamed out, "can someone get a mop, we have to clean up all this bird shit off the stage." There was no doubt, the audience was treated to the best of humor, some of which was rehearsed and some which was off the cuff, most of which would never see the light of day after the final editing.

The next act had been on the strip for years, reserved for bachelorette parties and women who wanted to get out of their homes and have a great time, "Thunder Down Under," an Australian strip troop. Each one a hunk with six pack abs, they pranced around the stage to the western song, "Save a Horse Ride a Cowboy." Before they began dancing they announced a disclaimer that the performance was rated for the general audiences and this wasn't their true Las Vegas act. In spite of not completely disrobing, they were great dancers, candy for the eyes, and when Tony decided to join the troop halfway through the song, it became incredibly funny. There was the host of the show, at sixty something, sporting a black cowboy hat, black vest, tight blue jeans and boots, dancing with the strippers, and disrobing both his hat and vest.

The mood reversed with the crooning of Jerry Tiffe, known for his Frank Sinatra impersonation. Tall and lanky, his voice was smooth as silk as he sang, "That's Life," leaving the audience in awe of his ability to imitate the original sounds flawlessly. Kelly Clinton, a stunning red head, who headlined her own show, belted out a humorous song about her lust for bald headed men. This was followed with the Motown sounds of, "Spectrum," singing a melody of Frankie Valli songs. Dressed in bright red jackets, with sequin embellishments, sparkling white tuxedo shirts, and black bow ties, they exploded with energy on the stage. There was no doubt the last act of the show was truly sensational: Sidro's Armada, a classically trained Spanish guitarist. With just a keyboardist and a singer, his brilliant guitar playing brought the audience up out of their seats for a standing ovation .His nimble fingers strummed the guitar with adeptness and speed unlike anyone else, creating a full bodied melodic sound. It was brilliant.

Tony thanked the guests and closed the show with a song he had written and produced, "Las Vegas, the Greatest Town Around." And he meant every word of that song. A bittersweet moment, he quietly said,

"I wish my mom and brother were here to see this commemorative show," and then love of his life, Josette, proudly walked onto stage and handed him a large spray of deep red roses. Tony didn't cry, he would save that for later, he would cry out of sadness for missing his brother and he would cry for joy that he had been given a chance at love. His passions consumed him, making him the performer that everyone loved and could relate to. Genuine, endearing, kind, and altruistic, people were drawn to him and once allowed into his circle of friends, it was like a spider's web: no one ever left.

Orange and black balloons marked the season of Halloween when the crowed streamed into the Railhead Theatre and took seats near the stage. Another packed crowd, everyone was buzzing with anticipation for the imminent appearance of the Mayor. Armed with water and a variety of freshly mixed alcoholic beverages, the crowd was prepared for the duration of the filming which notoriously ran over the scheduled hour. In so many ways it seemed as though a hex was thrown onto the show, with most everything going a bit awry. Tony appeared in a bold gray plaid jacket, and failed to remember the guests appearing on the line-up, but with a little coaching from Ron Garrett, his announcer and sidekick, they re-taped his entrance three times. Live, the humor was reality blasphemy, there was so much the world missed when unable to see the host of the show falter and then recover with off the cuff jokes.

"I was all hot and bothered when I came out tonight and now I feel like a lover who has already been spent."

There was a ruffling of the black velvet curtain as stage hands emerged totting bar stools for the Mayor, Carolyn Goodman, and her husband, the ex-Mayor, but the problem was the guests were already ensconced on stage, being interviewed by Tony, who from the corner of his eye waved the stage hands off and then underneath his breath wondered how he would edit out that stunt. The three spoke into the microphone for several minutes, and Ron announced that the tape wasn't rolling and none of the presentation had been recorded. They would have to begin again. Carolyn, who was blessed with a great sense of humor, strutted backstage to begin again and then yelled out,

"It's Friday, can we get this done? It's martini time!"

Tony, undeterred with the mess, kept wryly commenting on the value of an excellent film editor. With another rousing round of applause, Mayor Carolyn Goodman, and ex-mayor Oscar Goodman, returned to the stage and during the middle of reading the proclamation, an uninvited comedian, costumed as President Clinton, boldly walked onto the live performance making jokes comparing the Goodman's to the Clintons. Tony kept his cool as his eyes searched for Ron, who would hastily remove the intruder should things turn bad. After two lackluster jokes, he departed, and the presentation continued. Rare, but the cool host was blushing as the proclamation words, "Las Vegas Ambassador of Entertainment" were recited. October 25, 2013 was named the official Tony Sacca Day in the city of Las Vegas. Even though this was his seventh proclamation from the City of Las Vegas, it felt like the first. Smothered with kudos, he was truly humbled by their sincerity and appreciation for his services to the city. Tony turned to the mayor and sang a version of, "The Lady is a Tramp," changing the lyrics to, "The Mayor is a Champ," as a dedication to her, and then he thanked both the Goodman's,

"They make everyone feel so special." Oscar then added to the presentation by knighting Tony as "The Ambassador of Entertainment of Las Vegas," a most auspicious title. In the past, Oscar had given Tony the key to the city and today was another acknowledgement of his services and dedication to Las Vegas. All Tony could think about was how he wished his mom, dad and brother could have been alive to share the award, they had framed his life and he would have loved to have shared that moment with them.

Anthony Rais, a marionettist, was the next guest to take the spotlight, with his startling and rare performance. He stood still and patiently waited for the music to commence, until Tony had to scream out,

"Put on the track!" Another faux pas that would surely be edited out. Using twenty strings, and a profound classical music sound track, he brought the puppet puppy to life, pulling the strings so delicately that it truly seemed real. Anthony even had the puppet blow up a balloon and then sail gracefully through the air, an act never seen before. Later, Tony joined them and sang, "Send in the Clowns," which was his best vocal performance of the day. As he sang to the clown, the emotions captured in his voice were fraught with soul as he brought the audience to another standing ovation.

The performance ended with an upbeat sound as Sam Riddle, a famous western singer and his entire band took over the stage. What Tony hadn't accounted for was the fact it took the band a half hour to set up all of the instruments. Not wanting the audience to become bored he spent the time adlibbing jokes, a talent few could attest to having, and then he grabbed his secret tool, his puppy Coca who was asleep in the dressing room. Getting, "oohs," and, "ahhs," Tony showed off, commanding the dog to pray, and then accepting a slathering of kisses to his cleanly shaven face.

It was worth the wait when Sam appeared in his torn jeans, black cowboy hat, and black western shirt. With one short word, his rich voice filled up the entire room, as he sang two upbeat melodic songs that he had written.

When the audience finally filed, out there were constant sounds of laughter combined with chatter as one gambler summed up the program.

"The mistakes were the best part of the show. I'll be back next week."

And many familiar faces returned the following week as Pia Zadora co-hosted the show with Tony. She was stunningly beautiful in a black sequin ensemble, and she surprised the audience with her loquacious humor and bantering. With memories from her time as a serious actress and ballad singer, it was a refreshing side that few had been privy to see. Since moving to the city, she had taken up residence at Piero's, the most exclusive gourmet Italian restaurant in town, singing several nights a week. After taking a fifteen year hiatus to raise her children, she was itching to get back into the biz. As a child actress, she grew up in Hoboken, New Jersey: she toured with Frank Sinatra, performed in the original, "Fiddler on the Roof," and, "Hairspray," Broadway productions, and acted in several movies. She won a Golden Globe and was nominated for a Grammy: her multifaceted background had led her to a city where all of her talents could be exploited.

As she chatted with Tony, he was quick to respond to her sexual innuendos with sharp witticisms of his own.

"Do you know what Tony spells backward? Y not? You know I have big feet and everyone knows about men with big feet."

But this time Ron who was keenly aware it was a timeout for

commercials, responded,

"I think what you have is a big imagination," which garnered a lot of laughter and lay the topic to rest as the countdown to live began again.

Tony Miranda, the master drummer, was the next performer. He had played with bands around the world: he was renowned, but never selectively displayed for his talent. The applause continued for five minutes straight as he banged away to the Rocky theme. Behind him came Laura Schaffer, a true home grown talent, with a gift for sultry, sensual singing. Home at the Bootlegger, one of the oldest nightclubs in town, she played weekly to a devoted packed house. She was exceedingly beautiful, with a perfect model's shape, when Anthony Bourdain came to town to film his special for CNN, it was she who caught his eye, and accompanied him as he investigated the intriguing spots of the city.

He ended the show with Barry Manilow's, "All The Time," which was a testament to the true talent harbored inside Tony's persona. There was no cheating the camera when his face reddened as he sang the passionate lyrics in the song: he was a believable and credible talent. After fifty years in the business, he never takes a day in his life for granted, nor does he take the audience, the stage hands, his colleagues, crew, or guests for granted. He is genuine to the core, wears his heart on his sleeve, and perhaps that is why he has survived. People simply love him.

The Christmas show was the highlight of the year, particularly 2013, where Denise Clemente was the spotlighted entertainer. The Las Vegas Review Journal paid tribute to the show and to Denise in a lengthy article, running a column on the opening page of the, "Living Section."

"This afternoon, old friends Tony Sacca and Denise Clemente plan to sing, 'Let It Snow' at Sacca's annual, 'Merry Christmas Las Vegas' show in which they have both performed most of the past 27 years. But it never sounded better than it will this time- no matter how it comes out. 'This year is really special to me,' Clemente says. 'If you'd asked me a couple of months ago, I never thought I'd sing again.' After a life threatening heart attack with endless complications, she got her voice back and returned to singing. Sacca's Christmas TV special at 2:00 pm today at Boulder Station is a local TV institution. Part of the money it raises compensates Clemente for lessons she gives to students who don't have the money, but are really interested in singing."

Although the weather may have been frightful across the rest of the nation, in Las Vegas the thermometer read a balmy 62 degrees while the stage hands hurriedly put together the elaborate holiday set. There were several towering evergreen trees, candy canes hung by the chimney, huge toy soldiers, stuffed teddy bears, snowmen, and animated white reindeer threaded with twinkling lights. The plush green velvet curtain, along with the talented lighting effects of the stage director, created the quintessential Christmas backdrop. The packed theatre sat in quiet anticipation as the Michael T. Orchestra warmed up the audience with a melody of Christmas songs. Ron Garrett announced Tony Sacca's 28th, "Merry Christmas Las Vegas Show," and the audience exploded as he buoyantly appeared in a red velvet jacket, bow and vest, singing an upbeat song. The program was dedicated to the Las Vegas Young Entertainers Foundation, which provided instruments and private singing and dancing lessons to underprivileged children.

There was nothing more exciting than to be a part of a live filming of a television show, especially one that would be seen across the nation on NBC, The Retro Station, and hundreds of local cable stations. With an eclectic line-up of entertainers, the program appealed to most everyone who wanted to see the spirit of Christmas on their television sets or streaming on their tablets.

He introduced the marionettist, Anthony Rais, and Tony was kissed by the handmade puppet while he looked directly into the camera wishing for it to become real just like Pinocchio. As Anthony replaced the puppet back in the bag, Tony reached back into the same bag and pulled out a real dog that licked his face and smiled for the cameras. The entire audience, "oohed" and, "ahhed" at the adorable scene: magic had been performed before their eyes. The line-up included a group of the Young Entertainers, singing and strutting to a western carol, Genevieve, a world class singer, Rick Michael, a comedian, and singer/teacher Denise Clemente. After her rendition of Carol King's, "Merry Christmas Darling," she ushered her prime student, Angelo Mulinari, onto the stage. He grabbed the microphone and the bubbling, rising star sang, "All I want for Christmas" with finesse, as he added falsetto and vibrato to enhance the classic tune. The applause rang out for the teen, there was no doubt in anyone's mind that Denise was creating a new star. Pia Zadora added a sultry sound to, "Santa Claus is Coming to Town," and ending the show on a high note, The Bella Strings, a quartet of young women, played electric violins while accompanying the host to another Christmas classic. After he took his final bow, Tony thanked the entertainers, the band, the stage hands, and his right hand assistant.

All was well that ended well, a great season had come to a fruitful ending.

Tony talks to the Saccettes during a show

Las Vegas Rocks ®

1966 – Caesars Palace opened in 1966 with Andy Williams and Phil Richards as the opening entertainment acts. The hotel cost $25 million to build and open, a sum that was quickly made up by the success of the hotel. This is the dawn of the "Las Vegas Mega Resorts."

Tony appears with Chazz Palmintari of A Bronx Tale at the annual San Gennaro festival

CHAPTER 19

There was a less jovial mood when the first show for the new year was in full production mode; syndication would change the viewing spectrum from capturing the local audience to a nationwide audience and everything had to be perfect, timed accurately, and come off as extremely professional. Even though Tony had twenty-eight years of hosting and producing entertainment television under his belt, he too was feeling the pressure of the first show. The band struck the opening notes and Tony bounced out onto the stage singing, "Johnny B. Goode," and thanked the packed audience for coming. The first guest, Darren Dowler, lead singer for, Paul Revere and The Raiders, showed his soulful side by singing a southern blues song while picking on his bass guitar. He grew up in Florida and gravitated to rock and roll, but added comedic impersonations to his act, a rarity for a serious singer. The audience was treated to an original song he had written for his family that will be included in his new release in the late spring of 2012, and his latest is a movie about a group of rock stars. It's moments like that which catapult, Las Vegas Rocks Variety Show into a different realm of the ubiquitous variety shows aired: to be able to witness top talent preforming live, original music, presented first. His performance was so heartfelt that when Darren was finished, the audience stood up and cheered: the song, his style, and voice were ardently stirring, and he had moved the audience to tears. Some had seen Darren perform as the other half of, "The Righteous Brothers," after Bobby Hatfield passed away. As a fitting tribute, Tony and Darren sang, "You've Lost That Loving Feeling," which again brought the audience to their feet, it was exquisitcly performed, but, as things go on live television, the cameras were not rolling and just as the guest had said his good-byes, he was called back to re-sing the song. The second time around was even better than the first, and when Darren started to leave, an audience member shouted out,

"One more time," which made everyone chuckle.

The city boasts several boutique sized theatres, with state of the art lighting and acoustics, which are used by playwrights and producers as springboards for testing out new shows. The cast of, Love Story, a new theatrical production, were the next guests. Two striking women and a talented Italian operatic singer, they previewed several numbers that were part of the program. The play centered around Bill's piano bar, while the singers told the story of love through a series of songs spanning from the 1930s to the present decade: from sad, to humorous, to angry, to tender, all genres of love were included under the umbrella of love. George Dumont's strong vibrato resonated throughout the theatre filling up every inch of space as he sang an Italian classic and a Broadway tune, and then the full cast ended with, "I Want To Know What Love Is," one of the more contemporary numbers in the upcoming original production.

Even though the filming was over, the audience sat quietly and anticipated more entertainment. Tony walked back to center stage, grabbed the microphone, and announced the show was over and they could leave: and that was live television. It was through the magic of editing, that the audiences seated in front of their television sets would know exactly when the show was over, but it was a whole lot more fun to see it live. He smiled and waved good-bye and walked backstage to thank the guests for appearing and for their stellar talent. Once the audience had departed, and the musicians had packed away their instruments, Tony took a moment and returned to the stage. There was no doubt in his mind that the first show would be successful and serve as the standard from which the rest of the season would be compared. His life, and the manner in which he defined his life was wrapped up in the reflection as dubbed, "Las Vegas' Ambassador of Entertainment," and he was determined to prove to himself and the world, his right to the auspicious title. That day, and for the rest of the season, he would offer up preeminent talent, giving not only the city and state, but now the entire country, insight into the hidden treasures laying one layer below the headliners, those whose genius compared to the top names listed on the marquee, but rarely were given the spotlight to shine outside of the venues they were performing.

Most performers never fulfill their dreams of riding the waves to greatness, and seeing their name installed in the walk of stars, or performing at the most prestigious venue in the city, but these have all come true for Tony. Having pure talent was only one of the dozens of attributes paving the way to performing at the Smith Center in Las Vegas. More than raw talent, it's the sustainable audience, a long history of entertaining, and a demand for excellence, which has allowed him the opportunity to showcase his artistry. The ultra-modern facility opened in 2012 is the most esteemed home to the performing arts in the state, nick-named the Carnegie Hall of the West. Situated in Symphony Park, near downtown, the sprawling campus houses several sizes of venues, and caters to a multitude of artists. In March 2013, Tony's show commanded one of the smaller intimate settings for his one man show, backed by Michael T's ten piece orchestra.

After shoring up all the talent for the upcoming variety television show, and placing several cold calls to potential sponsors, Tony heard the front office door click open, and the all too familiar footsteps of Gary Anderson, his musical arranger. Gary slipped into an empty chair, sporting a rare smile as he dropped the finished arrangements onto the cluttered desk. Quietly humming an original arrangement, he waited resignedly for Tony to finish his call, before humming the music even louder.

"All done," Gary announced pointing to the pile, "and ready for the performance of your life. I think you will like how I put the melodies together and changed the tempo on the last couple of songs. We want to go out on a high note, and a strong brass sound. With that ten piece orchestra, I wanted to use their sounds to the fullest extent, and if I must say, I think you will be happy with what I have come up with."

"You know, I'm always happy with what you come up with, now just keep on humming." Tony grabbed the sheet music, got up, and began pacing as he reviewed the song list and the brand new arrangements, and the two of them began humming together.

"I really like what you have done, especially with the additional band instruments, but I think we will need a few extra rehearsals." Tony opened his email and sent a message to Michael T., the bandleader, asking for extra rehearsal times; he knew Michael would respond, it was just a matter of when. Getting the cluster of musicians together when each of them had their own agenda was tough, but they were loyal and they all knew what was at stake for the upcoming performance. The Smith Center was the crowning glory of a lifetime achievement as a performer, regardless of the part they were to play, every instrument and every sound played an important role in insuring the success of the show, they could be counted on, they would all rise to the occasion, even when it meant cancelling shows, or playing at other venues. That Sunday afternoon was carved for Tony Sacca, and they wouldn't let him down at the peak of his career.

Unlike most lounges, the Smith Center's dressing rooms were lavish, comfortable, with adjustable lighting, full length mirrors, and the walls painted in warm shades to act as a calming environment before the headliner took to the stage. Tony glanced in the mirror for the hundredth time and rechecked his hair, straightened his tie, looked at his pants to make sure they were free from dog hair, and then made sure his fly was zipped. Inserted in his pocket was a tiny list of the songs to be performed, he had never needed or used one in the past, but then, he had never played in such a prestigious hall and the small crutch was helpful. The stage manager gently rapped on the door announcing five minutes to curtain time, and his heart raced up a couple of notches. It was show time.

The theatre lights went from dim to black while the band silently took their positions, and then Tony climbed up on a stool, waited for Gary Anderson, his longtime conductor and musical arranger, to commence, nodded, and a single spotlight showered down from overhead. He began by singing his original song, "Listen To My Heart." A powerful love tune, it left the audience in awe as they almost forgot to clap. Beads of sweat trickled down the side of Tony's cheeks, the worst part was over, he had broken the ice, sang the song without a glitch, every note was in tune and in sync with the orchestra, it was time to have some fun. He took a dramatic step backwards, changed into a jacket while Ron formally announced Tony's name, and then the anticipated applause filled the theatre. "Dancing In the Street," "Together,'" Natural Man," and, "Ease On Down The Road," opened the first set followed by a medley of a cappella songs harmonized with the Saccettes. It was brave to sing with naked voices after the explosion of sound from the orchestra, but it was also Tony's way of displaying his versatility as a vocalist. The next set was filled with 70s songs: a medley that paid tribute to Barry Manilow, "The Prayer," an Italian ballad that paid homage to his roots, and Vintage Vegas songs, to pay tribute to the icons of entertainment who had once graced the showrooms in the city. The show ended in an upbeat tempo as Tony sang his original songs, "Las Vegas Rocks," and, "Las Vegas, The Greatest Town Around," while a short series of photos flashed on the screen as he paid homage to his family. The cabaret was pounding with applause when he took his final bows: his life, his body of work so beautifully displayed, so heartfelt, and so filled with talent. Fifty years of entertaining reached one of the high points not only for the audience, but for the man singing those songs. Although he was standing alone as he took his final solo bow, on his shoulders, silently suspended and unseen by the naked eye, were the vestiges of his brother, smiling down from the heavens, sharing in this moment with his twin.

There was an after party at his favorite Italian Bistro where friends and colleagues bestowed endless rounds of flattery as they sipped on their favorite glasses of wine.

"I feel like I'm at a funeral, with people talking to me as if I have come and gone, as if today's performance was my last hurrah. 'It's the pinnacle of your career,' so many said, funny, I don't feel that way. For me it was another performance, but the Smith Center topped the list as the finest venue I'd ever performed at." Surrounded by loved ones, they kissed and hugged him, and toasted him until the last drop of wine had been drained from the bottles. Although there was still a void in this heart for his family and twin brother, tonight and for the rest of his life, he would always see his glass as half full. If some wine spilt, he would always have the tenacity to reach for a new bottle, because that's how Tony sees the world and lives his life.

As he fell into bed, he reflected back on the life he was fortunate enough to have lived. Some old Willie Nelson song lyrics came to his mind, "To All the Girls I've Loved Before, who traveled in and out my door, I'm glad they came along, I dedicate this song, to all the girls I've loved before." Yes, in so many ways women had made his life pleasurable beyond his wildest imagination. Perhaps as they read his memoirs, they will know who they were, and that they haven't been forgotten. Time marches on, loves come and go: he was finally able, and lucky enough, to find the one. He looked over at the other side of the bed as the quiet sounds of his lover filled the room and his heart with joy. His life partner had arrived and was snugly tucked beside him. Taking a deep breath, his eyes calmly closed, as his dreams took him back to the basement of his home where it all began.

The next morning he awoke, dressed, drank one of his insanely healthy juiced concoctions, and entered the office, it was another day, and a full calendar: people to meet, places to go and songs to be sung, and he was the one who would be singing them, until he could sing them no more.

Morgan Fairchild was interviewed by Tony when she appeared in the Las Vegas production of Mrs. Robertson

Las Vegas Rocks ®

1969 – Elvis Presley opens at the International Hotel, now known as the Las Vegas Hilton. The International opened in the 1969 on Paradise Road off the Strip. This was the first of the three-wing hotel design that would later be used for the MGM, Mirage, Monte Carlo, TI, Bellagio, and Venetian.

Tim Conway talks with Tony during a press conference in Las Vegas

CHAPTER 20

"There are times and places when just the right things happen for the right reasons. Now in my early sixties, I'm able to tell my story. Still young enough to remember every detail, I'm old enough to have enough details to remember. I could have taken the easier, more secure road, maybe followed in my father's footsteps and become a butcher, but that is not how I, nor he, imagined my life to be. Becoming a performing artist, where I often wondered where my next meal was coming from, allured me, and my brother. Our father wished for talented children, and once he realized he had them, pushed us into the direction of performance art. Perhaps he was unhappy and saw his own business as unexciting, but there was something inside him that instilled the belief that his twin sons would be entertainers, and that was exactly what we became.

I have lived a long and fulfilling life, and after three bad marriages I was l lucky enough to find the love of my life, Josette. It was time for a real vacation: we received two tickets to the Polynesian Islands from Josette's sister. Josette, her sister and spouse, and I would take a well-deserved respite from decades of work. At the end of January, when most of northern Europe and America are experiencing winter, we departed Los Angeles seeking the comfort of warmth. We landed in Tahiti and then headed on to Bora Bora. At the end of the very long flight, it all seemed worth it as the plane descended onto the tarmac. The water was so crystal clear I could see the fish, some even jumping out of the ocean. The sea breeze was warm and moist with a tinge of saltiness, and everything smelled fresh. This was a place I could truly relax, unwind my mind, and allow new ideas that had been simmering for years to come to the surface. It had been so long since I had been on a true vacation, it took a couple of days to grasp the concept of total relaxation.

"Even though I have travelled extensively, this country of Bora Bora is one of the most beautiful places I have ever seen: the people were so kind, the flora and fauna so unusual, and the beaches were crescent shaped with white sand. This paradise was heaven on earth. The weather was perfect, with highs in the low eighties during the day, and a constant sea breeze in the evenings, we never needed an air-conditioner. At night, the windows to our room were always open, allowing the cool air into the room. As we toured the islands, I began to see why Josette had brought me here. Both she and her family are from France, and this country, French Polynesia, is filled with French culture. A lot of the food, road signs, art, clothing, and retail stores were French, as was the language. She was on holiday, but in her comfort zone. We spent the days using a variety of transportation to investigate every nook and cranny on the island.

If we weren't walking, it was a boat tour, or bicycling, or driving a small rental car, or sailing on a catamaran: each provided a different insight into the island. I began my days rising with the sun, and instead of juicing and rigorous exercise, I walked down to the beach, rolled out a towel and read. It was my story I was reading, and as I read, I could not believe it was my life. I hadn't written the words, I left that to the professional, but what I had done was open up my heart and soul and tell my life as it was. At times it brought tears to my eyes, or made me realize how shallow I had been, or made me laugh, but most of all it brought back the love I had been blessed to experience: the wonderful family I have had, and I thanked God for all that be had bestowed upon me, pointing me in the right direction, although at times I didn't listen. I read about my loves, my sexual escapades, my career, my family, and my businesses and again thanked God for the spirit of joy he had given me in life. As I closed up chapter five, I grabbed my towel, strolled back into the room, and lying there on the bed was the best gift of all, a love that is so overwhelming and encompassing, it can only be explained as a gift from heaven above. Yes, I had made mistakes, and my history of three divorces didn't sit well as a record of love when the vows I had taken were till death do us part, but once love had evaporated from the marriages, it was death. As I looked down into her closed eyes, I felt that God had made me wait, once I had experienced too many mistakes, when true love knocked on my door, I would know it and never take it for granted or destroy it. Josette is such a love.

"After getting our sea legs from the long flight, the four of us took a boat tour around the main island. It was mandatory to wear sunglasses because of the powerful rays of the sun, without them we were told our eyes would burn. Luckily at the tiny wharf, they sold custom French designer glasses at a local super market directly across the street, and I was the only one who had to purchase a pair. 'The reflection of the sun upon the water, will burn your eye lids,' Josette translated as the captain spoke in French.

"Walking across the road, I told myself I wasn't going to phone home, that I needed a complete break from work, but I was drawn to my cell, my own addiction. There was a text message from Ron who told me to call the office on an urgent matter, he was too heartbroken to break the news to me. I returned his message and insisted upon the news, however bad it was. I was shocked to hear the words that began with Denny Copper, my longtime friend and mentor in television production. At sixty-five, he had died in his sleep of a heart attack. I went numb, and my heart began racing, I could hardly catch my breath. Collapsing onto the floor of the market, several people came to my rescue thinking I had had a seizure. Denny's life had intertwined with mine for so many years, we loved and trusted each other. As a reader you can see that he was so much part of my life, I had taken him for granted: it wasn't until that moment that I realized his name had been left out of my story. Shortly after I had moved to Las Vegas and began producing the live shows he was so much a part of me that I didn't single him out in all these hundreds of pages of my life.

"Denny Cooper was my mentor in the television production business. We met in 1986 when I was desperate and in need of completing my Christmas show, I had run out of money to finish the project, and when I was introduced to Denny and told him the situation, his response was, 'no need to worry, I will make sure this gets done.' From that moment on Denny and I had pioneered the video television production business in Las Vegas. He was brilliant and knowledgeable on every aspect of video production, lighting, electronics and a master in computer technology. His personality was very passive-aggressive which was counter to mine, which is aggressive. We were together at every location, he was the backbone of my production business. We were the perfect dog and pony act for so many clients. Although we pursued outside projects on our own, we were there for each other every step of the way. We travelled around the globe producing numerous projects. He was always so proud of me, I guess he thought of me as his alter ego, I was the front man and he was the guy in the background that got things done. Together, we won many awards for outstanding film production, the plaques that hang on the walls of my office, we shared together. We were soul brothers and cared for each other unconditionally. We fought over details; he was a perfectionist, but when we would sit and watch the final product, we were always in agreement. I guess that is why we have all those awards. Twenty-eight years is a long time, a lifetime to share with someone, and now I feel very much alone. A part of my heart was taken away from me on that third day in Bora Bora. I believe the spirit of my buddy will stay with me until I meet him again. Denny, if you are listening, I thank you for your love, for your friendship and your dedication to our shared success.

The five minutes that passed as I tried to regain my composure, seemed like a day. With the assistance of a clerk, I stood up, dried my eyes, purchased the sunglasses and walked back to the wharf. I was happy I had the shades to hide my eyes, I didn't want to ruin the day for the others, so I kept the heartache to myself until Josette and I were alone at the end of the afternoon. We did the all day tour, and staring out over the endless miles of soothing aqua blue-marine ocean was probably the best thing I could do as memories of Denny flooded my mind.

Later that day, after I had showered, drank a glass of ice-cold Sauvignon Blanc, I shared my sadness with Josette. She knew Denny, and she knew how important he was in my life. She held me and wept and shared in my misery. Ever the positive uplifting one, she reminded me that we were going out to a nightclub, and I would be asked to sing. She knew that would cure my temporary depression.

"The restaurant that hung off the side of a hill overlooking the water was huge and held over five hundred customers. There was an expansive bar, dining area, and a large dance floor with a complete band playing the entire evening. Most of the better restaurants don't open until seven and stayed open into the middle of the night. Nine is the usual hour to dine. We sat at the outside bar overlooking the ocean, spent an hour sipping away on fine French wines, and then were shown our table. Shortly after we ordered, I was asked to sing and I was only too happy to oblige. With a full band and several excellent glasses of wine, I had plenty of back-up courage to get up in a foreign country and perform. I sang, "Fly Me to the Moon," but when I sang, "Beyond the Sea," in French, I got a huge applause. The manager was so impressed he sent two bottles of his best wine over to our table and handed me his card. The idea of returning to this glorious island certainly had me looking up."

Tony with Steven at his home during a conversation about booking Steven Seagal as a singer and guitar player in Las Vegas

Las Vegas Rocks ®

1973 – The MGM Grand Hotel and Casino opens. It was the world's largest hotel with a Florida style jai alai fronton that allowed pari-mutuel betting, the same as what's done in horse racing. In 1985, Bally's buys the MGM Grand.

Tony's souvenir "Las Vegas Rocks Musical Clock" was chosen as the best souvenir for 2011

CHAPTER 21

One could hardly write a book about Las Vegas without a Chapter 21, the sacred winning number in Black Jack. Tony lived and gambled in the city along with friends, family, colleagues, and of course, the endless stream of tourists. It is a psychological high and form of excitement that is hard to describe. Winning money, regardless of how much or how little, is fun and exhilarating: but when you lose, you walk away still having had fun. It is the raw unknown, the anticipation of the possibility that draws millions to the machines and the tables. It is the glamour, the flashing lights, the constant music, the beauty and grandeur of the lavish casinos that creates this unsurpassed aura surrounding gambling. Tony's favorites are Black Jack, roulette, poker and 3-5-7, but there are always new games invented to entice the gambler in all of us. Since the city draws tourists from every point around the globe, the games reflect hundreds of cultures, there is something for everyone on the gaming floors of the major casinos.

Although gambling is the brick and mortar that originally built the city, there is so much more than the extravagant edifices lining Las Vegas Boulevard. There are in fact lavish casinos on the outskirts of the town, North, South, East and West: resort style hotels and casinos attracting the tourists who are seeking quieter less harried experiences of the strip. The desert beauty surrounding the valley holds its own unique experience. Red Rock Canyon is an unusual sight to behold with its clay colored mountains. It's a great way to spend the day tromping through the footpaths, or rock climbing. There is Lake Mead with the Hoover Dam, and the newly opened highway spanning the dam, a truly spectacular view. The Grand Canyon, is a hop skip and a jump away and can be seen by helicopter, or by car. A visitor coming to the city has so many options, with the draw of the millions of sparkling lights dotting the strip. From the glamour of the star studded nightclubs, to world championship golf courses, to rustic horse rides through the desert: it is a town for all ages.

"When I first arrived, I felt like a pioneer, the town was small, barely three hundred thousand people and through the years, I have watched it blossom into a metropolis of over two million people. To see casino after casino being imploded making room for larger casinos, to watch the hospital and health care systems expand, the colleges emerge, the springing up of churches, private schools, the development of super highway infrastructures, and the expanding business opportunities, reminds me every day that I had made the right choice. I took a chance on Las Vegas, bet my lucky numbers on Keno and came out a winner. As you may well be aware, my life's course would have altered if I would have moved to New York instead of Las Vegas: or Puerto Rico for that matter. I chose Las Vegas. I have now have lived half of my life in Las Vegas. It has become my home, my work place, my playground, but most importantly the community in which I survive. Over the years I have been introduced to, and have become friends and associates with, those who have influenced my existence here on earth. I wish to thank the following people who have enriched my life and helped to shape my success.

"Over 15 years ago I met Rudy Ruettiger from the block buster movie, 'Rudy,' and his wife, and now partner, Cheryl. Not only did I have an opportunity to work with him, but we became bubbies. We realized that we had a lot in common, his father was a factory worker living below middle class standards, who loved his family and wanted the best for them as well. Rudy and I have had many talks on dreams, beliefs, determination, no turning back philosophy, lots of hard work, and a constant striving to achieve our goals. When I would feel down, I would call him and in his own way he would fill up my tank with his effervescent ideals, reminding me of my goals. Thank you Rudy for touching my life, as well as the world.

Just as this book was about to go to print, one of Tony's best friends had passed away: it is a fitting legacy, that David Brenner, 78, be remembered in this story. During the course of the Las Vegas entertainment shows, David Brenner was a favorite, and often interviewed, subject. Tony and David had become close friends over the years, and he had helped Tony write the production, *Vegas: The Story*, a history of the city, set to myriad of mixed media. Both entertainers had grown up on the streets of South Philadelphia, and they ran in the same circle of Las Vegas based entertainers, although David was best known for his television appearances on, *The Tonight Show*.

In Norm's column, Sunday, March 16, 2014, in, *The Las Vegas Review Journal*, a full two columns was devoted to David's passing.

"Brenner was considered the father of observational humor. His health began declining about a year ago, according to Brenner's longtime friend, Las Vegas entertainer, Tony Sacca. Sacca said Brenner sacrificed his career in his later years to raise his three sons, Slade, Wyatt, and Cole. 'During a custody battle, a judge raised the issue of Brenner being on the road so much. So Brenner settled in Las Vegas in order to keep his kids,' said Sacca."

"I will never replace his friendship: he was kind, caring, and generous. He was truly one of the funniest persons I have ever met, he always had a joke, and there wasn't anything he couldn't find humor in. He just needed a word or a topic, and he was off and running with off-the-cuff jokes."

"Charo, an international sensation, is a true artist. We met when she appeared in Las Vegas and eventually became close friends. I thank her for co-hosting the PBS special, and helping to make it a rave success.

"I thank Anthony Quinn, for allowing me to interview him and hang with him.

"I thank Steven Siegel for requesting to talk with me and letting me book him in Las Vegas.

"I am grateful for the wonderful opportunities that Las Vegas has afforded me: they have so profoundly affected my life.

"I thank my production crew, my office staff, the entertainers, and the people of Las Vegas who have supported my career, the television shows, and my production business. I am forever indebted for your support.

"And last but not least, thank you Las Vegas!

"These are a few of my mantra's by which I live my life:

"Do not search for opportunity in the distance but recognize and embrace it right where you are.

"With each adversity there is a seed of an equivalent or greater benefit when using a positive mental attitude.

"You can fool yourself until you die, but you can't beat honesty with a lie.

"After thirty, exercise is not an option.

"If you think you can, or you think you can't, you are probably right!

"Yesterday has gone forever, tomorrow will never come, but today is yesterday's tomorrow within your reach"

ADDENDUM

The huge body of Tony Sacca's shows have been archived, and are available for viewing. Many of the stars have since died, leaving behind rare film footage of their lives captured intimately by the camera. Historians, news networks and various media have used many of the sequences to embellish and uncover insights into the lives of these world famous stars.

Plans are in the works to air many of these interviews through the program, "Vintage Vegas."